THE BOYD GANG

PETER MARTIN ASSOCIATES LIMITED

Marjorie Lamb and Barry Pearson

THE BOYD GANG

Canadian Cataloguing in Publication Data

Lamb, Marjorie, 1949–
  The Boyd gang

ISBN 0-88778-145-4

1. Boyd, Edwin Alonzo. 2. Crime and criminals - Ontario. I. Pearson, Barry. II. Title.

HV6809.06L3   364.1'55   C77-001023-7

© Marjorie Lamb and Barry Pearson

ALL RIGHTS RESERVED

No part of this book may be reproduced or utilized in any form or by any means, electronic or mechanical including photocopying, electrostatic copying, recording or by any information storage and retrieval systems without permission in writing from the publisher, except for the quotation of passages by a reviewer in print or through the electronic mass media.

Design: Michael Solomon

Peter Martin Associates Limited
35 Britain Street, Toronto, Canada M5A 1R7

United Kingdom: Books Canada, 1 Bedford Rd., London N2
United States: Books Canada, 33 East Tupper St., Buffalo, N.Y. 14203

To Gertrude, Rhena, and Don

ACKNOWLEDGMENTS

The authors wish to express their deepest thanks to the many people who assisted in the making of this book:

Our close friend, Les Rose, who gave us the idea, and whose help with the research was invaluable to us;

Oleh John Rumak, the head of our research team, whose persistent and creative efforts in assembling the background material was an integral part of getting this story down on paper;

Jim Caverhill for helping with the interviews and giving moral support throughout. Also Ron Wisman, Michael Rose and Linda McKennit.

Kathy Vanderlinen, Michael Solomon, Peter Martin and Carol Martin;

The two chief players in the story, Edwin Alonzo Boyd and Staff Superintendent Adolphus Payne (Retired), upon whose recollections we relied for accuracy, detail, and many juicy tidbits that were never revealed in the newspapers of the time;

Dorreen Mary Frances Boyd (now Pace) for her lively and lengthy correspondence with us. We thank her for her insights and for another viewpoint on the events;

David Helwig who read our manuscript and gave us much good advice;

Lloyd Anderson, Selina Appleby, Harvey Blackstock, Doug Creighton, Jack Gillespie, Big Jack of the Horseshoe Tavern, Harold Jukes, Father John Kelly, Allan Lamport, Bill Macrae, Arthur Maloney, Alex McCathie, Billy O'Connor, George Pate, Maurice Richardson, J.J. Robinette, and Jocko Thomas, for giving generously of their time to submit to interviews and share their knowledge with us;

Those people who cannot be mentioned by name, but who provided us with a great deal of important confidential information;

Sgt. Ernie Pollock of the Metropolitan Toronto Police Museum who deserves special thanks for assistance with research and photographs; also P.C. Alex Robertson and P.C. George Cowie;

Inspector E. "Bud" Blight and his staff;

The John Howard Society;

The National Parole Service, especially Edwin Boyd's parole officer, whose co-operation and advice we greatly appreciated;

The Ontario Arts Council who contributed financial assistance to the authors;

Finally, our love and thanks to Frances, Elizabeth, John, Marlien and David, who gave us support and encouragement during those long days of researching and writing.

INTRODUCTION

It's early in 1975, and we have no intention of writing a book. But things happen. Our friend Les Rose, a film director, accidentally unearths a news item about some gangsters who were captured in a barn outside Toronto in the early fifties. Good feature film material, we think. Another friend, freelance researcher Oleh John Rumak, appears on the scene, and we start rummaging through old newspapers and taping interviews with policemen, reporters, lawyers and others who remember the escapades of the Boyd Gang.

By July, our modest mound of research has grown into a mountain. There are sidelights, intrigues, counter-plots, anecdotes and exciting stories by the dozen, and eventually we realize that we can't cram them all into the screenplay. Somehow the notion of writing a book takes possession of us—not a particularly reasonable notion, considering the fact that we aren't prose writers or journalists and that this yarn deserves the expertise of an Isabel LeBourdais or a Trent Frayne. We need the advice of a professional, somebody who will tell us to get lost. Maybe then this lunatic idea will stop nagging us.

Our only connection with the publishing world is somewhat tenuous—two telephone calls made months earlier to Peter Martin, on an unrelated topic. We decide to invite him to lunch. He meets us at a restaurant on Yonge Street, and before the meat loaf arrives we pitch the idea.

We don't know it at the time, but Peter Martin is something of a guerrilla fighter in the Canadian publishing jungle. He responds to our idea like a rebel leader about to stage a strike on the capital: "The Boyd Gang! And a movie! Let's do it!" Peter's enthusiasm has an electrifying effect on us. His few words launch us on a year of sleuthing, adventure, and typewriter cramp.

We track down sources one by one, we unravel scores of puzzles, mysteries and questions lobbed at us by the mass of printed and recorded material, and we haunt the Metropolitan Toronto Police Museum.

Early in 1976 we are ready to approach Edwin Boyd for an interview. Still on parole, he has built a new life for himself and is living under a cover identity. Our only means of contacting him is by letter, forwarded via the Parole Board. We devise the letter with great care, being perfectly open about our research and the nature of our intent in seeking an interview with him. We wait anxiously for a reply.

Several weeks later the reply comes. Boyd is not interested in co-operating with us. No reason is given, but we suspect that he is worried about jeopardizing his parole. Our disappointment is crushing. By this time we are obsessed by the belief that our work will never be complete unless we are able to meet face to face with Boyd.

Painstakingly, we and our research team begin to establish personal contact with members of Boyd's family—those whom we can locate. Two months later, short of cash and worried about rumours that two other groups of filmmakers are working on scripts about the Boyd Gang, we are ready to give up and complete the book on the basis of what we have. Suddenly Oleh, our tenacious researcher, drops in our laps the name, address and telephone number of Edwin Boyd's eldest son.

There is no guarantee that he will talk to us or that he will lead us to Boyd. Flying west to see him means more expense and more delay. We ponder over alternatives for nearly eight minutes, then we walk over to Air Canada's office on Bloor Street and gamble the plane fare.

Boyd's son is surprised to receive our telephone call. He seems openminded, but wary. We refer to our previous contact with the Parole Board, and he tentatively agrees to meet us and hear our story.

We like him immediately. Genuine, straightforward, willing to listen, he is nevertheless anxious about the effect that the publicity from the book and the movie will have upon the family. We talk to him for more than six hours and let him inspect the partially completed book manuscript and the screenplay treatment. He agrees to speak to his father's parole officer. No promises.

We wait. Then a telephone call. "He'll see you."

The parole officer expresses his concern about one point. It is essential that Boyd's cover not be blown. We suggest that the best guarantee is our ignorance of his new identity and present whereabouts. It is necessary then, but also appropriate, that we should meet Boyd in a "hideout" apartment somewhere in western

Canada, and that during the two days of continuous interviewing we should know him only as Edwin Alonzo Boyd.

Back home in Toronto we transcribe the interview tapes into 188 typewritten pages which contain many of the answers we have been hungering for. But even now that the book is finished, some puzzling mysteries remain.

Why did Boyd, a war veteran with a good record, a family man with an apparently settled life, suddenly take to robbing banks as a career? Why did Steve Suchan, a talented man with ambitions to become a classical violinist, walk into a shop one day and trade his violin for a .455 Smith and Wesson revolver? Why, several years later, did Suchan, seemingly unprovoked, use that same gun to shoot down a Toronto Police officer?

There don't appear to be any final answers. Edwin Alonzo Boyd recalls that he saw himself "going out" in a spectacular gunfight like Jimmy Cagney in *White Heat*. He loved to read about himself in the papers, and he delighted in his public popularity as much as any ascendant politician.

Although his character was shaped by many forces, he seemed to have been influenced as much by the myth of the gangster — something he experienced only at the movies — as by anything in the "real" world; in 1951 and 1952, the Boyd Gang itself was created as much by popular imagination as by life.

Now, twenty-five years later, the facts that we have uncovered and assembled here seem so much stranger than myth, the tragedies more immediate and profound, the triumphs more stirring and unlikely, that we are no longer tempted to sit in judgement upon them. Neither are we tempted to justify our motives for writing *The Boyd Gang*. The most appropriate comment comes from Edwin Boyd himself: "Yeah, I thought it'd make a good story. I even thought of writing it myself."

Toronto, November 1976

EDWIN

1

In Toronto, the year really begins in September. Summer holidays are over, students have returned to classes, and the Canadian National Exibition, known to Torontonians as the "Ex", is winding up.

Friday, September 9, 1949 was the last full banking day before the close of the C.N.E. on Saturday. At ten o'clock, when manager George Elwood unlocked the doors of the Armour Heights Bank of Montreal, he had no idea that in just over an hour he would take part in events which would mark the beginning of the most flamboyant and notorious crime career in Canadian history.

It was a slow morning, and Elwood welcomed the chance to tackle the rough ends of paperwork accumulated during the week. He knew that he and his staff would be busy later on, not only with the usual lineup of people waiting to cash their Friday paycheques, but with customers dropping in to withdraw enough money for a final fling at the "Ex".

The accountant sat comfortably at his desk, absorbed in figures. The stenographer concentrated on her typing, and Joyce Empey, the teller, served the few early morning customers, oblivious to the alarm button at her foot and the loaded Ivor Johnson revolver just a reach away in her drawer.

Although the $2,300 in her cash drawer was nearly equal to Miss Empey's total annual income, it did not occur to her that anyone would risk robbing a bank for it. Prices had risen steadily since the end of the war and $2,300 would barely buy a new car.

George Elwood glanced up from his papers. It was 11:02 a.m. The only customer was a man who had just entered, a man who looked as though he might have come in straight from the dentist's chair. His face was puffed out around the mouth, and he appeared to have some sort of pad or clamp on his lower jaw. Elwood felt only vaguely uneasy but decided to serve the customer himself.

"May I help you with something?"

Without replying, the customer handed him a folded cheque. Elwood turned the cheque over to see if it was endorsed. It was - with the words: *Hold-up—would you like to be a dead hero? Fill bag with money.*

For a moment, Elwood was startled. Then he looked at this slight, shabby figure standing in front of him. He elected to try a bluff.

"Are you kidding?"

The man reached inside his windbreaker and pulled out a black Luger automatic pistol.

"I'm not fooling," he said quietly.

The bank manager looked at the face under the low fedora. He noticed the eyes particularly. They were "real inward" eyes.

George Elwood turned to Miss Empey, handed her the note, and told her to do as it said, hoping that the young teller would have the presence of mind to press the alarm button. She didn't disappoint him.

Almost as if she were acting out a well-rehearsed role, the teller slowly and deliberately opened the cloth bag which the bandit handed her, at the same time pressing the alarm with her foot. She resisted the impulse to hurry. She dropped a fistful of bills. She thumbed through a pile of twenties. How long would it take the police to get there? It seemed like ages since she had pressed the button. In fact, less than a minute had passed. How much longer could she stall?

A moment earlier, the stenographer had glanced up and seen the robber, his profile turned toward her as he faced the teller's cage. She too had pressed the alarm. Then she watched, silently marvelling at Joyce Empey's brash stalling.

In her cage, as she slowly filled the canvas bag, the teller could smell the faint odour of whisky coming from the man who held the gun on her. He did not appear at all the stereotypical hardened criminal. There was something slightly annoying about being robbed by this scruffy-looking man with liquor on his breath.

In fact this small unprepossessing man with cheeks distended in disguise was the veteran of several escapades far more daring than this simple holdup. A commando in France during the war, Edwin Alonzo Boyd had served his country well. But the career on which he was now embarking would bring him far greater fame, attention, and money, than his military exploits had ever done.

"Don't press any alarm," warned Boyd. The teller's deliberation was making him jumpy. "Hurry up!" he snapped at her. "There's going to be a lot of dead people around here if you don't."

Across the street, salesman William Cranfield was happily closing his briefcase as he completed a successful business deal. He straightened the lapel of his blue pinstripe suit and stepped outside. As he strolled to his car which was parked a few steps north of the bank, his thoughts were on the weekend and the warm weather.

Inside the bank, events were proceeding so quietly that the accountant, eight feet from Joyce Empey, did not realize a robbery was in progress until it was almost over. But he saw the teller hand a canvas bag to the robber, who then backed out the front door.

On the street, Cranfield climbed into his car. Just as he put the key in the ignition, a stranger appeared at the driver's door and yanked desperately at the handle. The door was locked, but the man waved a pistol in Cranfield's face and forced him out of the car. Bewildered, Cranfield backed up and stood at the rear of the car, where he was startled to find himself the near target of several shots being fired by a man he knew very well—George Elwood, the bank manager.

About a foot and a half from Cranfield, a bullet zinged into the trunk just above the right bumperette. Cranfield stared incredulously at the bank manager. "What the hell are you doing!" he blurted.

"It's a holdup!" shouted Elwood. Cranfield ran for cover without bothering to look at the fugitive sitting in his car, vainly cranking the starter motor.

Having fired all six shots of the teller's revolver, Elwood ran back to the bank to get his own firearm and Boyd decided to take to his heels. In his haste he dropped a twenty-dollar bill on the front seat of the car, almost as if to pay Cranfield for the inconvenience.

At this moment, responding to the alarm, a North York Police cruiser had already turned onto Avenue Road, and was speeding north toward the bank. Also closing in on the area were officers of the Ontario Provincial Police and the Toronto City Police. A roadblock had been thrown up on Yonge Street to prevent the robber from leaving the city. A score of officers began a methodical combing of the streets surrounding the scene of the crime.

In public school Boyd had been a red ribbon sprinter, but now as he ran north up Avenue Road, the liquor he had consumed prior to the robbery inhibited both his speed and agility. When he turned the corner at Dunblaine Avenue to cut across a yard he fell on the lawn, spilling wads of currency onto the grass. Scrambling to his knees Boyd scooped the money back into the bag, leapt up and fled to the rear of the yard where he vaulted a fence and escaped to the next street.

On Haddington Street, a woman was playing in the front yard with her baby. She was amazed to see a man speed past her, cutting through her property with barely a glance in her direction. In the next block, two women were chatting in a driveway as Boyd came through from the back alley.

"What are you doing in my yard?" asked one of the women indignantly.

Without hesitation, Boyd answered, "A friend of mine was supposed to be working around here somewhere washing windows. You wouldn't have seen him, would you?"

"No I haven't seen any window washers, but I'd advise you to stick to the streets, and not go cutting through people's yards."

As Boyd quickly walked away, his money sack stowed in his windbreaker, the woman dispatched her thirteen-year-old son to follow on his bicycle.

Jogging toward a bus stop Boyd soon became aware of the cyclist behind him. What did this kid want, anyway? Boyd slowed down. The boy slowed down. Boyd turned a corner, the boy pedalled after him. In exasperation Boyd finally turned, faced his pint-sized pursuer and glared at him.

With a swift back-pedal the boy braked his bike, locked eyes with Boyd for a second, then did an about-face and rode back home to his mother. Boyd continued toward the bus stop.

By this time the police were organized into units for checking cars, stores, streets and public transit. Six suspects had already been rounded up when the call came in that a suspicious character had been arrested from a Toronto Transit bus.

Boyd was by habit a meticulous planner, but he made several errors in his first bank robbery. Normally a non-drinker, he had taken a huge slug of Irish whiskey to calm his nerves; instead it had made him shaky on his feet. He had allowed the teller and everyone else in the bank plenty of time to turn in an alarm. He later learned that surprise and immediate command of the situation would keep bank employees away from alarms long enough to allow him access to the cash drawers. His biggest mistake had been his failure to provide for a getaway vehicle. His clumsy attempt at the theft of Cranfield's car taught him the importance of planning ahead.

Despite these errors, Boyd had made one move that worked to his advantage – he robbed a bank close to home. It was a practice he was to use successfully in later robberies.

As the bus he had just missed receded in the distance, Boyd checked his watch. It would be ten minutes before another bus came along this route. His truck was only a few blocks away on Avenue Road. He looked up the street and behind him. The pesky kid was gone. Only a few neighbourhood pedestrians sauntered about the streets. It was a pleasant morning, sixty-one degrees with a slight breeze, a nice day for a stroll if you weren't too busy. Boyd walked the rest of the way to his truck.

By the time the police had reluctantly let the last of their suspects go, Boyd had driven the six blocks to his house at Eglinton and Duplex Avenue, counted his take, and called it a day. He had escaped with $2,200.

Two years and hundreds of thousands of dollars later, Edwin Alonzo Boyd signed a statement which in part read:

> After the robbery the Bank Manager fired several shots... I went to get in a car, but I was too drunk, so then I just staggered down a side street, and over some back fences, and made an escape. This was my first attempt at bank robbery. I wish now that I hadn't of been successful.

2

As a child, Edwin Boyd was devoted to his mother. He strived to please her in every way. Being only average in scholastic ability, young Eddie sought parental approval and pride by excelling in music and athletics. With diligent practice he soon became a superior sprinter and jumper. Later he acquired stacks of books on physical fitness as he progressed into weight-lifting and muscular development.

At Earl Beatty School in Toronto Boyd was a soccer player on the school team, and for years his picture hung in the hall of the school. But the source of his greatest pride was the fact that he mastered the mouth organ and earned a place in the YMCA band which won a world championship at the Canadian National Exhibition.

His family was very religious, and Edwin attended both church and Sunday School regularly. Once Edwin and some friends were challenging each other to walk on a spiked metal fence. Boyd slipped and broke his wrist. His father, who didn't believe in doctors, called Oliver Crockford, the faith healer. Crockford looked at the boy's wrist, which was twisted in an S-shape, and prayed over him.

Boyd reports: "Two days later, I could walk on my hands and turn handsprings. My dad said, 'It's a miracle.' He told everybody that the Lord had healed my wrist, and I suppose he had, because I really had a break."

Thomas Glover Boyd, the father of the four young Boyds, three boys and a girl, was for twenty-five years a well respected constable on the Toronto City Police Force. Born April 2, 1914, Boyd was named after his paternal grandfather. Thomas Boyd was a decent man but very tough, and Edwin got along best with his mother. She, in return, lavished affection on her eldest son.

When Mrs. Boyd died, Edwin, then fifteen, became despondent. The bottom had dropped out of his world. The children were farmed out to different homes, and went their separate ways. With no one but himself to glory in his accomplishments, Edwin soon dropped out of school.

"He took his mother's death hard, and he got so you couldn't talk to him," his father told friends. "He wouldn't let anyone into his confidence. He may have been emotionally confused with it all. But you had to give him credit for having a mind of his own, and being as good as his word if he ever made a promise."

By this time, the Depression was on. Jobs were scarce in Toronto and Boyd headed west to look for harvesting work. He "rode the rods" across the country several times, once taking his next younger brother Gordon with him. But he wasn't always successful at finding a job. "We were lost in the shuffle," says Boyd. "There were too many guys who were already experienced, going back to places they'd been before."

Finally, Edwin, who was then eighteen years old, got work at a relief camp—six hours a day for six dollars a month. He was helping to build the Trans-Canada Highway at Nipigon, Ontario.

After a long, hard winter, Boyd had saved thirty dollars. "Geez," he thought, "this is terrific. This is the most money I ever had in my life." He and his friend Duke decided to go on strike. "Where are you going?" asked Duke. "I don't know," said Boyd. "Anywhere west—Port Arthur maybe."

Boyd worked his way west, mostly bumming from generous people when he could. Duke introduced him to the prostitutes of Winnipeg. He did a little harvesting in Kelvington, Saskatchewan. He learned how to panhandle from a wrestler in Calgary.

Times were tough, and Edwin was young and inexperienced. In 1933, at the age of nineteen, he made his first appearance in the files of the Royal Canadian Mounted Police. Even then he thought of himself as a swashbuckler and a hero. When he was picked up for vagrancy in Edmonton he gave as his alias the name John Wilson Harkaway, after the fictional hero Jack Harkaway, popular with boys everywhere at the time.

Boyd was convicted of the offence, and given a choice: twenty dollars and costs, or six weeks in jail. He went to jail. "That was my first contact with that kind of thing, and I thought it was quite a unique experience," says Boyd. "I enjoyed it."

Wandering from job to job in the west, he was again picked up for vagrancy and begging, in Saskatoon, Saskatchewan. This time, under the alias John Gerald Adams, he was sent to Moosomin Jail. For Boyd, the experience was not too distasteful. "I spent ten glorious weeks there," he later recalled. Moosomin is where I learned to do a back somersault in the air."

On his release, Boyd attempted to find work in the United States. Kept in custody overnight for violation of immigration laws, he was deported under the name Herbert John Hardley.

In August 1936, Boyd and another man, hungry and jobless, walked into a Calgary restaurant. Neither had any money but they ordered a meal of stewed beef, listed on the menu at forty cents. For dessert, Boyd indulged himself with an ice cream dish called a Rainbow Special. His companion settled for a banana split.

When the restaurant proprietor demanded payment, Boyd offered to work off his debt, but the prorietor was adamant. "Too many of you guys have been pulling this stunt. I've gotta make an example of you." And he called a policeman.

In court the judge was not sympathetic. "I can understand that you're hungry, and you want a meal," he told Boyd. "I don't blame you for that. But a Rainbow Special and a banana split?!"

Boyd and his pal went to jail for three days for obtaining a meal by fraud.

In the context of the period, Boyd's various escapades had been more unlawful than criminal. Thousands of men were out of work during the Depression. Many had turned to begging, and a few weeks of jail time was not considered a total disgrace. Many so-called vagrants of the Depression era in fact went on to successful and rewarding careers when the economy recovered.

The time he spent in jail did nothing to deter Boyd from his life of drifting and riding the rods. One night, about a month after the restaurant episode, he and a buddy hopped off a freight and found themselves near a lonely service station. It was two a.m. "I wonder if there's any money in the cash drawer," Boyd's buddy mused.

Feeling perfectly safe, they broke the washroom window. Boyd wriggled through, looked around and had just filled his pocket with a dollar's worth of pennies when he spotted a police officer passing by. When he heard the policeman squeezing through the broken washroom window, Boyd hid under a desk in a pile of rubber boots.

"This was lack of experience," Boyd said later. "I should have thrown the office chair through the window and followed it. Instead I squeezed in underneath the desk, and the policeman came in and looked around and looked around, then telephoned that somebody had broken into the service station. Then he sat down in the office chair and put his feet up. He started opening the desk drawers and whatever he found he put in his pocket. He found a lighter — that went into his pocket. After that he's sitting there with his feet on me, and he flashed his flashlight on a couple of times. Then all of a sudden his eyes focus and he realizes that it's not rubber boots he's got his feet on. 'Hey, come outta there,' he says."

According to the official record Boyd had committed twenty offences of break, enter, and theft. Boyd's recollection of what happened is at variance with this account.

"They were just cleaning their blotter and using me—I was stupid! I didn't know what I was doing. There was no lawyer furnished. You just went into court and somebody said, 'Mumble-mumble-mumble —guilty or not guilty?' You couldn't even understand what he was talking about. I said, 'Not guilty.' And the Crown Attorney said, 'You can't do that. You have to say "guilty".' I didn't know what you were supposed to say, so I said, 'Guilty.' He said, 'That's better.' When I got to Prince Albert I wasn't there for one thing, I was there for about twenty things. And I didn't know what to do."

During his days as a hobo, Boyd had served an apprenticeship in crime. At the penitentiary in Prince Albert, Saskatchewan, he absorbed all the scams and dodges of a journeyman criminal.

Boyd hated working on the outdoor farm gang in Prince Albert. It was freezing cold in the winter. "My nose would freeze every time I walked out the door," he remembers. He wanted to work indoors, but such a request would not normally be granted. Boyd decided to make the warden *want* him indoors as much as he wanted to be there.

Boyd wrote an anonymous letter to the warden, saying that he had overheard Edwin Boyd and some other prisoners plotting to escape in a few days when they were outside. The very next day he and his pals were called inside, given brooms, and told they were on the indoor cleaning gang.

Boyd spent two and a half years in the penitentiary. In March 1939, when he came before the warden to receive his ticket of leave, there was very little left in him of the naive and enthusiastic youngster who had marched with the YMCA band ten years before.

They gave him ten dollars and a suit of clothes. "The clothes pulled this way in one spot, and the opposite way in another spot," says Boyd. "They looked horrible. The shoes were real stiff, army boots cut down. They were comfortable enough, but they would not stay on my feet. And the tie — the first rainfall it shortened up about one-third. It wrinkled up and almost vanished."

Boyd's father had arranged a job for him, so the warden gave him a train ticket to Toronto. He stpped over for several hours in Saskatoon and saw a Dorothy Lamour movie. When he got to Toronto he went to work in a dairy, slinging cases and loading wagons.

Boyd lived with his father, across the road from Charles Templeton's church, and continued to practice his father's religion. His father took him to see a Dr. Jackson, who so influenced the young Boyd that he began taking ice cold baths every morning and running to work every day. Dr. Jackson gave lectures at the Masonic Temple, where Boyd saw him take off his clothes and reveal his eighty-year-old body to be as healthy and svelte as a twenty-year-old's.

Boyd's father had Edwin eating great quantities of Dr. Jackson's Roman Meal. Although Dr. Jackson advocated the use of ice and snow on the bare skin, Boyd decided that cold baths were preferable for keeping his body youthful.

Edwin joined the militia and devoted one night every week to it. He had disliked the strict military discipline in the penitentiary, especially the silent system which prohibited the prisoners from speaking to each other or to the guards except by special permission. But the militia was different. He and his buddies were called upon to guard the Welland Canal when the locks were in danger of being blown up by enemy agents, or so it was feared.

Boyd soon worked himself into a responsible position. As Hitler and Mussolini discussed the terms of a political and military alliance, Boyd's militia unit, the Queen's York Rangers, disbanded so that the men could join regiments going into training for war. Ironically, world events were offering Boyd the best opportunity he'd yet had to make something of his life.

Boyd joined the Royal Canadian Regiment, First Division. By skill and temperament he was ideally suited to his infantry assault training. Although at five-feet-seven and 140 pounds Boyd was not a big man, he was tough, agile, and well-coördinated. He excelled in hand-to-hand combat, having had some experience with judo as a young boy.

Since his mother's death, Boyd's life had been nearly devoid of affection or romance. Drifting from prison to prison and city to city, his few involvements with women had been casual encounters, soon forgotten. But his father had told him that he might meet some interesting women overseas, and when war was declared Boyd was delighted to be posted to England.

His first few months consisted of familiarization and training. But by June 1940, Boyd was ready when his regiment crossed the channel to France. They landed at Brest on the Atlantic coast while the evacuation at Dunkirk was happening in Belgium to the north. Suddenly, orders came that they had to get out of the country. They were told to ditch all their equipment, head for the harbours, and get onto the first boat they saw.

Boyd and his comrades drove their vehicles into a vacant field and began to smash their gas tanks and motors. For Boyd it was as a "rip-roaring time" until all the vehicles were ruined, gasoline was running out everywhere, and then "some nut went and threw a match in it".

The thick black smoke soon brought the Germans to investigate, but Boyd and his unit were on their way back to Brest. Though shaken by their near escape, some of the Canadian soldiers thought the war was over and began throwing away their guns. Boyd kept his revolver, listing it as missing. It was a souvenir he would take back to Canada when the war was really over.

When they finally got back to England they were put in barracks at Aldershot. It was several weeks before they were outfitted with new vehicles and weapons. Boyd was well aware that the higher officials were not impressed with the Canadian soldiers for disposing of their weapons.

In Aldershot, Boyd and his pals finally had time for a little social life, and Boyd soon found himself entangled in an affair with a schoolteacher from Guildford, less than ten miles away. The woman accepted a marriage proposal from Boyd, but when her former boyfriend returned on leave from Tunisia she changed her mind. Boyd was philosophical about the event, and decided to take dancing lessons.

His regiment was posted to Reigate. A few miles away, in Red Hill, dancing lessons cost half a crown. One rainy evening, Edwin was driving through Reigate on his way home from his lesson when he noticed a small, pretty, dark-haired young woman hurrying along the main square.

Boyd stopped and asked if he could give her a ride, since it was raining, and soon the two of them were happily laughing and talking together.

She told him her name was Dorreen Mary Frances Thompson, and she was twenty years old. Her charming accent and lovely face enchanted Boyd. He had never met a woman quite like her.

Dorreen had grown up in the town of York in northern England. Her childhood ambitions were to become a veterinary surgeon and to learn to play the piano accordion. Although she hadn't achieved either goal, she was happy.

"We had an angora rabbit, a budgie bird, and a great big dog, a Saint Bernard," she recalled. "And of course I collected all the stray dogs and cats in the neighbourhood."

Because her mother had veen very ill when she and her twin sister were born, Dorreen was raised by her grandmother. The four children in the family were brought up as staunch Roman Catholics. At the age of fourteen Dorreen entered a convent with the intention of becoming a nun. At eighteen, the Sisters of Charity allowed her a month to decide whether to take her vows.

"We could have taken vows to work unto death or to pray unto death," said Dorreen. "I was going to choose work. My name was going to be Bonaventure."

Skilled in embroidery and homemaking arts taught in the convent, Dorreen Thompson decided she would rather have a home and children. Later she confessed, "That's all I've ever wanted out of life."

After leaving the convent Dorreen became a parlourmaid in the home of Lord Louis Mountbatten. "We wore black dresses, starched white collars and cuffs and apron, and a little cap. I remember what a time we had, getting those caps right."

Boyd was fascinated by this vivacious young woman. Dorreen was also interested and the two became immediately inseparable.

Dorreen didn't know that Boyd had already applied to his commanding officer for permission to marry the schoolteacher from Guildford. Since the request was still on the books, Boyd filled in Dorreen's name.

Dorreen and Edwin give different accounts of these first few weeks. Dorreen thinks it was two weeks before she was ready to marry him. Says Edwin, "I met her on Friday and we got married on Tuesday."

The ceremony was a quiet, hasty, war wedding. "We were married in the registrar's office," remembers Dorreen. "I wore a pink dress under a grey coat, and I had no flowers." Seven or eight days in London was the extent of their honeymoon.

They set up houskeeping in one flat after another, but eventually Boyd was transferred to Brighton, and Dorreen, now pregnant, stayed at Red Hill, thirty miles away. On one off-duty day, Edwin and Dorreen went to visit Dorreen's family. Her grandmother told Dorreen how much she liked Edwin, but with prophetic insight warned, "You'll never know what that man is thinking. He's as deep as a drawn well."

The young Boyds delighted in the off-duty hours they spent together. His rediscovered zest for life soon brought out the old recklessness in Edwin. "I used to go home every night and drive back in the morning if I could get away with it. I'd get somebody to cover for me." One time Boyd was given a seven-day leave. Dorreen hated to let him go when it was up.

"Stay another day," she begged him. "They won't notice you're missing." Boyd, feeling that he wasn't important enough to be missed, agreed to stay.

Two days later he was marched up in front of the major and asked to explain his absence. His lame explanation that he had forgotten what day it was did not satisfy the major. Boyd was stripped of his rank and put on latrine duty.

When word came down from headquarters that anyone who volunteered for the new Provost Corps would be given training and one stripe immediately, Boyd was one of the first in line. He was trained on a Harley Davidson motorcycle, and learned how to put the squad through their drills. It wasn't long before he had earned two more stripes, and was once again a sergeant.

In July 1941, during a particularly heavy blitz, Dorreen gave birth to their first child, a son. She was proud of the fact that her father was a veteran of the first war, so as soon as she was able, she enlisted in the Auxiliary Territorials as a dispatch rider. Her brother and sister also enlisted, and her father joined the Eighth Army in Palestine.

Sometimes when Dorreen was out on her motorcycle she would take her speedometer off and go to visit Ed. Often they kept in touch by letter. In 1942, Edwin was away when their second son, Edwin, died in early infancy. Ed wrote to Dorreen:

> Your words tell me of your precious love for me and all about the heartbreak of having our baby son snatched away. However, darling, it was better that we hadn't a chance to get to know him as we knew our oldest boy, because it would have been harder that way. We still have our very deep love for each other.

They were soon together again, and Dorreen was happily into her third pregnancy. A twin herself, Dorreen was not surprised when she gave birth to twins, a boy and a girl. Says Edwin: "I sat in on their birth because it was with a midwife. They did everything at the house. It was the first time I'd ever seen a birth. It was quite interesting."

Dorreen's memory of the event is somewhat different. "He was in the house when I had the twins. He was outside the door, and when he heard me moan and let out a scream, he fainted. My grandmother helped him."

Robert* and Gordon, Edwin's younger brothers who were also stationed in England, often took time off to visit Dorreen and the children.

Wrote Ed, "Dearest Brownie," (a nickname referring to her lovely dark eyes), "I hope you are not having a bad time with my brothers... As for me, my love, I passed my general exams with 94 per cent."

On D-Day, June 6, 1944, three Canadian divisions joined the Allied troops in the invasion of France. The beachhead had already been established by the time Boyd's division arrived two days later, but Boyd took pride in being part of the war effort, and distinguished himself along with hundreds of his fellow soldiers.

Still, his thoughts were of home and family. He wrote to Dorreen in July:

> Well darling, this is our first baby's birthday and I am still not reunited with you. I pray dearly for us and do hope it comes true.
>
> I'll bet Gordon [Boyd's brother] and Trudie will go crazy

*Pseudonym

over our children. Gee, I'd like to see you and the kids! Well, I managed to find a mobile laundry, have a bath, and get a clean towel and shirt today.

His cleanliness and tidiness were points of pride for Edwin, and for Dorreen, who often commented on how annoyed her husband would be if he couldn't have a clean shirt.

The couple dreamed of a peaceful and secure home. They wanted a place of their own, and decided to move to Canada. Dorreen packed late in 1944 to take the children to Edwin's father's home in Toronto. Just before she left, she received another letter from Edwin:

I haven't drawn any pay since I was over here. I am saving for a certain young lady's wrist watch. Well, dear one, kiss the babies for me. Tell them daddy wants to see them very much before they leave for Canada. All my love, Eddie.

In April 1945, President Roosevelt died of cerebral hemorrhage. Vice-President Harry S. Truman became president of the United States. Mussolini was caught while trying to escape to Switzerland, and was executed by partisans. Hitler committed suicide. Goebbels, the Nazi propaganda minister, and his wife poisoned their children and committed suicide. The world was in turmoil in April 1945, and Edwin Boyd wrote to his wife:

We're lucky people to have such a real love in our hearts as we hold for each other. Some day we'll be very happy in each other's company, more happy than anybody has ever been before.

By mid-May, the Allies had declared victory in Europe, surrender had been signed in Berlin, and Edwin Boyd was on his way home.

One of the first things he did on arrival was to buy the watch he had promised Dorreen. She remembered, "He never cared for jewelry or spent much money on it, except for my watch and ring." (To please Dorreen's parents, she and Edwin had remarried in the Catholic Church. Although their children were raised as Catholics, Edwin never became a true convert.)

Boyd's father had remarried and was living with his evangelically religious wife in the elegant Toronto area of Rosedale. Dorreen and the children had been staying with them while Edwin waited to be shipped home. When he arrived, he found a small wartime house on Eglinton Avenue in north Toronto and they began a new life.

Years before the term was invented, Edwin Boyd was a "liberated father". Dorreen recalled his cheerful assistance:

> He'd think nothing of changing the twins' diapers or minding them for me or helping with the dishes. He's always been thoughtful and helpful that way.

During the war years, hundreds of small factories and industries had shut down as production switched over to wartime needs. Now with thousands of servicemen returning home, jobs were neither plentiful nor easy to find. Many veterans had fallen behind in skills or education. But Edwin Boyd worked hard to support his wife and family.

His first job after the war was with the Toronto Transit Commission. He began on June 4, 1945, and before long both his brothers worked there too. Edwin was a motorman, or driver, and on weekends they put his brothers on the same train with him. Gord liked talking to people, so he was the conductor. Robert was in the trailer and pushed the bell when people wanted to get off. Says Edwin: "Sometimes he'd push the thing anyway, just to see me stop. And then he'd laugh."

At that time the new subway was under construction south of Bloor Street. Had Boyd stayed with the TTC for another year or two he would have become a subway driver. But according to Boyd, Dorreen wasn't happy with the hours he was working and urged him to quit. (Dorreen disputes this, describing the job as well-paid and clean.) Whatever his motives, Boyd left the job in March 1946.

At one point he talked a baker into hiring him as a pastry cook. Another time, gambling on his good looks, he tried to get a job as a photographer's model but was unsuccessful. In May 1948 he was reduced to seeking work as a janitor.

While Boyd began to grow bitter toward the country he had served in the war, toward the society that wouldn't let him forget his past regardless of the penalty he had paid, and toward the people he saw daily who were better off than he, his devotion to Dorreen never wavered.

When Edwin's stepmother fell ill, Dorreen volunteered to go and look after her for a few weeks. The brief but painful separation precipitated a flurry of correspondence:

There must be something wrong with my brain to let you go away. Coming home is like walking into a morgue. I went to a movie, even if you did keep intruding on my thoughts. We love you very much.

Even when he was worried or lonely Boyd managed to exhibit a playful sense of humor. One of his notes to Dorreen was written as if from their cat, Berky, and signed with a smudged paw print. "You know something," he wrote, "this house doesn't seem as warm since you went away."

Boyd began to save some of the money he was making from a series of odd jobs. Frustrated by his family's economic situation, he searched constantly for ways to make more money. For a time he worked for a window-washing service. When the job was finished, he started washing windows on his own.

But one day Boyd read a newspaper article about a mentally retarded sixteen-year-old boy who had walked into a bank, pointed a gun at the teller, and walked out with $69,000. He read the article again. It seemed ridiculously easy. If a mentally retarded teenager could rob a bank, Boyd, with both brains and athletic ability, could certainly do just as well. The retarded boy had been caught, but he hadn't been trying to escape. He just walked away down the street.

Boyd began to formulate a plan. He didn't tell Dorreen what he was thinking. For several days he walked around the Bank of Montreal's Armour Heights branch. He looked in the windows. He cashed some cheques and asked for change. He memorized the interior of the bank, planning where he would go and what he would do.

The layout of the bank was perfect. He had a Luger pistol, brought back from the war, lying in a drawer at home. He would put on a little face make-up to make sure he wasn't recognized.

Thus carefully disguised and fortified by a tumbler of whiskey, Edwin Boyd entered the Bank of Montreal that warm September morning—a morning that George Elwood, Joyce Empey and the rest of the bank staff would remember for many years.

Dorreen later told reporters: "Eddie always did have a soft spot in his heart for the Banks of Montreal. He always said they were laid out so nicely for a holdup."

The day after the robbery, encouraged by the fact that he hadn't been apprehended, Edwin Boyd set out to test the success of his disguise. Carefully dressed, Boyd walked brazenly into the bank and took his place in the line of customers before Joyce Empey. With a flash of his gleaming white teeth, Boyd handed her a twenty-dollar bill and asked for change. He watched her carefully. Would she know him? Cheerful and courteous, and without a flicker of recognition, Joyce Empey counted out his money. Boyd smiled again. He was home free.

This was Boyd's second meeting with the pretty young teller, but it was not his last. The next time Joyce Empey saw Edwin Boyd she knew him at once. It was two years later, and Edwin Boyd had graduated to the big time.

3

What had possessed Boyd to go back to the scene of his crime, to tempt fate, risk detection, or at the very least, suspicion? He had had a bad scare. Not only had he narrowly escaped apprehension, he had almost been shot by George Elwood. Perhaps that was part of the thrill. As Winston Churchill put it, "Nothing in life is so exhilarating as to be shot at without result."

Boyd had mixed feelings. The robbery, although frightening, had brought him a much needed injection of funds for his home and family. Christmas was coming. The children were growing and always needed new clothes. Dorreen, patient and loving as ever, deserved better than he could earn by ordinary means.

His job was routine. Before the war Boyd had led an unconventional life which though hardly distinguished was not dull. Where there had always been excitement and adventure there was now only monotony and habit. He might have survived without the money, but the spirit of danger and the love of sport lured him back.

By the beginning of 1950 the take from the robbery was running out. The idea of robbing another bank preyed on his mind. He had been lucky the last time. This time he would be smart.

He chose the Canadian Bank of Commerce at St. Clair and O'Connor Drive. He discovered that the manager always went upstairs to his suite over the bank during his lunch hour. This left only two employees in the bank. This time there would be no stumbling around in the street, making himself a target—this time he would do it right.

His previous getaway attempt had been a fiasco — he would not risk that again. But, obviously, he couldn't drive his own truck right up to the door of the bank. It was bright red and had "E.A. Boyd" lettered on the door.

January was cold. As Boyd went about his daily routine he began to notice that many people left their cars running when they went into stores on small errands. An idling automobile was easy pickings. He could steal a car to use in the holdup. The problem was what to do with it. If he just parked it somewhere it was likely to be found before he was ready to use it. He would have to take it to his own garage and risk keeping it there until the time of the robbery.

On the evening of January 16, 1950, Fred Care had to make a stop on his way home. Pulling up in front of Cedarvale Motors on Eglinton Avenue West, Care decided against turning off the motor. The night was cold and he'd only be a minute. It turned out to be a much longer minute than he had anticipated. As he walked out of the shop he was stunned to see his car being driven down the street.

Edwin Boyd had again narrowly escaped. He hurried to his garage without further incident. It was risky to leave the car there, but he heaved a sigh of relief as he closed the doors on the stolen vehicle. He would wait one full day to see if he had been followed before using the car in his latest plan.

Boyd had learned a great deal from his first robbery. He knew several tricks that worked, and he knew even more that didn't.

He stuffed his cheeks with cotton and carefully reddened his entire face with rouge. The bank was empty except for two employees, a teller and the accountant. Like clockwork, the manager went upstairs for his lunch at 12:30. Boyd had discovered that writing his holdup note on a cheque was an effective method of catching the bank staff off guard. He handed the teller the note along with his cloth bag, at the same time pointing his pistol at the two employees.

"Fill it up," said Boyd, pushing the gun further into the cage, nearly touching the teller. "Hurry up!"

From the newspaper accounts of his previous robbery Boyd knew that the revolver used by the bank manager had come from the teller's drawer. He wasn't going to be caught out that way again.

"Where's your gun?" he demanded.

Timidly, the teller replied that she didn't have one. Not about to allow them the opportunity to chase him as he tried to escape, Boyd ordered the two empolyees into the bank vault, threatening them with his gun. The accountant pulled the door closed behind them.

It was only a few seconds before they heard the robber leave. They rushed out of the vault. While the teller ran upstairs for the manager, the determined accountant grabbed a revolver from his desk and ran outside.

Boyd had parked his getaway vehicle right outside the bank, and as the accountant looked around the street that cold, windy afternoon, he observed a 1949 Ford car, bluish in colour, heading west on O'Connor Drive at a high speed. He jumped into his own car, which happened to be nearby, and gave chase. He watched the getaway car until it crossed Woodbine Bridge and then lost sight of it.

Boyd realized that his pursuer had gotten close enough to take down the licence number. He stopped the car and took off on foot.

Seconds after Boyd abandoned it, a policeman discovered the car with its engine still warm and the keys swinging in the ignition. But Boyd had disappeared. The vehicle was taken to the East York Police Station for fingerprint examination, but no prints were found. Fred Care claimed his car that afternoon.

Boyd had obviously had another close call. For a novice he had not done badly. If he had stopped then, chances were good that he might never have been caught. But the lure was too strong, and the prey was too easy. With two successes behind him, the latest netting $2,862, Boyd felt more confident than ever.

Later, even Toronto's Mayor Alan Lamport complained that banks were practically sitting ducks. In a newspaper interview he denounced the banks for failing to protect their money adequately.

We can never have enough policemen if easy money in banks lies around. Men read in the newspapers how thousands were stolen from a bank and how the getaway was fairly easy, and they see a way to get enough money to last them for a couple of years.

Unfortunately, Boyd's money did not last that long. By summer he was broke. But now he realized the foolishness of his previous holdup methods. Banks were easier to rob than he had imagined but he knew he'd been lucky. What would he have done if the employees had resisted? What if other customers had come in while he was in the middle of the robbery? How could he control more than three or four people and still guarantee his escape? What he needed was a partner.

The perfect partner would be a man who was easily led, needed the money, had experience robbing banks, but was not necessarily too smart. With luck he would be fast on his feet and at ease with a weapon.

Those were the ideal qualifications, but Boyd could hardly take out a classified ad to find his accomplice. All he could do was latch onto the nearest available candidate, a man named Howard Gault.

Gault did not exactly meet Boyd's specifications. He was older, slower, and had never robbed a bank. But he was an amiable fellow and needed the money. He had once been a guard at Burwash Reformatory and was familiar with weapons.

Gault's brother once said of Howard, "I think the term as guard at Burwash didn't help any, as he often said the inmates had a good time."

As a young man, Gault had been forced to marry his pregnant girlfriend. He always felt resentful and eventually left his wife and two children. His brother felt that this action was the result of Howard's having inherited some money on his mother's death. "It went to his head," he said.

Howard took a house in Parry Sound and found work as a guard at Burwash, but still hoped to be reconciled with his family. The reconciliation never came about. Gault's brother speculates: "When his daughter was married he realized that everything was over as far as he was concerned, and I guess he went completely wrong. He isn't bad at heart.... "

Gault left the reformatory, apparently suffering a nervous breakdown. He travelled west to Winnipeg for a rest, then took a job harvesting on a farm. Later he tried mining in northern Ontario at $300 per month, a rather good wage for 1950. Drifting back to Toronto Gault found himself short of cash, and in company with Boyd.

By this time, Boyd's *modus operandi* was fairly well established. However, he was constantly refining his techniques. Late in the evening of July 30, 1950, a woman parked her new green Ford convertible in a Dominion Store parking lot. Half an hour later when she returned, it was gone. Boyd and Gault were travelling in style.

The next afternoon Richard Barry, teller in the Dominion Bank at Dufferin and Glencairn, was working at his desk when he heard heavy footsteps in the bank. Continuing his paperwork, he did not look up. The next thing he heard was someone ordering, "Everybody get back against the wall!" Still he didn't respond. Barry thought it was a joke.

When he finally did look up, Boyd was in front of him with the black Luger pointed directly at his chest.

While Gault herded the group of bank employees into the cellar, Boyd jumped over the counter and into the teller's cage. An agile and practiced jumper, he was soon famous for leaping bank counters to take control; this act in fact became the trademark of a genuine Boyd robbery.

When the bank staff found they were alone in the cellar without their assailants, they immediately rang the alarm, which was connected to a bell in the grocery store next door.

The manager of the store heaved a sigh. This wasn't the first time that blasted alarm had gone off. Something was always making it jangle, much to the manager's irritation and his customers' bewilderment. He was supposed to phone the police as soon as he heard the signal, but he didn't want to appear foolish if it were another false alarm. On the other hand, you couldn't just ignore it. The grocer sent his delivery boy to the bank to see what was up, meanwhile going about his business. The boy returned almost at once.

"There's nobody there," he reported. "The bank's empty!"

The grocer realized there must have been a robbery. He telephoned the police at once but was too late by several minutes. Boyd and Gault were blocks away, sitting in a garage counting their money.

The take was $1,954, and the bonus was a .38 calibre Smith and Wesson revolver, property of the Dominion Bank. They split the money evenly but Boyd allowed Gault to keep the revolver.

Not long after the holdup, a lineup was held by the North York Police. Mr. Richard Barry was called in to see if he could identify the person or persons who had robbed the bank and forced the staff into the celler. One Peter Marino was at this time under arrest on another charge of armed robbery. As a result of Mr. Barry's identification, Peter Marino was convicted of the robbery of the Dominion Bank.

At Marino's trial, a woman testified that Marino had been working in her store at the time of the holdup. Unfortunately, she was Marino's sister, who was not considered an impartial witness. Even so, the defence attorney protested the Crown's evidence: "I argued until I was black in the face that it was a miscarriage of justice to take the uncorroborated evidence of one person who identified him, but I was turned down."

Vehemently protesting until the end that he had been framed, Peter Marino was sentenced to ten years in Kingston Penitentiary, concurrent with sentences on other charges.

This not only cleared the books for the police, it left Boyd and Gault more or less free to carry on without suspicion.

Boyd now began to review all his original reasons for taking on a partner and to question the value of including another person in his plans. The most obvious problem was that in order to obtain the same return for his efforts, he either had to double the take from each robbery or attempt twice as many of them, which would have doubled the chance of being caught. He found he was depending on the money from his robberies as though it were regular income; he couldn't afford to jeopardize this major source of revenue.

A second problem was that any association increased the risk of being tracked down should the other person be suspected or caught.

Then there was the additional danger of things going wrong when another person was involved. A partner might panic or make a wrong move during a robbery, or he might brag about it later to friends or get drunk in a bar and show off.

All these problems for a mere thousand bucks? *I don't need 'em*, thought Boyd. *I am going back to working by myself.* And so he did. But at his very next holdup, a partner would have saved him a lot of grief.

It was two and a half months since Boyd and Gault had made their successful getaway. The police still had no reason to suspect Boyd, and he didn't draw attention to himself. He decided to have another go at it alone.

On October 11, 1950, he walked into the parking lot of the Capitol Theatre and drove out in a 1947 Chev. He drove straight to the Imperial Bank of Canada at Avenue Road and Fairlawn. Brandishing a pistol in the teller's face, Boyd announced his intentions.

Mr. W.H.G. Smith, the branch manager, was sitting in his office looking through the glass partition into the bank proper. Seeing a man with a gun threatening the teller, Mr. Smith called out, "What's going on?"

Boyd was startled, but quickly recovered. He hadn't expected a third person to be in the bank. Waving his gun, Boyd motioned Smith to come out of the office.

At that period in Canadian banking history, banks were perhaps more concerned about their money than the possible danger to their employees. All bank staff, and especially the tellers and managers, were not only asked but expected to actively resist any robbery attempt. There were few recriminations if risks were not taken, but daring and even foolish acts of resistance and pursuit were not uncommon.

Having been shot at by the Bank of Montreal's Mr. Elwood and pursued by the Bank of Commerce's Mr. Church, Edwin Boyd was well aware of the hazards of his chosen vocation. When Mr. Smith of the Imperial Bank refused to come out of his office, Boyd should have turned tail and fled. Instead he decided to forge ahead.

Waving his gun, he repeated his demand. Almost without hesitation the manager ran to his desk and grabbed his gun.

At this point, accounts of the events differ. The manager told police:

I got my gun from the drawer and stepped to the doorway leading from my office into the bank. As I did so, the bandit opened fire at me and fired three shots and I fired one in return. The man then ran out the side door and made his escape.

Boyd claims that the manager fired first, and he merely "returned fire". He also says, "I only fired two shots. I didn't try to hit him, I only wanted to scare him."

Police later recovered two bullets from the south end of the bank, one on the floor, and one embedded in the wall. The bullet from the manager's gun "had embedded itself in the north wall so deeply I was unable to retrieve it", noted the sergeant who investigated the holdup.

Considerably shaken, and not a penny richer, Boyd returned the stolen car and walked home.

4

Boyd must have given careful thought to this latest debacle and its implications. He was sure he didn't want to kill or wound anyone – in the bank he had fired high and wide, taking care not to risk hitting the manager or staff – but it was evident that the bank personnel were quite prepared to kill *him* if they were given the opportunity.

Boyd realized that no matter how much money a bank might have, it wasn't worth getting killed for. He could end his criminal activities now and his family would be safe. No one would be the wiser; not even Dorreen knew about the robberies. Every week Boyd was careful to take home about what he thought he might have made washing windows.

When he suddenly came home with a new second-hand car, he told Dorreen that he was making regular payments on it. He had, in fact, paid cash from one of the robberies.

"My idea was not to make any kind of display," says Boyd, "and it wasn't to do anything different. The most I did that was different was

I was able to take the family out to better dinners, go to more shows, or have an evening out as a group."

He couldn't keep his secret forever. One day he emerged from the bathroom after scrubbing the makeup off his face. Dorreen confronted him in the hallway.

"I just heard about the robbery on the radio," she said.

"What about it?" asked Ed.

"It was you, wasn't it?"

He had to admit that it was. To Boyd's relief, Dorreen was neither angry nor shocked. She knew that they needed the money. She knew that Ed would have a hard time finding any job that would pay as well. But she worried about the danger of her husband's new occupation and hoped he would find a good job soon. She later recalled that Edwin would promise to reform. Perhaps he was trying.

On November 9, 1950, Boyd signed on with the City of Toronto Works Department on the street repair crew. The job was temporary, the pay only $1.10 an hour (considerably less than the hourly rate for robbing banks), and the tedium often seemed unbearable. But Boyd persevered, hoeing after the burner, scraping smooth the freshly laid hot asphalt, breathing the acrid smoke day after day.

Boyd's friend Gault was also taken on the crew, and the two men had many a secret laugh, wondering what their co-workers would think of their unorthodox avocation.

While Boyd toiled away at his honest, though dirty and unrewarding, job, Christmas and New Year's came and went, and the world around him changed. Newfoundland became Canada's tenth province. Canada adopted the North Atlantic Treaty. Ireland had severed her last ties with Britain by leaving the Commonwealth. "Axis Sally" and "Tokyo Rose", the infamous wartime propaganda broadcasters, had been convicted of treason and sent to prison.

But Boyd had not changed. He thought of his several successful robberies, the ease with which large sums of money could be aquired. He thought of the house he wanted to build on his lot in Pickering. He thought of his dirty and demeaning job.

He decided he was still a bank robber. When he went back to his chosen profession, he didn't tamper with the successful elements of his style.

He stuffed his cheeks with cotton. He reddened his face with lipstick. He carried his Luger. But now he had more confidence, more poise, and he was developing a flair that was unmistakable.

On March 19, 1951, when Boyd appeared in front of her cage wearing an engineer's hat and brandishing his Luger, Joyce Empey couldn't believe her eyes. It was the same bandit who had robbed the branch two years earlier.

This time he gave her no opportunity to stall or turn in the alarm. With incredible agility he jumped up on the counter and into the teller's cage, forcing Miss Empey away from the cash drawer while he cleaned it out himself.

Now Boyd was swifter, more assured, and much more alert than he had been the day George Elwood had emptied a pistol at him during his first escape from the bank. This time Boyd had an added advantage: Elwood was absent from work.

Quickly scooping up the money, Boyd snapped at the acting manager, "Don't push any alarms!" The man disregarded Boyd's warning and pressed a nearby button, but ruefully told reporters later, "It was all over in less than a minute and half, and there wasn't anything more I could do."

The newspapers gave the robbery front page coverage. The brashness of a thug who would hit the same bank twice provided a good angle to hook readers. The Toronto *Star* reported that "officials said he stole $6,000 and fled in an automobile which was last seen speeding at seventy miles an hour toward the city".

Flamboyant as he was, Boyd had more respect for the facts: "I got about $2,900, although the bank people said a lot more, but that is not right. I took this car right back to the spot where I got it. I don't think the owner knew it was used."

Perhaps the $2,900 was enough to satisfy his wants for the time being. Perhaps Boyd was again attempting to settle into an honest life. In any case, he kept his job with the city for another four months. Then on July 31, as he toiled away behind the burner, a passing truck angled too close and grazed him with a fender, knocking him down.

Boyd's shoulder was numb, but he wasn't too concerned until a policeman suggested that he go for a checkup at the hospital. The doctor probed him in several places, then announced that there was nothing wrong with him. But the pain worsened, so Boyd quit his job and applied to the Workmen's Compensation Board for benefits. When his claim was refused, he protested that they had cheated him. He later told Mayor Lamport that the treatment he received at that time caused him to return to crime.

Had Boyd's work situation been more encouraging, perhaps he would not have been so willing to take the risks involved in robbing banks. But the balance sheet was convincingly one-sided. He had been successful at crime, unsuccessful at employment. His job with the City, when it was full-time, netted about $500 a month; his last bank job—a few minutes of nervy action—had brought in almost $3,000.

For a time Boyd was preoccupied with the fulfillment of a long-held dream: owning his own home. He had acquired a Department of Veteran's Affairs lot in Pickering, just outside Toronto, and had begun to build a cement block bungalow on it. Although he was now out of work he had saved enough money to allow him to spend a comfortable summer working on the completion of his house. Boyd did most of the work on the house himself. According to Dorreen, he was "a jack-of-all-trades. He could do anything, fix plumbing, a car, anything."

During the spring and summer of 1951, while Boyd was immersed in the domestic atmosphere of cement blocks and roofing shingles, a gang of high-rolling bandits armed with submachine guns staged a series of Bonnie-and-Clyde-style holdups in and around Toronto.

One week after Boyd had hit the Bank of Montreal and threatened Miss Empey for the second time, armed bandits held up the Bank of Commerce in Colbourne, Ontario. The manager refused to open the vault, and was hit over the head. Three men escaped with $5,000.

The same thugs repeated their pattern of robbery in Woodbridge on May 10, and Mitchell on May 28, both small towns outside Toronto. In early July, as though taking a leaf from Boyd's notebook, the three struck for a second time at the Royal Bank in Woodbridge, exactly two months after their first success there.

The intrepid manager refused to open the vault. One of the bandits, all of whom wore Hallowe'en masks, ripped the telephone cord from the wall, while the others helped themselves to $6,000 in the tellers' cages.

There was no attempt to hide the fact that it was a repeat

performance. During the first robbery, one of the thugs had stood guard over Thelma Bell, a member of the staff. On July 9, he looked around at the staff, ordered them to hold up their hands, and then asked, "Where is Miss Bell today?" Miss Bell was not working at the time.

After a shootout with local police, during which one of the group was wounded, the robbers were reported to have made a rendezvous with two blondes in another car.

Boyd knew no more than what he read in the newspapers but was intrigued by the methods of his colleagues in crime. He had no idea that within a few months he would have extensive opportunity to compare notes with them, and that the conferences would take place while the government provided free room and board for them all.

Impressed with these accounts of armed robberies staged by a small gang, Boyd decided to form his own attack group. He called on his old friend Gault. He conscripted a third man and the three of them laid plans. They would hit the Lansing branch of the Dominion Bank on Sheppard Avenue.

Prior to that day, except for their distressing tendency to fire at him and give chase, bank employees had been relatively well behaved and had offered Boyd few problems. This time some unexpected quirks of human nature introduced new variations into the usual scenario.

It was a Saturday morning, September 1, and Boyd knew the bank closed at 11:00 a.m. He had watched a young female clerk every day for a week as she went out to a local grocery store, bought something for lunch, and came back to the bank. Today was no different, except that the manager was away getting married, and his replacement was inexperienced.

At 11:01, Helen Butler left the bank, and Boyd and his companions waited for her return. When they saw her coming back, they went into action.

Miss Butler later reported: "A very dirty man, who looked as if he might have been unloading coal earlier, waved a revolver under my nose, pushed me and told me to get into the bank." She did as she was told.

Unfortunately, she didn't move fast enough for Boyd, and he tried to hurry her up by grabbing her blouse as he forced her into the manager's office. The flimsy material tore in his rough grasp—an incident that made such a strong impression on Boyd that he later apologized for it.

While Boyd herded Miss Butler, two customers and the acting manager into the vault, Gault guarded the door. The third man, imitating Edwin's flashiest manoeuvre, leapt over the counter into the teller's cage.

The sight of the guns and the rough commands were too much for one staff member who had just returned to work after a nervous breakdown and a bout with pneumonia. "I ran into the cage nearest the door and dropped to the floor," she said. "I pretended I was fainting."

When Gault stepped into the cage to clean out the cash drawer, he couldn't resist a jibe at Boyd. "You're slipping," he called out. "Here's one of the staff on the floor. You better hurry up."

But the woman was no threat to the gang. "They didn't pay any attention to me after that. By that time I was so scared I almost had a real faint."

As they sped away in their stolen car, the thieves made a quick reckoning of their take. They were elated. It was the largest amount yet realized by Boyd, a total of $8,029.70. Abandoning the car in Hogg's Hollow on the outskirts of Toronto, the trio drove home unmolested in Boyd's truck.

Many months later, Robert Boyd,* Edwin's younger brother, was charged as the third man in the holdup. But in an ironic postscript to the story, the effectiveness of the disguises was proved and an extraordinary piece of good luck befell the younger Boyd.

The following Saturday, September 8, Miss Butler and another woman employee left the bank in the morning to go to a local restaurant. Conversation from a nearby table attracted their attention. One of the voices was strikingly familiar.

Could it be one of the thieves from the week before? After a hurried conference, they decided it was. The excited amateur detectives trailed the man outside and copied down the licence number of his truck.

Police later arrested twenty-six-year-old Francis Daniels* and placed him in a lineup for the two women to view. Both identified

*Pseudonym

him positively as the man who had held the gun on them at the rear of the bank.

Daniels was held in jail for a week. His firm, absolutely convinced of his innocence, posted $5,000 bail. When he was later cleared of the charges, he was so enraged he threatened to sue both women for false identification.

Unnerved by this threat, the women decided not to identify anyone at a subsequent lineup which included both Edwin and Robert Boyd. One of the women told the court, "I felt I had done enough damage by identifying someone."

In the absence of other evidence, the proven unreliability of these witnesses destroyed the Crown's case, and Robert Boyd was found not guilty on this charge.

By now Edwin Boyd was hooked. Robbing banks was too easy. He wanted to make a career of it. One day a bum stopped him on the street trying to panhandle a dime. Boyd said, "Why don't you get it the same way I do?" "How's that?" asked the bum. "Robbing banks," said Boyd, looking him straight in the eye. The bum stumbled off down the street, shaking his head, but Boyd had nothing but contempt for him.

> Those days were over. The Depression was finished, and the war was over, and there was lots of money floating around. I didn't bum as I used to in the Depression years. My way of living was robbing banks.

But Dorreen was anxious to settle down and live a normal life. She still loved Edwin very much. She had hopes and dreams for him, dreams that would never come true.

> If only he'd turned his mind to other things, he could have been the head of his own business in no time. He had the brains and the organizing ability. And he doesn't gamble. I don't think he's ever been to the race track.

But the race track is not the only place a man can play the odds. With five successes and one attempt under his belt, Boyd was used to gambling his freedom. On the morning of October 16, 1951, he was getting ready to make his seventh try.

> About 12:00 noon, me and Howard were sitting in my truck on north Yonge Street. About a week ago we planned to hold up a

store or something. Howard brought along his gun, and I brought my gun also. We drove around the city looking for a place to hold up.

Without thinking, Boyd pulled up in front of the Armour Heights Bank of Montreal that he had hit twice before. Suddenly they noticed the accountant peeking out the window at them. Boyd realized at once that he'd been recognized and wanted to call it quits for the day, but Howard goaded him into trying another bank.

We decided to hold up the bank at Lawrence and Yonge Streets. We drove to a parking lot opposite the Fairlawn [movie theatre] and stole a Chev sedan.

As a method of disguise, Gault carefully removed his false teeth, wrapped them in a somewhat soiled handkerchief, and left them on the seat of the truck. Boyd, who wore a bridge of four front teeth, did the same. Leaving the truck in the lot, the pair drove the sedan to the Dominion Bank.

Several unpredictable factors contributed to the outcome of Boyd's seventh bank attempt, but the most significant was his choice of Gault as an accomplice.

They were a mismatched pair from the beginning. While Boyd was an advocate and model of physical fitness, Gault was slow and overweight. Boyd had a stable and quiet family life; Gault was undisciplined and erratic. Boyd had learned to be cool and self-possessed, regardless of how nervous he was; Gault was excitable and easily rattled. In this instance, Gault proved to Boyd the folly of choosing bad companions.

At 12:45 p.m. Boyd and Gault entered the bank. Boyd jumped up on the accountant's desk. "Don't anybody move!" he yelled. "This is a stickup. We mean business."

The reaction was one he'd encountered several times before. "I thought he was fooling," said the bank manager, "but not for long. They made us all line up and told us not to move our heads."

One customer was fascinated by the cotton in Boyd's nostrils and his piercing, beady eyes. He looked like a monster, she thought. "Quit staring at me," snapped Boyd.

While Boyd herded the staff to the rear of the bank and kept them covered, Gault climbed into the two tellers' cages and cleaned out the drawers.

With his attention divided among Gault, the door of the bank, and the huddled employees, Boyd failed to notice Mrs. Adelene Jamieson, secretary to the manager, edging near the accountant's desk and pressing the alarm switch.

Mrs. Jamieson, whose late husband had been a bank manager, didn't think she was heroic, "just lucky, that's all". She didn't like the idea of two hoodlums walking out with a lot of money that didn't belong to them. When she noticed that one of them, undoubtedly Gault, seemed nervous, she decided to try for the alarm.

In previous holdups Boyd hadn't outsmarted the alarm system, he'd merely been lucky. It was betting against the odds to count on an alarm not being turned in while a robbery was in progress. And it was playing a long shot to count on the police always being too far away to show up before he could make a clean getaway.

Despite what Dorreen told the press, Ed Boyd *was* a gambler, a big one. This time his luck ran out.

In number 12 Police Station the alarm rang. The dispatcher immediately radioed all cars. Police Constables Walter McLean and Frank Skelly were patrolling in the vicinity and arrived at the bank within a minute.

Unnerved by Gault's slowness, Boyd had backed out of the door first. He didn't see his partner trip, drop the bag of money and stop to pick it up, but he did see Constable McLean across the street. Boyd made a dash for his car; so did McLean. They collided at the door and "the policeman landed on the road". Boyd jumped into the car and gunned the motor.

McLean drew his revolver and fired as Boyd pulled away from the curb. Boyd bobbed from side to side in the driver's seat, tramping on the accelerator in a desperate attempt to avoid the shots. A .38 slug slammed into the metal of the trunk, but Boyd wheeled the car away fast enough to escape.

Meanwhile, Skelly, sprinting down the laneway behind the bank, was already gaining on Gault who was fleeing across a vacant yard toward a used car lot eighty yards north. Skelly shouted to Gault to stop, but to no avail.

A third policeman arrived on his motorcycle in time to stop the footrace. He drew his revolver, leapt from his Harley-Davidson, and joined the chase.

> I saw . . . Gault running. He had this revolver . . . a .38 Smith and Wesson, in his hand, and a shopping bag in the other hand. He was wearing a cap and dark glasses. As I ran I fired some warning shots in his direction, and shouted to him to stop or be shot.

Gault may have been slow, he may have been unlucky, but he was no fool. He stopped. He dropped the revolver and shopping bag containing more than $12,800, and raised his hands.

Despite Gault's incompetence, Boyd had escaped. If his partner had been a seasoned criminal, his luck might have held, but Gault cracked readily under police interrogation.

Within half an hour, police radios crackled with orders to pick up a suspect in a red Chevrolet panel truck, licence 39650-C, with the name "E.A. Boyd" lettered on the sides.

Twenty-five minutes later, two detectives spotted Boyd's truck and followed it for several blocks. At gunpoint, they forced him to pull onto the shoulder of the road.

For Boyd there was no bluff that would work now. He might as well throw in his cards. In the waistband of his trousers, the detectives found a fully loaded .9mm German Luger with the action cocked and the safety catch applied.

"How did you get my number?" asked Boyd. "Did you get my pal?" While the officer searched his truck, Boyd told him, "You won't find any money there. My pal got it."

They didn't find any money in his truck but they did find other incriminating evidence. Detective Lorimer listed the following items in his notebook:

> 1 pr. of rubber gloves, 1 commando knife, one holster, several lengths of sash cord, a quantity of .9mm ammunition and .38 ammunition, 1 box of mascara, 1 lipstick, a towel and face cloth, a bar of soap, 1 black jack, 1 extra clip for Luger pistol, 3 road maps of greater Toronto.

In an excess of zeal, the officers also confiscated Gault's false teeth. Fortunately for him, the missing dentures were delivered to his cell a short time later.

The following day a squad of police officers, some of them carrying shovels, arrived at Boyd's home on Rosebank Road in Pickering. Dorreen could do nothing but stand by unhappily while they searched the house and dug up the back yard. They failed to unearth the loot they were searching for, but the newspapers reported that they did collect some evidence:

> ... several masks, some full face, which had been made to simulate the appearance of missing teeth. Another mask had a moustache painted on it. Also found were various types of makeup and rubber gloves.

While officers were raiding Boyd's home for evidence, detectives at the police station had identified the revolver found in Gault's possession as the property of the Dominion Bank at Dufferin and Glencairn. Gault confessed that he had held up that bank in July, and that Boyd had planned the heist. "Boyd did all right while he was working alone," a police officer told the *Telegram* that day, "but his operations started to go haywire when he got an accomplice."

The wave of robberies committed in and around Toronto by Boyd and others during 1950-51 was unprecedented. Local politicians and law enforcement agencies were justifiably concerned, and Toronto Police Chief John Chisholm appointed one of his top officers to investigate, Sergeant Adolphus "Dolph" Payne.

Payne was a tall, heavy set man with red hair, a slow, methodical manner of speech, and an engaging grin. He came from the small town of Orono, near Peterborough, and his temperament was classic rural Canadian—while friendly and ingenuous, and a great respecter of "common sense", he had an innate shrewdness and tenacity. He was the kind of character Gary Cooper might have played in a movie of the era.

Payne and Boyd first met on October 16, 1951. Their meeting was without fanfare, although circumstances were casting them as leading players in a drama that eventually captured the attention of the nation. Nevertheless, it was not a routine investigation. Closing seven big files on bank robbery was an important piece of policework, and Payne attacked it with characteristic patience and thoroughness. Boyd was questioned for a total of twelve hours. When the interrogation was over, Payne was ready to take Boyd into court on all seven occurrences, as soon as he had put the accused man through the tedious procedure of lineup and identification by bank staff and other witnesses.

Through his interrogation, Payne was able to balance the scale of justice a bit. The robberies Boyd and Gault confessed to included the one for which Peter Marino was already serving a sentence, and another for which the innocent Mr. Daniels had been remanded following identification by the two bank employees. Authorities immediately cleared the charges against Marino and Daniels.

Edwin Boyd was taken to the Don Jail to await his preliminary hearing. His string of luck had been broken, and as he marched through the stone corridors toward his cell he must have felt defeat—as though this were the final chapter in his personal story. In fact, it was only the prologue; the real beginning had been written just a few days earlier, and its protagonist was a princess.

LENNIE

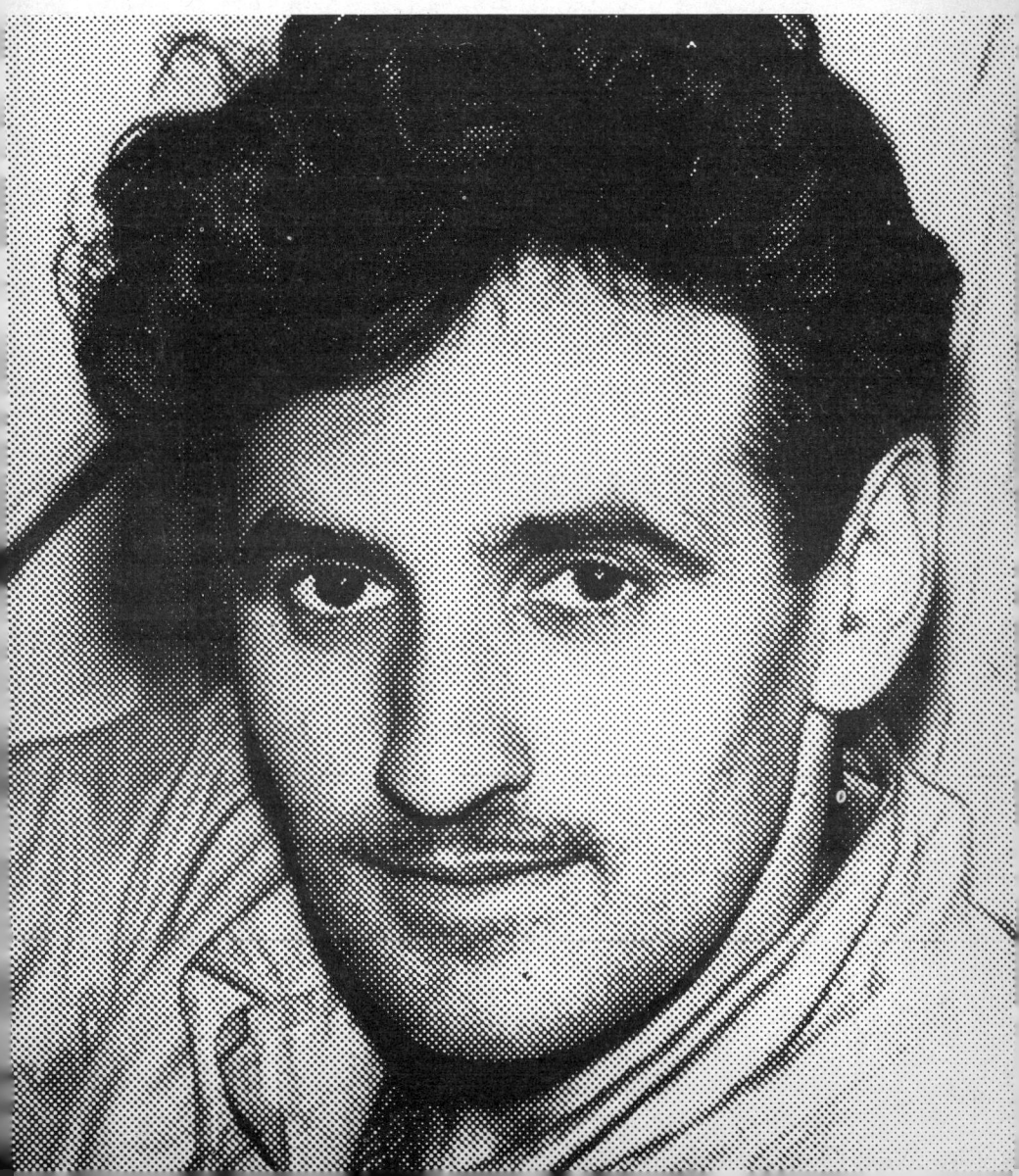

5

Toronto was alive with excitement. The young Princess Elizabeth, daughter of King George VI of Britain and the Commonwealth, was in Toronto with her husband Philip, Duke of Edinburgh. Toronto's population was still largely Anglo-Saxon, and there was no question about the treatment accorded British royalty. Only the best would do.

It was Saturday, October 13, 1951, and the crowds were often ten deep along the royal couple's parade route. Nearly every policeman in Toronto was on duty, lining the streets in anticipation of the enthusiastic greetings of the well-wishers and spectators. One of the biggest crowds of the day was on Broadview Avenue, where extra police and troops had to be brought into service for the occasion. Across the Don River Valley, 53,000 people waited in Riverdale Park.

Behind the high stone walls of the Don Jail, yards away from Broadview Avenue, plans had been made long in advance for a very special celebration of the royal visit.

A heavy backlog of appeals forced a record number of prisoners, destined for Kingston Penitentiary, to wait in the Don Jail. Guards had been watching carefully for any signs of a breakout attempt. If such an attempt were made, it wouldn't be the first.

In 1866, when the Don Jail was completed, Toronto residents were outraged by its grandeur. A great many citizens considered criminals the scum of society deserving nothing better than a dungeon. Some Torontonians were of the opinion that the new "Palace for Prisoners" was so spacious and modern that the occupants would be delighted to spend their days in its comfortable confines. However, experience proved otherwise.

The first prisoners kept in the institution were rebel Irishmen captured in the Fenian raids and led in shackles to their cells. For the next century, escape plots hatched within the walls of the prison matched in ingenuity and determination the jailers' attempts to keep prisoners locked away from the world.

The Spellman Gang of 1896 were the first to escape, followed by Frank McCullough, who drugged his guard, and Norman Neal who sawed his way out in 1926. Guards had searched Neal, and found five saw blades cached in his cell. Moved immediately to a different cell, Neal produced yet another blade and five days later sawed his way out.

In 1930, four young men went over the walls on blankets tied together. In 1934, a nineteen-year-old boy who couldn't bear the thought of spending his five-day sentence for shopbreaking in the Don, went over the wall on a rope thrown in by an accomplice. Once free, he jogged through nearby Riverdale Park in his undershirt and shorts. Passersby thought he was a marathon runner out practicing, and left him to flee unmolested.

The same year two other prisoners hacked through the roof of the jail, not long after a previous attempt had been foiled and extra guards put on them.

Throughout the thirties, several men had escaped by walking away from their assigned jobs outside the walls or slipping out the front door when delivery trucks came in with groceries.

Allan Baldwin, convicted in 1944 of bank robbery, beat his guard with a lead pipe and strangled him, escaping from the prison hospital. When caught, he was convicted of manslaughter.

An acrobatic effort by the Polka Dot Gang ended in failure after a valiant attempt. They overpowered two guards in the exercise yard and hoisted each other up the wall pyramid-fashion. Armed guards met them at the top and they were forced to go back down the same way they had gone up. Sergeant Edmund Tong, who was later to figure prominently in the Boyd Gang saga, was responsible for the eventual breakup and capture of the Polka Dot Gang.

Interspersed with escapes from the Don Jail were episodes of drug traffic, bribery, murder, and corruption. By 1928, Toronto city council was asking for a provincial governmental investigation into the administration of the jail. A grand jury called the prison "a disgrace to the city". The investigation was shelved, but various outcries were raised every few years complaining about the laxness of security, the riots, death and scandals. Every year jail reforms were mentioned, but postponed to accommodate more pressing needs. Meanwhile prisoners continued to cut, saw, sneak, bribe, bludgeon and break their way out of the old Don Jail.

Prisoners might have been less enthusiastic in their attempts to escape from the Don had they been acquainted with its history. From the time of the first escape until the day Princess Elizabeth arrived in town, not one prisoner had escaped custody permanently. Some were captured within minutes or hours, some were out for days and a few lived on the lam for weeks, but every fugitive was eventually escorted back to the jail.

But in prisoner Leonard Jackson's cell block the inmates weren't concerned with history. Their main interest lay in the details of the royal tour schedule. The bars of their cell windows had already been cut with a hacksaw blade and patched with soap and shoe polish. The escape would be simple.

As soon as Princess Elizabeth and the duke passed, Jackson and several of his cronies would slip out through the windows and escape along the Don Valley, merging unobtrusively with the confusion of the cheering crowds.

The guards at the Don Jail had been accused of every kind of stupidity, error, cunning, disinterest and corruption. But the pay was low and the work tedious most of the time, dangerous the rest. Good help was hard to get. On the second floor corridor where several notorious criminals awaited transfer to Kingston, the guards were not especially well-trained or competent. But several days before the princess was scheduled to pass by, they discovered the cuts in the bars.

Detectives from the Toronto Police Department were called in to investigate. Every prisoner was searched but no blades found. The source and the hiding place of the blades remained a mystery to officials for five months.

Although Leonard Jackson was disappointed, he knew there would be another chance. The next time he'd do it right, and he wouldn't wait long for the opportunity.

Jackson had been born Leonard Stone in 1923, the son of a Jewish mother and an English father. His older brother and sister had been born Jacksons in his mother's first marriage. Her second marriage had produced three Stone children. When Lennie was six years old his mother took the children to live in Niagara Falls. Perhaps to prevent any stigma arising from the use of two names in a small community, it was decided that they would all adopt the name Jackson. Lillian Jackson established her own business as a hairdresser in Niagara Falls and was successful enough to provide a reasonable standard of living for her family.

Lennie's formal education was a mixture of disciplines. He attended the Church of England Sunday School as a boy. For a while he went to night classes to learn wood carving, and made a taboret which stood in his mother's living room for years. By the end of the eighth grade Lennie had had enough of conventional education.

At fourteen he got a job as a farm labourer, adding his meagre wages to the family income. Although a fun-loving teenager, Lennie could not have been described as wild. He didn't drink, and didn't go out with girls until much later than his peers. His favourite pastimes were picnics and swimming.

The police chief of Niagara Falls never saw Lennie's name on his books. In 1931, a break and enter conviction against his brother Sam Stone (as he gave his name) was the first hint of trouble in the family. Sam was sent to Victoria Industrial School in Mimico, Ontario. Lennie was young and impressionable and perhaps idolized his older brother too much. It wasn't many years before he followed in Sam's footsteps.

In 1937, Sam was sentenced to two years in Kingston Penitentiary on various charges of shopbreaking and theft. The same month Lennie was picked up a few thousand miles away in El Paso, Texas. The charge: violation of immigration laws. He was deported back to Canada.

But the wanderlust in Lennie was not so easily quelled. Living on odd jobs, travelling and eating when and how he could, Lennie wandered through the United States during the Depression.

While Edwin Boyd was learning the ropes in the Prince Albert Penitentiary, Leonard Jackson was arrested for loitering, sleeping in public, and immigration violation everywhere from Texas to New York. These were all minor offences, but Lennie was picking up a few tricks that Boyd already knew. One rule of the trade they used in later years with a good measure of success: when apprehended by the law, give any name but your own. In Waycross, Georgia, Leonard Jackson became for a few days Robert Kent, hobo.

Jackson returned to Toronto when the war broke out and at seventeen joined the Royal Regiment of Canada. Al Bird, later instructor at the provincial police college in Toronto, served in the army with Jackson during the war. It was he who taught Lennie how to shoot, but as far as he was concerned, Lennie was "just another soldier". Constable Bird told the *Telegram*: "Jackson wasn't any better shot than any of the other soldiers."

Jackson was overseas for more than four years. During this period he was plagued with recurring attacks of bronchitis, hay fever and asthma, and spent many days and nights wheezing and sniffing in an effort to breathe. It was a great disappointment to him that his asthma forced him to miss the raid on Dieppe. In 1944 he was finally discharged from the Royal Regiment because of his illness.

Leonard promptly joined the Merchant Navy. Here was action and adventure, and he loved it. At one point his ship was torpedoed and he spent several chilly hours in the water; he was eventually rescued, cold and wet but unharmed. His fate was not to die in the service of his country. When the war ended the following year, Jackson went home to Ontario.

Finding little to do in Toronto and even less in Niagara Falls, Lennie went travelling again. Although he'd had a little trouble with police on his last tour through Canada and the United States, he had enjoyed the adventure. Of course, there was no question about his mode of travel—Lennie Jackson rode the rods.

The day in 1948 that changed Lennie's life forever began casually enough. Hanging around the train tracks at the foot of Strachan Avenue in Toronto, Lennie planned to hop the next westbound freight to anywhere. Wherever the train was headed was sure to be more exciting than where he was now. Of course one had to be careful not to be seen by any of the police or railway supervisors, but sometimes a casual employee would close his eyes if he saw you waiting for a train with no ticket. Not that you could hang around the station. You had to be a little way down the track and hop on just before the train got up speed.

The whistle blew, and a train chuffed out of the station. Lennie started to run alongside. The train was going faster than he had calculated. He'd have to hurry. He grabbed for the railing and swung his foot up. His toe barely caught the edge of the step.

The rest happened so quickly he didn't have time to panic. The weight of his body lurching off the step caused him to lose his grip on the railing. With a thud he hit the ground. Gasping to catch his breath, Lennie felt a dull throbbing in his ankle.

By the time he could look up the train had passed. On the sooty ground beside the tracks Jackson saw his bloody, lifeless left foot. Shortly after, in hospital, he was given a clean amputation just above the left ankle.

For six months he languished in bed, first in hospital, then at his mother's home. When he finally felt well and confident enough to go out on an artificial foot, he decided he needed some skill to make an honest living.

The Department of Veterans' Affairs offered a program of vocational training. Influenced and encouraged by his mother, Jackson took a six-month course in hairdressing. Once qualified he went to work in his mother's shop.

Hairdressing was steady, but it wasn't exciting. There was little to interest him in Niagara Falls. His brother Sammy, known to police as Sam Stone, was no sooner released from Kingston Pen, where he had served a six-year sentence for armed robbery, assault with bodily harm and intent to escape, than he was back in for shopbreaking and theft. His older sister Mary was now Mrs. Mitchell, but at that point she and Lennie had little in common.

For a while, Lennie patiently washed, curled and combed the heads of the ladies who patronized Lillian Jackson's hairdressing salon. When he grew restless he would talk to his older brother Ben.

Ben felt that Lennie's attitude had changed since his accident. "I know he found it difficult to work in my mother's store," he said. "He complained to me the constant standing on his artificial foot hurt him." He became moody and irritable. When his mother finally asked what was bothering him, Lennie hung his head in his hands.

"He wasn't happy because his chums had been killed in the war," recalled Mrs. Jackson. "He said he planned to leave and he did."

Toronto offered the attractions and distractions Jackson was looking for, and he soon found a job as barboy in the Horseshoe Tavern.

Toronto was just beginning to expand as a cosmopolitan city. When the Horseshoe opened in December 1947, it was only the fourth open bar in Toronto. The Silver Rail had been first followed by the Club Normand and the Metropole, where Billy O'Connor led his group in nightly entertainment.

O'Connor had introduced the popular song "Slow Boat to China" in Canada, and sang a special version for Torontonians, entitled "Slow Boat to Centre Island". The Liquor Board had strict regulations about entertainment in bars and O'Connor recalls that there were no singalongs allowed.

> We had to do novelty songs. We put new lyrics to old songs for comedy. . . . We'd do something a little blue, but you couldn't get rough. The words all had double meanings.

By the time Billy O'Connor began playing in the Holiday Tavern at Queen and Bathurst Streets, Toronto's nightlife had become a little more exotic. It was here that O'Connor met Leonard Jackson's sister, Mary Mitchell, who was working there part-time as a hostess.

> She always made sure the boys in the band and myself had a drink when the customers weren't sending them up . . . a very, very nice girl. . . . She always had immaculately done hair, a lovely dresser, lots of dark clothes, earrings and necklace. She was classy and beautiful, and very well-spoken. I always felt she was above the Holiday Tavern.

Mary Mitchell had a friend, Ann Roberts, a model, who stayed with her on weekends. Born Audrey Ann Warburton in South Shields, Durham, England in 1927, Ann had been married at the age of nineteen. When she and her husband arrived in Toronto on the first day of 1948, their marriage was already shaky. By June they had separated. "Shortly after that my husband sued for divorce, and this divorce was granted and became final in May 1951. This divorce was a mutual agreement on the grounds of my having committed adultery. I did not defend it."

Mary used to drop by the Horseshoe Tavern quite often to see her brother. One day in May 1950, she brought along her friend, Ann. By September, Lennie and Ann had set up housekeeping in an apartment on Sackville Street. Lennie's job at the Horseshoe paid only about fifty dollars a week, so Ann continued to work as a model.

At that time the Horseshoe was a small establishment: the bar and the dining room each seated seventy-five people, and the music was not yet country and western for which the tavern eventually became famous. In the early years it was a gathering place for moguls of the garment industry. Clothing manufacturers would come in with beautiful models on their arms.

"Big Jack", a waiter at the Horseshoe since the day it opened, remembers Jackson with affection. "Lennie was the type of guy everybody got along with. We got along real well. We never had an argument."

Jackson wasn't at the Horseshoe long before he knew its steady customers. His friendly manner and ready smile made him a favourite with patrons. He drank little and was known to disapprove of off-colour stories, but was fascinated by the group of regulars who sat at the back of the tavern.

Included in the group were such well-known thugs as Frank Watson and Eddie MacDonald, and others carrying large money rolls in the packets of flashy suits. They always pulled up in huge new cars, spent a lot of money and left generous tips for the boys at the Horseshoe. Sometimes they would come in every day for a week, but never in the evenings.

In the motley mix of types who frequented the tavern, one man was recognized by all. The moment the door opened and "The Chinaman" walked in, all talk of criminal activities ceased. "Hi Tong. Buy ya a drink!" someone invariably called from the back of the room. And Sergeant of Detectives Edmund Tong would pull up a chair.

Tong was a Welshman and ex-rugby player who had worked his way up through the ranks of the Toronto Police Department. His straight black hair and Oriental-sounding name soon earned him the nickname, "The Chinaman". A big man with florid complexion, Tong was well-liked by his colleagues and even by some of the criminal types he dealt with every day. He had a reputation for having more underworld informants than any other man on the force, and he would never say a word about any of them.

Jack Gillespie, who worked with Tong, remembers him as a

tenacious investigator with a wide circle of acquaintances. Says Gillespie:

> Tong gave everybody a fair shake, but he was never rough.... He used to watch criminals from taverns. He knew all the crooks and prostitutes and so on all over town. He was always slipping five dollars to some rounders down on their luck—he couldn't afford it, he had a family to support.

Gillespie would go along with Tong when he was looking for someone, but Tong wouldn't tell even his partner where they were going or how he knew where to go. When an unsavoury character came up to Toronto from the United States, Tong would know about it as soon as he arrived, if not before. "Come on Reilly," he'd say to Gillespie, "let's go." "Where to?" asked Gillespie, but Tong just put on his coat and smiled. And Gillespie, who was called Reilly by no one but Tong, would hop in the car and the two of them would drive over to some tavern and wait outside.

When his target came out of the tavern, Tong would follow the car, then signal it to pull over. "Hi Mike," he'd say, "how ya doing?" And Mike would know that Tong knew he was there and would be watching him. This was Tong's own method of preventive medicine.

So it wasn't unusual for Tong to stop in and have a drink with the Horseshoe Tavern gang. As Gillespie remembers: "Tong would go and sing a few bars of a song in a tavern with some rounders, and a few hours later he'd be locking them up."

Through his job at the Horseshoe Leonard Jackson became acquainted with representatives of both sides of the law. He was an assiduous student. It was soon obvious who had the money, the clothes, the cars and the women. It didn't take long for Jackson to make his choice.

On July 2, 1951, Lennie Jackson and Ann Roberts moved to a cottage at Musselmans Lake, northeast of Toronto. On July 10, Jackson left the cottage to meet three men, one of them Frank Watson, whom he knew from the Horseshoe Tavern. Their destination: Woodbridge, Ontario. This was not the first trip the group had made to the town; on May 10 they had driven to Woodbridge and come away with $9,646.

Now on this hot July morning Hugo Abel, operator of an egg

grading station at Woodbridge, stood in line with his $500 for deposit in the Royal Bank of Canada. Mr. H.N.Smith also carried a roll of bills from a local business. It was 10:15 a.m.

As Jackson and his friends entered the bank, they pulled their black Hallowe'en masks up over their faces. Dressed in coveralls, they were almost unidentifiable. However, when one of the bandits asked for Miss Bell, the staff knew immediately it was the same gang that had robbed them two months earlier.

"Stay where you are!" came the rough command as one of the men yanked the telephone off the wall. The others pointed their guns at manager Glen Newans, demanding that he open the vault. Newans nervously pretended he couldn't work the combination. The gunmen became impatient and held their revolvers to Newans' head. With amazing bravado, the manager convinced them he couldn't open the vault.

Time was running out so the thieves grabbed the cash from the tellers' drawers. Mr. Smith, as soon as he realized what was happening, nonchalently stuffed his roll of bills down the front of his pants. Mr. Abel was not so lucky. One of the gang grabbed his $500. "Don't worry," said the robber, "the bank will be responsible."

The three turned to leave, almost colliding with a customer just coming in the door. "Turn around!" demanded the gunman, pointing a .45 colt at the man's stomach. The customer was too stunned to move. Jabbing him with his gun, the robber ordered him out of the way. "I wasn't going to argue with a .45," recalled the customer. "It would blow a hole in me as big as a tin can."

Fortunately for him, he had the presence of mind to close his fist around the ten ten-dollar bills he carried and quietly put his hand in his hip pocket. Unfortunately for the bank, the thieves escaped with more than $6,000.

As Jackson and the group jumped in their waiting getaway car, the bank manager and a young accountant grabbed the bank guns and ran outside.

The alarm from the bank rang in nearby Henderson's Drug Store. There the clerk, following instructions to the letter, immediately phoned the police. The phone rang once, twice, three times; it continued to ring. Where was the operator? Why wouldn't she answer?

The thugs were now speeding towards Thistletown with Newans and the accountant in hot pursuit. Cutting in and out of traffic in the small town, the gang took to the sideroads.

When the operator finally answered the clerk's call, the response was swift and precise. Provincial Police from Aurora and Port Credit were now setting up roadblocks in a ring around the whole area. Two inspectors who were still investigating the May 10 robbery rushed from Toronto to the scene of the crime. Already police were questioning every motorist anywhere near the bank. The roadblock routine had been worked out since the previous holdup in case of another attempt, but obviously they were too late.

The first holdup had involved some shooting by the gang—fortunately no one was injured—but this time the robbers were so well organized they simply sped away and disappeared.

Newans and the accountant never got close enough even to read the licence number of the getaway car, and the prevailing confusion resulted in the car being identified first as green, and later as gray.

A local farmer reported that he had seen two blonde girls, wearing slacks, sitting in a car parked on the seventh concession. Speculation in the newspapers was that the girls had supplied the gunmen with a second car for the escape. This spicy item added fuel to the growing public interest in the daring and flamboyant style of bank robbery becoming increasingly common.

Jackson, who had previously owned only second-hand cars, turned in his old black Pontiac with "extras" and was now driving a 1950 metallic blue Oldsmobile Rocket. Lennie couldn't resist the impulse to display his sudden wealth. He returned to the Horseshoe Tavern to show the staff.

The boss had offered Lennie more money to stay at the Horseshoe, but it soon became obvious that the tavern could no longer afford him. Big Jack remembers:

> After he left here for a while, he pulls up in this big Oldsmobile, flashing a big roll. He never said nothing about how he got the money. . . . The gang didn't come in so much after they made their money. The heat was on. They were good customers, good spendors, good tippers. What they did was their business. We knew they must have been a racket, naturally.

It was about this time that Ann Roberts first met a friend of Lennie's, Steve Suchan, whom she knew only as "Val". Suchan arrived at Musselman's Lake one afternoon and stayed several hours. Although she hadn't met the man before, it seemed to Ann that Suchan was a very close friend of Lennie's. It was only much later that she learned what their real connection was.

On July 26, Jackson left the cottage early in his big blue Oldsmobile Rocket. On the seat beside him was a Thompson sub-machine gun.

6

It was a hot and muggy summer day in the marsh-farming village of Bradford, forty miles north of Toronto. Constable Reginald Wilson of the Ontario Provincial Police was off duty that day, July 26, 1951. He was out for a stroll.

The staff of the Bradford Bank of Commerce felt secure in their excellent circumstances. Directly across the street from the bank was the Bradford Police Station. Constable Wilson lived in the apartment above the bank. The bank windows faced Highway 11 and Holland Street, virtually the centre of town.

Around 2:00 p.m., Wilson observed a man pacing nervously between the bank entrance and a parked car. Wearing a striped railroader's cap, dark glasses, gray cotton gloves, and spotlessly clean overalls, the stranger was glaringly conspicuous.

Wilson casually but quickly walked up the outside staircase to his apartment. Without even acknowledging his wife's curious questions, he grabbed his revolver and loaded it.

Inside the bank, the holdup was going smoothly. One teller had quickly locked up her cash drawer when she saw what was happening, but the thieves were undaunted. Two men vaulted the counters and blocked off three tellers' cages. A third man guarded the staff and customers, forcing them to lie on the floor.

"What the heck is this?" demanded the bank manager, but he too went down on the floor when he saw the guns.

The entire staff remembered being impressed by the size of the weapons the thieves carried, but none could guess the calibre.

One woman customer with a small child fell to her knees and began praying. As the accountant raised his head, the leader of the gang shouted, "Keep it down. You're seeing too damn much! What do you think this is, a play or something?"

Jimmying the tellers' drawers with screwdrivers, one thief seized $4,200, which he put in his carpenter's apron, the other, nothing. Teller J.A. Rose, who was out to lunch, had emptied his cash drawer before leaving. The thieves began to panic. The third teller had a large sum of money in his cash drawer, but it was never touched.

"Let's get out of here," shouted the leader, and all hell broke loose on the streets.

A bank customer reported: "Just as they were leaving, one of the tellers came to his feet from behind the counter, and a shot was fired that went through the glass just over his head. We all stayed in the bank until the shooting was over."

A woman walking on Holland Street was grabbed by the arm and pushed by a man rushing out of the bank. Terrified, she raced away as soon as he slackened his hold.

Constable Wilson ran from his apartment and was greeted by a hail of bullets. Four shots whistled over his head. One smashed into the doorjamb, inches from his chest. Crouching low to avoid being hit, Wilson heard another bullet plow a furrow into the stucco wall.

Two locals watched the action from inside the hardware store. "Someone ran in here while the gunfight was on," recalled one, "grabbed a baseball bat and threw it at one of the gunmen. There were lots of shotguns here but it happened so fast no one had a chance to grab one."

Still shooting and cursing, the thieves jumped in their car and tramped on the gas. With a sickening crunch they hit the side of a panel truck parked on the street. Throwing the car in reverse, the driver swung around the truck and roared away.

But the momentary delay gave Constable Wilson a chance. He fired four times, each shot slamming into the fast-disappearing vehicle. One shot, he thought, might have hit one of the men. His last two shots went wild, and the getaway car pulled out of sight.

Tearing down the stairs, Wilson leaped into his car and raced away in hot pursuit. Speeding south on Highway 11, he came to within a quarter-mile of the fleeing vehicle but was unable to catch it. Police cruisers were already on the scene in Bradford, but were too late to help in the chase.

The bullet-riddled sedan, which proved to be a stolen car, was found parked on a sideroad, the engine still hot, with no trace of the gang who had abandoned it and fled in another vehicle.

The gang split the loot and separated quickly. Lennie Jackson went home to Musselman's Lake. Within hours he and Ann Roberts had packed their bags and left the vicinity. Their home was to be a cottage in Paradise Camp at Orillia, Ontario.

By the following day, police were already holding one man on a vagrancy charge, hoping to connect him with the case, and were extending their search to Musselman's Lake. Obviously in receipt of information, they told newspapers the thieves might have a hide-out somewhere in the resort area.

Perhaps fearing police were closing in on him, or estimating that his chances were better in the city, Jackson left Ann at the cottage and headed for Toronto.

Unknown to Jackson, Detective Tong had been relentlessly working on his case for months. In late January, Jackson and his gang had robbed the Dominion Bank at Dovercourt and Davenport in Toronto and had escaped with $10,000. Tong had been assigned to the case immediately, and had been working undercover ever since. Within hours after the robbery he had arrested two men, Louis Stavroff and Tony Brunet, who were already serving fifteen-year prison terms.

On July 28, two other suspects were arrested on Jarvis Street in Toronto. In a raid on their rooming house, police found two walkie-talkies radios and highly detailed maps of the Bradford Bank of Commerce and surrounding area. The press began referring to the thieves as the "Numbers Mob" after police revealed that the gang may have used walkie-talkies for calling signals, much like a football team. They spoke of a "mastermind" who controlled the group from a distance.

The *Telegram* described the *modus operandi*:

After directing the operations at the scene of the robbery, the mastermind checks road blocks and escape routes, and radios the best road for the bandits to use.

Inspector John Nimmo declared:

We know these men are local thugs. They are well organized and have taken to using radio communication in an attempt to escape police. But they are not imported crooks, and there is no master criminal other than the ordinary leader of the **gang**.

Lennie Jackson was still at large. On July 30, 1951, the *Globe* reported that the resort hide-out tip, given police by two women, was false. That day, Detectives Tong and Gillespie with two other officers followed up information leading to an address on Roncesvalles Avenue in Toronto. Jackson was supposed to be on the third floor. The group went in with their arrest warrant. Much to their disappointment, however, the rooms were empty. Without much hope they trooped out of the house, some out of the front, some out of the back. "Just as we were leaving," recalls Gillespie, "who do we see coming up the lane at the back but Lennie Jackson!"

Spotting the police, Lennie fled down the back lane, Tong in pursuit and another officer close behind. With Tong gaining on him, Lennie knew he had to get rid of the evidence he was carrying. A car was parked in the lane, its windows open to the hot summer breeze. Without a backward glance, Jackson threw a paper-wrapped bundle in the front seat.

Even with one wooden foot Jackson was a fast runner. Tong chased him to Boustead Avenue. Jackson was fading. With a flying tackle, the ex-rugby player lunged for Jackson. The pair went down. A scuffle ensued. Lennie's face was cut above the eye. Struggling and protesting, Jackson was handcuffed and arrested. Taking no further chances with his slippery prisoner, Tong wedged Jackson in between himself and another officer in the rear seat of the cruiser.

About the same time that Jackson was taken to Toronto Police headquarters, another squad of city and provincial police were bringing in Frank Watson. He had been sleeping in his apartment when police handcuffed him "before he knew what was happening".

Jackson and Watson were charged with armed robbery of the Bank of Commerce at Bradford. Had Tong not seen Jackson throw the package into the car, he might never have recovered the $1,500 wrapped in paper; the owner of the car, it developed, planned to leave for Kapuskasing that afternoon.

Included in the list of robberies for which the men were under suspicion were banks at Mitchell, Woodbridge, Colborne and Pickering. If Jackson had confined his activities to banks outside Toronto, he would not have had the tenacious Tong on his trail and might have eluded capture far longer. Now he was held without bail and placed in police lineups for identification by bank employees.

Ann Roberts heard the news on the radio. She had never heard of Frank Watson and claimed she had no idea how Lennie was making a living, although "he always had enough money for our regular needs, and always had an automobile". Desperate, she could think of only one friend to whom she could turn for advice. She phoned Steve Suchan.

Anna Bosnich, Suchan's girlfriend, answered the phone and invited Ann to her house on Wright Avenue. Suchan was there when she arrived and seemed to know all about the situation. He told her Jackson had been sent to jail in Barrie, Ontario.

On August 21, Detectives Gillespie and Tong stood on the courthouse steps at Bradford. As Jackson was brought up to the courthouse, he paused on the steps, turned to Tong and said, "We'll get you. Your time's coming." Used to threats, Tong just laughed. Jackson entered the courtroom and was there committed for trial. Sergeant Tong did not give evidence.

By the time Ann Roberts, was able to go to Barrie, Jackson had been transferred to Toronto's Don Jail.

On September 25, Jackson was brought before the York County Magistrate's Court. Sergeant Tong sat at the Crown counsel's table directly in front of the prisoner's dock. Again Jackson was committed for trial. He was still held without bail.

Eventually, through Tong, Ann was allowed to visit Lennie at the Don Jail, and continued to do so twice a week. In her statement to police she said:

Up to the time of [Leonard's] arrest for bank robbery, I had never seen him with a gun, had never heard him talk about a gun, and had never seen him with a large sum of money. From the time I met Leonard until the time he was arrested we did not associate with anyone. When we went out we went out together, we did not have any visitors come to our home, and we did not receive any phone calls, although there was a phone in the house."

On several of her visits to the jail, Ann was accompanied by Steve Suchan. She was now living with Mary Mitchell and Steve would stop to talk to them as he picked up Ann and drove her back in his girlfriend Anna Bosnich's car. Anna was then four months pregnant with his child. Uninhibited by this circumstance, Suchan began showing increasing interest in the beautiful Mary Mitchell.

WILLIE & VAL

7

Steve Suchan was born Valent Kozak in 1928 in Czechoslovakia. He came to Canada with his mother when he was eight years old; his father had arrived several years earlier. His parents, Sam and Charlotte Kozak,* named him Valent because he was born on Valentine's Day. He later changed his name for fear of bringing shame to his family.

Val first lived in Smooth Rock Falls, a small mining town in Ontario. He went to public school in the country and then moved to Cochrane, Ontario for his high school education. Living in a boarding house on Arthur Street, he visited his parents when he could and wrote them letters about his progress in school.

His major interest was in playing the violin, for which he displayed a considerable talent. His classmates remember him as a quiet and timid boy. One fellow student described him as a "tight-lipped fellow, rarely speaking unless he was spoken to. Few people knew where he came from or where his parents were. His friends thought he had a sense of fairness. He was known to defend weaker boys from bullies at school."

Another classmate remembered: "He was such a quiet boy. Val was well liked by all the students. He was the kind of fellow who would go out of his way to avoid injuring anyone."

Once, he and some friends got hold of an old .38 revolver and went out to try some shooting. Val was very frightened, and wrapping his arms around a tree trunk, pulled the trigger with both hands. It was the first time he had ever held a gun.

As he grew more accomplished as a violinist, Val played first with the school orchestra and then with his equally quiet and shy

*Pseudonym

girlfriend, who accompanied him on the piano. The two played duets for high school graduations and parties.

In June 1946, feeling that Cochrane could offer him little more in the way of musical training, Val moved to Toronto.

Just out of high school and with no vocational skills, Val found a job with the Crystal Glass and Plastics Company. Alone in Toronto, he made few friends, but continued to study the violin. One person he came to know well was George Kindness, of George B. Kindness and Son, 5-A Walton Stret, violin-makers. Val frequently went to the shop for repairs and adjustments to his violin and would often exchange pleasantries with the proprietor. In 1949 he went to the shop to exchange more than pleasantries: he traded his violin for a .455 Smith and Wesson revolver and a little cash.

In a later statement to police, Mr. Kindness noted that Val "had seen this weapon, and about August, 1949, stated that he was going out West, and would like to dispose of his violin. Since that time I have had other dealings with [Suchan] in connection with violins, but have had no dealings with him in connection with firearms."

Kindness was careful to point out to police that he had complied with all necessary laws in making the trade of the revolver for the violin. He even obtained permission from the Ontario Provincial Police to make the trade. Val Kozak became the legal owner of a deadly weapon.

Val had been unable to make a living playing the violin, the only thing he enjoyed and could do well. Perhaps he was frustrated by the series of short-term, dead-end jobs he had taken since arriving in Toronto. In any case Val, now going under the alias Steve Suchan, began passing bad cheques.

On March 3, 1950, Steve Suchan was tried on six counts of fraud, attempted fraud, and issuing forged cheques. He was found guilty on all counts and sentenced to the Ontario Reformatory for three months on each charge, concurrent sentences. A naive boy of twenty-two when he went in, Steve Suchan left the institution having acquired a degree of criminal sophistication.

Nevertheless, he immediately set out to find a legitimate job, using his real name.

After working for two months in the shipping department of the Standard Chemical Company of Leaside, Val got a job at the King

Edward Hotel. On December 30, 1950, he became an elevator operator for $4.90 per day, working a forty-eight-hour week.

In October he had met Anna Bosnich, a real estate agent, on a blind date. Anna was separated from her husband and had an eight-year-old daughter. She enjoyed the attentions of the younger man, Val, and they began dating occasionally.

In February 1951, Anna bought a new black Monarch Sport sedan with extras such as wheel rings, heater, and undercoating. The total price, including gas, licence and glycol, was $3,003.81. She was obviously doing well in her business.

Val was promoted to doorman at the hotel. Although the pay was less, the tips more than made up for it. His relationship with Anna deepened.

Anna Bosnich remembers that they would go out to taverns and movies. "While with him I met a number of his acquaintances, but he would always introduce them by their first names, and I did not get to know their last names."

It was about this time that Val Kozak, doorman and struggling violinist, finally gave way to Steve Suchan, professional gangster. In the spring of 1951, he met Leonard Jackson at the King Edward Hotel. They became good friends, and soon Suchan was involved in Jackson's lucrative bank-robbing business. Unlike Jackson, Suchan had the advantage of not being known to police.

On May 9, 1951, three men armed with tommy guns held up the Royal Bank in Woodbridge. Two weeks later, Suchan quit his job. More robberies were commited over the summer.

Anna Bosnich remembers that Steve

> would not remain at home living with me all this time, but would stay for a day or so and then return to his own home. However, in the month of July, 1951, he did live at my home for three weeks, as he was under quarantine with chicken pox, which he had contracted from my nine-year-old daughter.

It was the end of July when Steve visited Lennie Jackson and Ann Roberts at their summer cottage. It was July 26 that Jackson and accomplices hit the bank at Bradford. A few days later, Jackson was arrested and Suchan went back to live with Anna.

It was then that he met Mary Mitchell. He was fascinated by her. His trips to the Don with Ann Roberts gave him ample opportunity to pursue his interest in Mary, and he began spending less and less time with Anna.

Mary often visited Lennie too, and sometimes would deliver a message to Suchan. It was Steve who obtained the bolt that Len needed to replace the one in the window screen they'd had to saw through. But Suchan was too nervous to throw it over the jail wall, and Mary performed the task for him. She put the bolt in a cigarette package, and when the prisoners were scheduled for their daily walk around the bull ring, an accomplice of Lennie's walked around stepping on all the cigarette packages until he found one that didn't crumple under his feet.

Suchan knew that escape was imminent. On the night of November 4, he should have been waiting at a prearranged apartment with the getaway car. But on that particular Sunday night, he succumbed to the charms of Mary Mitchell, and forgot about his appointment.

8

Oblivious to events outside the confines of the Don Jail, Leonard Jackson plotted his escape. In less than a month he had made his first abortive attempt. As welders worked to repair the bars, Edwin Boyd and Howard Gault were discussing plans for another holdup. A few days later, Boyd was ushered into the Don and became Jackson's neighbour. A new set of possibilities opened up for both of them.

The following week, a second fateful meeting took place when William R. Jackson (no relation to Leonard) joined Boyd and Jackson in their cell block. Willie was awaiting transfer to Kingston. Not as bright as Ed and Lennie, Willie nevertheless was a carefree companion who loved telling jokes, and kept the two entertained with stories from his criminal history.

William Russell Jackson was born in 1925, not far from where he was now incarcerated in the Don Jail. Confrontation with the law began early as a tough kid in Cabbagetown. By the age of twelve he had skipped so much school that the Children's Aid Society was assigned to supervise his activities. Within six months he was in reform school for theft.

At sixteen he was charged with vagrancy in Montreal. At eighteen he tried to steal a car, was caught and given a suspended sentence with two years probation. Thus far the authorities had been relatively lenient with young Willie, but when he broke probation within two months, he was sent to the Ontario Reformatory for ninety days.

By 1945 William R. Jackson had established the pattern that was to keep him in jail for most of the next six years. His specialty was robbery and his method was violence. He spent two years in the Manitoba Penitentiary in Winnipeg. In 1948 he was charged with three counts of robbery with violence and sentenced to three years in Kingston Penitentiary on each charge, concurrent sentences.

Released in early 1951 he went out and robbed an old man, beating him with a beer bottle in the process. He was sentenced to seven years in Kingston Penitentiary plus twenty strokes of the strap. On October 25, 1951 he was sent to Toronto's Don Jail pending an appeal of his sentence.

Thus Leonard Jackson, armed robber, Edwin Boyd, armed robber, and William R. Jackson, armed and violent robber, met and joined forces. None of them was anxious to stay in the Don, but how could they get out? Leonard Jackson just laughed as he tapped his wooden foot on the cold cement floor.

ESCAPE

9

In 1864, when construction was begun on the new Don Jail, little was known about the tempering of metal. Russian iron was used in the formation of the cell bars. This soft metal was quite easily sawn through, and had in fact borne the onslaught of dozens of smuggled saw blades over the years.

The first week of November 1951 was unusually cold for Toronto. Temperatures hovered below freezing, and a light skiff of snow covered the ground. Inside the jail, prisoners shivered in their unheated cells and piled on extra blankets at night.

In the second-floor corridor of the northwest jail block, Leonard Jackson, Edwin Boyd and William R. Jackson kept warm with a little exercise of their own devising—they patiently hacked away at a single bar on a window. The sawing was done surreptitiously in shifts. Each time they had to stop, the shiny cut was disguised with soap and shoe polish and the protective screen carefully replaced.

It was Sunday afternoon, November 4, a month after Leonard Jackson's first escape attempt. Eighteen prisoners occupied number three corridor. A new deal for prisoners, introduced recently at the jail, allowed the men to play cards and read before being locked in their individual cells for the night. Boyd and the Jacksons were hidden from the guard's view by the other prisoners who were creating plenty of noise and movement to divert attention away from the trio.

Boyd jammed himself into the cramped space between the window screen and the iron bars. Standing in a half-crouched position, he sawed feverishly at the bar. When the position became totally unbearable, his hip joint gave way and his leg buckled beneath him.

As Boyd's hip went through the screen, the glass hit the floor with a crash.

"What's going on down there?" hollered the guard at the other end of the corridor.

"Nothing," yelled a quick-witted inmate. "I was just opening the window and I stuck my broom handle through it. It's okay, I'll clean it up." The inmate started sweeping up the bits of broken glass and the guard left him alone.

Boyd heaved a sigh of relief.

At three p.m. chief turnkey Alfred M. Bennett came on duty. His first job at the start of his eight-hour shift was to inspect the corridors and be sure that all prisoners were present. Having satisfied himself, he carried on with his duties about the jail.

Throughout the afternoon the games and reading continued on. Every so often the guards would pass through or cast an eye over the group. Nothing seemed amiss.

Supper was at five. Before each meal the roll was called in each cell block to ensure that all prisoners were accounted for. The men began to assemble for the meal.

"Boyd, Edwin," called the guard. "Present!" came the reply. The guard did not look up.

Darkness was falling outside the jail. A cold breeze whipped up puffs of snow and laid them across the tops of the high stone walls. Streetlights and headlights blinked on and reflected off the slippery streets.

"Jackson, Leonard," called the guard.

There was a brief and deafening silence. The guard raised his eyes slightly from the list of names. Before he had time to see where the voice came from, "Present!" boomed out from the rows of hungry prisoners. "Jackson, William R.," bellowed the guard.

Outside on Gerrard Street, a car crept past the front of the jail. Pausing briefly for a look at the imposing facade, the driver continued around the corner into the night.

Inside the jail, the prisoners shuffled their feet impatiently. Supper was not noted for its gourmet delights but at least there was lots of it, and it was usually hot. Would this roll call never be over? Finally, with everyone accounted for, the men went down to eat. At 8:10 p.m. Alfred Bennett stopped in corridor three. Something was terribly wrong here. The screen on the third last window was broken loose from the frame. He thrust his hand through the opening. The window was broken. A bar had been sawed through. The corridor was open to the night.

With a swiftness born of long years of service, Bennett summoned a guard to lock the prisoners in their cells immediately. Another guard brought the slate with the names of the men assigned to this corridor.

This time when the roll was called, three men did not answer. The only sound was a cough or a laugh from another corridor, a key being turned in a lock far down the hall, or the scuffle of fidgeting feet as the prisoners in number three corridor looked out at their guards.

Sometime earlier that day Boyd and the Jacksons had gone from cell to cell, removing sheets from each one. When the sheets were finally knotted into a strong rope, the three men loosened the screen that they had carefully removed several times before.

The bar looked quite like all the others on the window. Only the three men knew its weakened spot. With a few more quick thrusts of the tiny hacksaw blade the bar was cut. Tying the end of one sheet around the remaining bars, the three wriggled out the nine-inch opening and lowered themselves forty feet to the ground.

With a soft thud Edwin Boyd landed in the exercise yard. He looked around. There were no guards in sight but that didn't prove a thing. They would have to hurry. With hearts pounding, the trio crossed the yard to the outer wall.

Leonard Jackson shivered in his light prison garb, but his mind wasn't on the cold. The men had brought a second rope of bedsheets and now made a loop on one end of its length.

The stone walls of the Don Jail were sixteen feet high. They were impossible to scale, and Leonard's wooden foot made any acrobatic effort unfeasible. Where the walls met at ninety-degree angles, their Victorian builders had seen fit to festoon the top junctions with decorative cornices. Beneath the shadow of one such ornament, the three prisoners huddled together.

Lennie faced the corner and bracing himself against the walls with both hands, stood spread-eagled. Boyd leaned forward and put his hands on Len's shoulders. Willie climbed up on this human scaffold.

With their home-made bedsheet lasso, he hooked the cornice at the top of the wall and pulled himself up, hand over hand. Boyd grabbed the bedsheet next and quickly followed Willie. Both of them stood on the wall and helped to pull Len up.

The three men looked over their shoulder as they crouched low to grip the cornice. One at a time they dangled their legs over the outside of the wall and let go. The drop was sixteen feet, and snow provided little cushion. The cold and damp was beginning to penetrate to their very bones. But not far away, an apartment offered warmth and protection, and the men hurried away from the jail.

When they arrived at the apartment and discovered that Suchan wasn't there, Boyd was furious. So far, everything had gone perfectly, but now some idiot was screwing up their plans. Len calmed him down and got on the telephone. Suchan arrived with the car a short time later.

On Humberside Avenue, George Hill looked up from his paper. Who would be calling on a Sunday night? He answered the phone. The call was for his tenant, the pretty English girl, Ann Roberts. Curious about what young man would be phoning her, Hill summoned Ann to the phone. The astonished smile that broke out over her face was hardly a clue. A few minutes later she rushed out the door, buttoning her coat as she ran.

Ann Roberts got out of the streetcar at Parliament and Gerrard, less than a mile from the jail. Fear mingled with joy as she saw Lennie Jackson in the front seat of the parked car. She hurried over. "When I arrived at the car, Boyd got out and I got in the front seat and I believe Boyd got into another car — I was too excited to notice."

A guard at the Don Jail phoned Toronto Police Keele Street Station. Without mentioning a jail break, he asked that the police check Leonard Jackson's Humberside address. Number four station was asked to check William R. Jackson's Winchester Street address. The station duty officer was curious about the request, and the guard admitted that three men had escaped. The chase was on.

Teletype messages clicked into all police stations. Border points were notified. Police began to comb the streets and question their sources. Detectives Edmind Tong and Adolphus Payne methodically began their investigations.

Speeding into the night, Lennie Jackson and Ann Roberts slipped out of Toronto travelling east to Oshawa. Stopping at a tourist cabin, they embraced at last in the darkness. As she reached out to touch her lover, Ann felt the long barrel of a weapon tucked into the waistband of his trousers. Fighting her curiosity she didn't mention the revolver. If it was loaded, that was Lennie's business. Tonight they would try to forget their desperate situation and think only of each other.

In Toronto, police and prison officials concentrated all their energies on a full-scale manhunt. Batches of pictures with descriptions of the fugitives were rushed from headquarters to all police stations. The police and sheriff's investigation convinced them that a saw had been smuggled into the jail. No trace of the actual blade had yet turned up.

On the west side of the city, Edwin Boyd and William R. Jackson settled down for the night in the softest beds they had known for weeks. Down the hall from them, in the landlord's kitchen, Steve Suchan conferred with his parents, Sam and Charlotte Kozak.

The Kozaks had moved to Toronto a few years earlier and bought a rooming house that was usually fully occupied by tenants. When the young couple on the first floor moved out, Steve Suchan arranged to take over the room. The change did not escape the attention of the other tenants.

Mrs. Jean French and her husband lived quietly on the second floor at the front. One condition of the tenancy was that Mrs. French be given free access to other parts of the house, including the telephone in the downstairs hall, and Mrs. Kozak's kitchen stove.

Jean French remembers the time two strange men came to occupy the room on the main floor:

> I was no longer allowed access to the rest of the house, including the use of the telephone. The door to the downstairs being kept locked, and many times when I went to use the phone, I could hear people moving around, they would not answer my knocking. The same applied to the use of [the] stove.

Another tenant remembers the change in her landlord and landlady. She used to talk to Mrs. Kozak and do laundry in the cellar. She felt that her landlady was glad of the company.

Then about the first week in November of 1951, their son Val brought two men to stay there. They had a room on the main floor next to ours. After they came I noticed a change in Mr. and Mrs. [Kozak]. They were no longer friendly.

The tenant often heard voices in the men's room, but the door was always closed. She observed Val's mother entering without knocking, and knew that she was cooking for the men and feeding them in her living room. ". . . and from this time on, they made it plain to me that they did not want me coming through the kitchen."

Four days after the escape, with Boyd and the Jacksons still lying low, the city was in turmoil. Two turnkeys at the Don Jail were dismissed for negligence, and the governor was reprimanded by Reforms Minister J.W. Foote for not seeing that his orders were carried out. One of the dismissed guards stated that at five p.m. on the day of the escape, he personally saw the prisoners at their supper. This was never confirmed by other guards.

The chief turnkey later testified that there were about 400 prisoners in the Don Jail at the time of the breakout, while facilities were meant to accommodate only 250. When asked by a lawyer if a guard could keep track of each prisoner's movements, the turnkey replied:

> It is impossible. There is no way of getting away from it. Each guard is responsible for his own. There are 400 brains working against me. What can I do?

Speculation began to grow that other prisoners had answered for the trio at the supper roll call. They might have escaped as early as 3:45 p.m. Prison officials thought that unlikely, since they would have been seen in daylight.

Newspapers called the escape the most daring in years. Police informed the public that Edwin Boyd, Leonard Jackson and William R. Jackson were dangerous criminals who "would shoot it out if cornered". Ontario Provincial Police offered a $500 reward for information leading to the arrest of the fugitives.

Reports began to filter into the police from ever-helpful public. An informant claimed that he became acquainted with two men who were living in a tree in Scarborough, on the east side of Toronto. The tree-dwellers were said to be in possession of a Luger and a shotgun.

A score of Toronto city, provincial, and Scarborough police swarmed through the area, but found neither men nor arms.

Vancouver police, 2,000 miles away, were on the lookout after hearing reports that the fugitives were headed west.

About ten p.m. the night after the break, Ann Roberts and Lennie Jackson left the Oshawa tourist cabin and continued driving east. They spent the rest of the night at a tourist camp in Kingston. The following day they drove on to Montreal.

While the royal tour was coming to a rainy close in Halifax, Edwin Boyd and W.R. Jackson lounged in Mrs. Kozak's cosy living room, enjoying her hearty meals. They were safe for a while. Lennie and Ann were safe and setting up house in Montreal. It was a relief to be free of the wretched Don Jail, but their problems were far from over.

Boyd had two mortgages on his Pickering house, and Dorreen had no source of income to make the payments. Mrs. Kozak had to have her rent. Lennie and Ann had rent to pay. Steve Suchan was living well, keeping both Anna and Mary reasonably happy, juggling presents and dates. Clearly they would all need some money soon. Of the entire group, only Willie R. Jackson seemed free of worry. This was a damn sight better than being in the joint, and the life-style of his new found friends seemed increasingly attractive.

A week passed, then two. Toronto began to settle down, complacent in the belief that the escaped convicts were hundreds, if not thousands, of miles away. Sergeant Tong continued his rounds of the hotels and bars, keeping his ears to the ground. Sergeant Payne methodically carried out his other assignments, always alert for the clue that would lead to a break in Boyd's mysterious disappearance.

When the break came, it wasn't by hints or clues. When the gang was next heard from, the news was relayed across the city within hours. Splashed across the front pages of the newspapers, spreading alarm among the citizens, was the report that the bank-robbing convicts were on a spree.

THE BOYD GANG

10

At 10:20 a.m. there were only two customers in the Bank of Toronto's branch at Dundas and Roncesvalles on the city's west side. Bank manager Brian O. Branston was on the telephone in his office. As he hung up the phone, he became aware of someone behind him. The intruder shouted, "Get up out of there," and grabbed the manager by the right shoulder, pulling him out of his chair.

Forced out into the lobby and behind the first teller's cage, Branston saw the members of his staff lying face down on the floor, and the menacing gun in his captor's hand quickly convinced him to do likewise.

The gang encountered no resistance as they cleaned out the cash from the drawers, throwing the money into wrinkled brown bags.

It was all over in a few minutes. And when the thieves finally left, $4,300 in their bags, no one was sure exactly what had happened.

The newspapers reported that five men had held up the bank. As written up by the *Telegram*:

> Two men manned the tellers' counters and two men stayed by the entrance. The fifth gunman, employees said, guarded the double-doored street entrance. The "toothless master mind" remained by the door and directed the holdup, shouting commands to his accomplices.

Testimony given in connection with the robbery was so confused that it was never ascertained exactly how many men participated in the theft. Newspapers reported five men, police believed there were four. Bank employees knew there were three, or four, or five, but no single employee was able to give a description of more than two robbers.

At lineups the following year, several bank staff identified William R. Jackson as having taken part in the robbery, and some picked out Edwin Boyd. One person thought that Leonard Jackson was "similar to" one of the persons who robbed them, and one even thought Edwin's brother Robert Boyd was "similar to" one of the thieves.

Police noted that the bank staff was extremely reluctant to attend police lineups, and it was only after a great deal of persuasion that they would agree to go. Mrs. Joan Robinson, they said, was the best of the witnesses.

Under cross-examination by defence counsel, Mrs. Robinson told the court that she went to three lineups.

Q. You attended one on March 27th, correct?
A. I don't know the date.
Q. Well, let us say that was the first one. Did you identify anybody in it?
A. No.
Q. Did you attend another lineup, May the 14th?
A. I don't know whether that is a correct date.
Q. Well, in any event, at the second lineup, did you identify anybody?
A. Yes.

At this point Mrs. Robinson indicated William R. Jackson, sitting in court beside a policeman.

Q. And what part did he take in the bank robbery?
A. He is the one that stood at the door.
Q. The front door of the bank?
A. Yes.
Q. Did he have a gun?
A. I don't know.

Later in the testimony, Mrs. Robinson was asked how long the office was from the front to back, and replied that it would be as long as the courtroom anyway.

Q. That is about what? Fifty, sixty feet? About sixty feet?
A. I don't know. I can't judge distance.

The defence attorneys proceeded to go through the details of the robbery, attempting to discredit the witness.

Q. How long were the men in the bank? Just roughly? One minute, two minutes?

A. I don't imagine they were in there any more than a couple of minutes anyway, but I am not much of a judge of time either.
Q. You are just a judge of faces, are you?
A. Well, I try.

Continuing with the process of identification of the robbers, the lawyer asked:

Q. Now then, you attended a police lineup on the 27th of March.
A. I don't know the date.
Q. You don't remember dates very well?
A. No I don't.
Q. But you attended. Well, you remember the month, sometime in March or April.
A. I couldn't even tell you that.

The defence lawyer then tried to cast doubt on her identification, assuming that the publicity given Boyd and Jackson was so great they would have been identified by anyone.

Mrs. Robinson's testimony revealed that a policeman had come to the bank before the robbery and showed the staff pictures of Edwin Boyd, and that after the robbery she had gone to the police station to look at more pictures.

Q. Quite a few?
A. Oh yes.
Q. They really let you look around?
A. Oh yes.
Q. Did you see any other pictures at any time after that? Did the police show you any pictures?
A. Not from the police.
Q. What pictures were you shown?
A. I saw all the pictures that came out in the daily papers.

Mrs. Robinson then went on to explain that she had read about the three men escaping from the Don Jail and had seen Edwin Boyd's picture in the newspaper.

Later in the testimony she was asked:

Q. Did you see any pictures in any papers?
A. I can't remember.
Q. What paper do you read?
A. The *Daily Star*.
Q. Do you remember seeing any pictures in the *Daily Star?*
A. I don't remember. I don't read very much besides the comics.

Although Edwin Boyd was committed to trial for this robbery the following year, he was found not guilty. Charges against Steve Suchan and Leonard Jackson were dropped, and only William R. Jackson was convicted on the charges. He was given twenty years, concurrent with other sentences.

About the time of the robbery, Leonard Jackson purchased a 1950 Oldsmobile in Montreal for $2,500. Ann Roberts was not working at that time. Another $2,500 went to a Toronto lawyer, but Ann "never did know who paid this money, or where it came from". She had sold the car Leonard owned when he was arrested. She got $1,300 for it, and had about $350 left when Leonard escaped from the Don Jail.

On November 22, two days after the robbery, Leonard Jackson suddenly got a prescription for eyeglasses. At the same time he began to grow a moustache.

In Montreal, Suchan registered at the Castle Tourist Rooms on Mountain Street, giving his name as J.W. Doyle from Timmins, Ontario. The following week, he purchased a holster for his gun at the Circle C Saddle Shop in Toronto. When police later collected the bill of sale for evidence, the purchaser's name read "Jim Doyle".

Ann and Leonard registered at the same tourist house, giving their names as Mr. and Mrs. Fred Wilson, also from Timmins, Ontario.

Willie Jackson was the happiest member of the group. "From then on," says Boyd, "you didn't have to talk to Willie about robbing a bank. He really felt good. The first time in his life."

Ten days after the bank robbery, life was returning to normal for most Torontonians. People still talked in the streets and the bars and the coffee shops about "The Boyd Gang" but not too many were worried about going to the banks and making their deposits as usual. No one thought the robbers would hang around Toronto waiting to make another attempt, or waiting to be caught.

On Friday, November 30, Sam Kozak went to work as usual. For two years he had been a sweeper in the north combine plant at the Massey-Harris Company and never missed a day. That morning at ten o'clock, he asked for a pass to leave the plant. He explained that he had some real estate business to attend to. At 11:51 a.m. his time card was punched out, and Kozak left work. When next his supervisor saw him, over a month had passed, and Sam Kozak had had a delightful vacation in the south.

While Kozak was requesting his pass, Albert E. Hockley, manager of the Leaside Branch of the Royal Bank, was just starting work for the day. It was the end of the month and many of the large industrial accounts would be in heavy demand for payroll obligations. Hockley saw to it that there was about $100,000 in cash ready for his customers.

At 11:10 a.m., Mr. Hockley rose from his desk, and began to usher a client into his office. Clerk Betty Cooley was working near the back of the bank when she suddenly heard somebody shouting near the front entry. She looked up to see a man in a dark coat, and immediately a man with a gun jumped up in front of her on a desk. He had come through the back door of the bank the same moment the shouting began at the front.

A third man charged through the door of the manager's office, ordering Hockley and his client into the clerk's space. Someone shouted, "Put your hands up!" The confused staff and customers moved slowly into positon, unsure of what was happening. The man at the back of the bank ordered the staff against the wall.

Perhaps because they might be seen through the window, the robbers changed their minds and ordered everyone to put their hands down again. One customer was slow in obeying and one of the robbers hit him on the arm with a machine gun.

Said manager Hockley, "He lined me up against the wall and every time I tried to get a look at him a gun was prodded into my ribs."

One of the bandits jumped up on the tellers' counter. He waved his hands around, and then jumped down on the floor in front of a cash drawer. "I thought," said a teller, "he was a drunken man, acting crazy or something."

Suddenly an incredible calm descended on the bank. With quick but cool precision, the men began to empty the cash drawers. One of the thugs was reported to have said to the bystanders, "All right, take a good look at us." Another told the staff to keep quiet, and they wouldn't get hurt. Said a stenographer, "He had a soft voice, but you could feel he meant business. The bandit smiled at me, the rat."

As the thieves coolly dumped thousands of dollars into their white pillowcase sacks, they conversed casually, as though, described the accountant, they were in a bar. Having filled his sack with money, one of the men turned to another, who was still pulling out wads of bills and stuffing them into his sack. "Do you think you've got enough?" he asked. "Yeah," replied the second gunman, "quite a lot. Looks like we did all right."

With quiet efficiency, the bandits finished their job and fled. Not one of the staff had had a chance to turn in the alarm. Said one, "It all happened so fast, you were bewildered." So, it seems, were the newspapers.

"Sten-Gun Five Stage Biggest Bank Hold-Up in History of Toronto," blared the Toronto *Daily Star*. Reported the *Telegram*: "Six cool gunmen pulled a payday hold-up of the Leaside Branch of the Royal Bank . . . "

One thing on which everyone agreed was that the robbery was the largest ever in Toronto or its suburbs. The final tally revealed that the thieves had made off with an incredible $46,207.13. The stolen getaway car was abandoned on Pottery Road, and Boyd, Suchan and the two Jacksons drove quickly back to the Kozak's house.

Within an hour after the holdup, clues began to filter in to police. Someone thought he had seen the master robber outside a pharmacy on the east side of Toronto. Cruisers converging on the area found no one. Six suspects were picked up in a west side tavern. All were released. Notes, letters, phone calls and messages led police on wild goose chases all over the city, but nothing led them to the quiet rooming house where four men sat around a table piled high with currency.

The same Friday, Prime Minister St. Laurent and Premier Frost discussed building the St. Lawrence Seaway. In Britain, Winston Churchill celebrated his seventy-seventh birthday with his family. Toronto Mayor McCallum was reproached by Alderman Nathan Phillips for a "listless" approach to traffic problem. The *Star* reported "18 Red Planes Bagged in Korea".

Boyd and the others knew that the police would be relentless in their pursuit. They had to lie low and keep out of sight. Lennie Jackson and Steve Suchan decided to head back to Montreal in a day or two. Boyd and Willie Jackson would stick around Toronto for a while. But first they'd split the loot.

Elated by their success, the four men were in a festive mood that day. Boyd noticed that the Kozaks were sitting watching as the gang exuberantly counted out the money: "Ten for you, and ten for you, and ten for you . . . " Mr. Kozak seemed to expect to be given a share for looking after these wanted men. Boyd agreed.

"What's your dad getting out of this?" Boyd asked Suchan, thinking they could each chip in a thousand dollars to give the old man.

"Oh," replied Steve, "I'll take care of it."

Boyd later discovered, much to his disgruntlement, that Suchan's method of "taking care of it" was to tell his father that he would get nothing, and too bad if he didn't like it.

Suchan and Len Jackson left to spend the night at Anna Bosnich's house. Boyd and Willie were bunking down at Kozak's, as if they were simply the new tenants. They shared a bedroom on the main floor.

"What are you going to do with your money, Willie?" said Boyd before they got ready for bed.

"I'm going to count it. Every hour on the hour."

"Yeah, but I mean where are you going to hide it?"

"Right under my pillow," said Willie, "and my gun right beside it. And my hand on the gun."

Boyd said that he would keep his money under the pillow, too, but when Willie wasn't looking, he slipped it into a cupboard in the bedroom. Later he gave Willie a bit of his philosophy on bank robberies.

"Look Willie, I know you like that money, and I know you maybe never had that much in one bundle in your hand, but there's lots of that laying around. There's more where it come from, so don't worry so much about it."

Willie laughed, but his reply was only half joking. "I'm going to worry about this every minute of my life until it's gone."

The next morning, Sam Kozak approached Boyd and said, "You know, I've been thinking. I've been worrying about you fellows having that money in my house. I'm afraid of what would happen if somebody sneaked into your room and stole your money. Or what would happen if the police came?"

Boyd knew he was right. "What would you do?" he asked Kozak.

"I've got a good hiding place," replied Suchan's father. It seemed a large cupboard in the hallway had a secret section, where a person could raise the floor and stash something in the wall.

Boyd kept about $3,000 in his pocket, which "didn't take up any space", and put the rest in the hiding place.

"How about putting yours there, Willie?" suggested Boyd.

"No sir!" replied Willie. "I'm not doing that!"

But finally Boyd talked him into it. Making faces and glaring at Boyd, Willie asked, "Do you know what you're doing?" Boyd reassured him.

"God," said Willie, "I had the money one minute, and now it's gone again."

"Don't worry," said Boyd, "it'll be safe."

The following morning, Sam Kozak left for Florida. Eddie and Willie's loot left on the same plane. Boyd got up to see what was for breakfast and was surprised to find Suchan there that early in the morning.

"Did you let the old man talk you into hiding your money in a place he had?" demanded Suchan.

"Yeah," said Boyd.

Suchan turned and spoke to his mother in Slovak. She answered briefly, then Suchan returned to Boyd.

"Go and see if your money's there," he said.

Suddenly Boyd's heart was pounding. He strode to the hallway cupboard. Willie was still in the bedroom. Boyd pulled up the piece of floor and pulled out the money sacks. They were empty.

"Just what I thought," said Suchan. "My old man's crazy, you know."

"You didn't tell us," said Boyd, unaware that Suchan had refused his father a share of the money. Boyd went to the bedroom.

"Willie, the old man took off last night with our money."

"What!!" willie bellowed like a wounded animal, then grabbed his gun and headed for the kitchen. He stomped in and snatched Mrs. Kozak's lapels, knocking her to the floor. Leaning on her chest, he pointed his .45 in her face.

"I-am-going-to-jam-this-right-down-your-throat, if you don't tell us where the old man is."

Mrs. Kozak was frightened, but managed to tell Willie in her broken English, "I don't know where he is. He just walked out the front door, and that's the last I've seen of him."

Boyd suggested that Suchan and Jackson might divide the

remainder of the loot four ways again, but Suchan would have none of it. He convinced Len that they should stay clear of Boyd and Willie for a while, so the two, who still had about $12,000 each, departed for Montreal.

Ann Roberts had been working as a hat check girl at the Famous Door Tavern on Yonge Street. On November 30 she disappeared from work, and never returned. A few days later, Mary Mitchell, who had been working as a hostess at the same tavern, went to collect her salary early in the morning. The manager was not immediately available, so she left without her money. She did not return.

Boyd and Willie never forgave Suchan for his father's duplicity. In a statement the following year, Boyd told Sergeant Payne that they had split the loot four ways, "but mine and one of the other fellow's was stolen from us that same night by a so-called friend". Payne: "Did you report this loss to the police?" Boyd: "Are you kidding?" Payne: "Anything else you wish to say?" Boyd: "I hope you catch the guy that took our money."

While Lennie and Ann, as Mr. and Mrs. Fred Wilson, booked rooms at the Castle Tourist House in Montreal, Suchan registered with Mary as Mr. and Mrs. Victor Lenoff at the Berkley Hotel. Not long after, Boyd and Willie Jackson arrived in Montreal. Although furious about the money, they still felt an allegiance to the group. Boyd registered at the Berkley Hotel under his wife's maiden name, Thompson, and Willie used his brother-in-law's name, A. Gibson, not realizing that this same Gibson would later be involved with Boyd in another holdup. The Boyd Gang settled in quietly in Montreal, living as "good citizens" and staying within the law.

To avoid bringing undue attention to themselves, the group members made few friends in Montreal. Lennie and Ann were discussing getting married, and talked over their problem with one friend, a Montreal taxi driver. The friend advised that since Ann was divorced, but without proper papers, it would take some time to arrange a marriage in Quebec.

Lennie suggested going to New Brunswick to see what the laws were like there. The young couple went as far as Edmunston, New Brunswick. There they discovered that the required papers for marriage would not be available for five days. They returned to Montreal.

Applying for a marriage licence, Ann registered as a "spinster". By then it was almost Christmas, and the wedding was postponed to allow a little time for festivities.

Steve Suchan rented a posh Côte des Neiges apartment for $145 per month. This was to be the gang's Montreal hideout, and Suchan optimistically signed a year's lease.

Also enjoying the festive season was Willie R. Jackson. He very quickly tired of sitting cooped up in his room at the Berkley Hotel. He had money now, although he had been robbed of about ninety percent of his original haul. Still he had more than he ever made rolling drunks.

Willie liked to get out and drink, living it up in nightclubs and bars. He was no longer a dead-end kid from Cabbagetown; he was a notorious big-time bandit, a member in good standing of the infamous Boyd Gang.

An ex-con friend of Willie Jackson's remembers the reputation he had:

Willie's a clown, a kibitzer, a laugher, a talker, a wheeler-dealer. He's a guy you wouldn't put anything past. He was funny just for what he said. He'd do anything on a bet or a dare . . . Not serious, but you know he has much more intelligence than he's obviously showing.

His friend remembers Willie's flair for being the centre of attention:

He was always trying to tell a joke, and never having the punch line right, never! You'd be laughing because you heard the joke, and you knew the punch line. I was at a party one time, and he's telling this joke, and he's laughing so hard before he got to the punch line that everyone's laughing, nearly wetting their pants laughing. And when he did get to the punch line, he didn't have it!

Willie "The Clown" Jackson, they called him: a guy who could have a whole room full of people laughing, and a guy who could go out and beat up an old man to steal his wallet. Willie Jackson: a loveable kibitzer to his friends, an habitual criminal to police.

On December 18, 1951, Willie R. Jackson was enjoying a Christmas drink with a female companion in a Montreal nightclub. According to Boyd, Willie could be "very gracious and polite" when he wanted to be, and had already been so gracious with this lady friend that he had stayed with her overnight, causing Boyd considerable anxiety that Willie might have been picked up. But by now Boyd didn't worry when Willie was away for long stretches.

On the night of the 18th, Willie excused himself from his companion, and went to the men's room. As he stood in front of the urinal, his suit jacket fell open. The man standing beside him took one look at the big .45 tucked in Willie's waistband and made a beeline for the telephone. The police arrived in a matter of minutes.

When Montreal police discovered that he was wanted in Toronto, Willie Jackson soon found himself back in the Don Jail. The pattern was familiar. Commit a crime, go to jail, serve your time, get out, have fun, commit another crime, and go back again. This time he had altered the pattern a little; he had escaped before serving his time, and the life he had led was better than any he had ever known.

But now Willie was back in the coop, and Christmas would be just a day like all the other days, waiting for freedom. Sentenced to an additional two years for escaping custody, consecutive with his seven-year term, he was immediately transferred to Kingston Penitentiary.

As soon as Willie Jackson was caught, the heat was on in Montreal. Boyd read about the arrest in a tiny article in the newspaper. The police would be asking around. Willie had friends who might know too much. With barely a backward glance, Boyd, Suchan and Mitchell checked out. Christmas would be more fun in Toronto, anyway.

On December 20, Mitchell and Suchan checked in at the Sunnyside Motor Hotel on Lake Shore Road in Toronto. Mary Mitchell was apparently well known at the Sunnyside, having "partied" with some other fellows there previously. On checking in, Mary told the managers that she had some friends coming in from out of town and requested the room adjoining hers. She was given rooms 48 and 50, and she paid all the bills.

The following day, Edwin and Dorreen Boyd arrived to occupy room 48. Mitchell and Suchan had been at the Sunnyside together before, but this was the first time for the Boyds. Mary introduced Dorreen to the staff as her sister, and the couple signed in as Mr. and Mrs. Smith from North Bay, Ontario.

Christmas, 1951. Negotiations had begun for a truce in Korea. The Toronto Maple Leafs had won the Stanley Cup for the sixth time in nine years. In the National Baseball League, young Willie Mays was rookie of the year and Stan Musial was champion batter. Movie-goers lined up for "The African Queen" and "A Streetcar Named Desire". In Toronto, Allan Lamport was elected mayor and, as one citizen put it, "dragged the city kicking and screaming, into the twentieth century".

For Edwin Alonzo Boyd and his family, only the present mattered, and the good times were what you made them. Christmas was for the children, so Dorreen and their three children spent the day with Edwin, Mary Mitchell and Suchan in the Sunnyside Motel.

The room clerk was kept busy taking ginger ale and other treats to the adjoining rooms. The children, fascinated by the moving pictures on the screen, spent hours in the motel lobby, staring at the TV. Christmas carols and Eaton's advertisements blared from the radios in the rooms. In preparation for the ritual gift exchange on Christmas Day, Dorreen bought some jewelry and a little Eskimo doll from the china bar in the lobby.

Dorreen remembers the day with fondness:

> It was a real family Christmas. The children were all there. We handed out the presents and even had a turkey dinner. The only thing we didn't manage was a Christmas tree.
>
> In the evening, Ed and I went to The Famous Door, and had supper there. It was nice but we both had the feeling we might be recognized at any minute, and that doesn't make anyone in our position feel very comfortable.

By December 28, Boyd felt confident enough to go back to his house in Pickering. He and Dorreen checked out of the motel. The confinement was hard on both of them, and Edwin became more daring. One night they decided to go out to a movie.

Dressed very conservatively, and with hat pulled down low, Edwin Boyd escorted his wife to the theatre. They scanned the streets carefully before moving out of the shadows. They stepped into the lobby. A policeman was standing with his back to them, facing the telephone. Dorreen fought off the instinct to flee. Edwin didn't bat an eyelash. "Two tickets, please," he said to the cashier, and the couple walked inside.

"You can't say he hasn't got guts," Dorreen once said. "Maybe he doesn't use them the right way, but he certainly has them."

New Year's Eve was spent at home. Ed bought a bottle of champagne and as the clock struck twelve, Dorreen and Edwin raised their glasses to each other and the future. "It wasn't the best New Year's we'd ever spent, but we both had high hopes for the future," remembered Dorreen.

Despite his heavy involvement with Mary Mitchell, Steve Suchan felt an obligation and a tenderness toward Anna, very soon to be the mother of his child. Their relationship had been stormy these last few months, and he would often leave her for weeks at a time. On Christmas Eve, he showed up at her door.

Leonard had called at her house a few days earlier and asked for Steve. She later noted that he "seemed surprised that [Suchan] was not there, and after wishing me a 'Merry Christmas', he left. At this time Jackson was wearing glasses, but I am not sure if he had a moustache or not."

When Steve dropped by on Christmas Eve, Anna made dinner for him and they had a brief but happy time together. When he left, he said he would be back soon, but the promise was not kept. Anna didn't see Steve again for a week. He had been away on a buying spree.

The Sportstown Grill in Buffalo was a favourite hangout for certain visitors from Toronto. The owner knew the two Jacksons, Wilfred and Leonard, and had been in crap games with Suchan and his father, Sam Kozak. On December 30, 1951, Steve Suchan and Mary Mitchell checked into the Statler Hotel in Buffalo. Registered as V.J. Lenoff and wife, they gave their address as Côte des Neiges, Montreal.

Suchan conducted a little business at the Sportstown Grill, made a few telephone calls, and they checked out again the next day. Arrangements and contacts had been made—now they would have to wait for the outcome.

"Happy New Year, Anna." Suchan was at her door again. The New Year, 1952, was only an hour old, and Anna was sick. She felt heavy and awkward and couldn't bear the thought of another emotional scene. She told him not to come back.

In Montreal, Ann Roberts was feeling excited. Lennie had been free for nearly two months. The incredible anxiety every time he went out was easing off. It was now possible to pick up a Toronto newspaper without seeing his face in it. Perhaps there was a future after all. Tomorrow they would be married.

The marriage licence listed the applicants as George Jackson Jr., hairdresser, of Niagara Falls, and Ann Warburton, model, of Humberside Avenue, Toronto. The witnesses were Montreal acquaintances – the taxi driver, a mechanic and a storekeeper. On January 2, 1952 at St. James the Apostle Church, Ann Roberts became Mrs. Leonard Jackson.

Things were looking up. Ann and Lennie decided to have a honeymoon. About a week after the wedding, they gave up their room on Mountain Street and headed west. They drove as far as Alberta and stayed away five weeks. Thousands of miles away from Toronto and Montreal, they managed to forget men like Tong and Payne. For a while, only the happiness of the moment mattered—until the money ran low.

On January 11, the telephone rang in Anna Bosnich's house on Wright Avenue. Her voice was soft as she answered, "Hello?" "Anna, it's Steve." He never failed to arouse some feeling in her, but she couldn't see him that day; she had an appointment with the doctor. The baby was due any moment. Steve promised to pick her up the next day.

The following day when Steve called for her, Anna was gone. She was in hospital giving birth to their son. Gone were his thoughts of Mary Mitchell. Gone were ruminations about Boyd and the gang. He was a father! Bursting with pride, Suchan rushed to the hospital. He stayed with Anna two hours talking tenderly about their son: what his name would be, whom he would look like, what kind of future he would have.

Later that night, Suchan and Mary Mitchell checked into the Hillcrest Motel in Toronto.

By Wednesday, Anna was ready to go home. Steve picked her up. Anna remembers: " . . . he called at my home every day the rest of that week until Saturday or Sunday, when he said he was going out of town. About two weeks later he telephoned me from New York."

But New York was not the first stop on Suchan's agenda.

11

Edwin Boyd was furious. He had the bank all cased, the date and time arranged, and a man to help them with the job. But Suchan hadn't arrived from Montreal at the appointed time.

"I told you I was going to get this job ready, and then you'd come down two days later and we'd rob this bank. What's the matter with you?" Boyd shouted into the phone.

"I thought you were fooling," replied Suchan lamely.

"You creep! I told you I was going to get this job ready and you heard me. Now you're saying you thought I was fooling. I don't fool about things like that!"

Boyd bided his time while Suchan drove all night to Toronto. When Suchan arrived, he tried to explain again.

"I really thought you were fooling," said Suchan.

"Jesus!" said Boyd. "I'm on the run. I have no money. You have your money. It didn't get stolen from you."

Boyd was still angry about the money he'd lost, and resentful that Suchan was so stingy with his share.

"Look," said Boyd, "I know very well that it's impossible to talk you into sharing evenly what you have, so how about helping us rob this bank?"

Suchan, who was spending money as if there were no tomorrow, was quick to agree. He could use the cash.

Suchan had brought Mary Mitchell with him from Montreal. It was exactly one month after Christmas. With Lennie still away on his honeymoon and Willie otherwise detained in Kingston, Boyd had recruited a third person to help with the holdup. Mary begged to be allowed to do something to help. Suchan pleaded her case with

Boyd, who was now the undisputed boss, and Boyd agreed to let her drive the getaway car.

The three men drove their stolen car to a supermarket and parked near where Mary was waiting in her own car. As Mary went into the store, the men headed for the bank. When she returned to her car, they were crouched on the floor, waiting for her. She couldn't believe it was all over so fast. But the newspaper headlines quickly confirmed that the job had gone off in fine style.

"Take Gun, Kick Clerk at Kingston Road Bank, 3 Flee in Stolen Car," reported the *Star*. The Bank of Toronto lost $10,400 and a .38 calibre Iver Johnson revolver, while one of the bank clerks suffered a kick in the pants for not obeying the order fast enough to get down on the floor. During the robbery, the bandits leaped over the counters and threw cash from the tellers' drawers into bags. A customer reported that one of the armed men was "looking directly at me and grinning!" The robbery had all the trademarks of a Boyd Gang heist.

Licence plates had been stolen from another car and attached to the getaway car. The vehicle was found abandoned only four blocks from the bank in a supermarket parking lot.

Three men were eventually accused of the robbery: Edwin Boyd, Steve Suchan, and Joseph Jackson, a brother of Willie "The Clown" Jackson's. In subsequent lineups, only one person was able to identify Joseph Jackson, and with little certainty. At the preliminary trial, Jackson was discharged before Suchan and Boyd were taken to trial.

Although the evidence was strongly against Boyd and Suchan (the bank's stolen revolver was found in Boyd's possesion and a list of figures corresponding to the bank's losses found in Suchan's effects), charges were eventually dropped against both.

The defence lawyer at the trial intimated that Boyd's notoriety made the bank manager's identification suspect. A bank customer who had picked Boyd and Suchan out of lineups admitted that she had been unable to furnish a description of the bandits immediately after the robbery. Boyd didn't know it at the time, but he was away scot-free.

The day after the robbery, Boyd's brother Robert applied for his 1952 licence, transferring the registration for his car, a 1949 Austin sedan, to Dorreen Boyd. This one simple act was to be a catalyst in a crucial chain of events in Boyd's life, but that was still nearly two months away.

On January 28, Suchan, under the alias Lenoff was back at the Sunnyside Motel, and two days later Boyd registered there under his new alias, Charles Hunter.

Around this time, Robert Boyd rented the garage of a Toronto house. The 1951 grey Nash sedan that he stored in the garage was registered to Charles Hunter of Côte des Neiges in Montreal. On February 8, the address on the registration was changed to Harbord Street in Toronto.

All the comings-and-goings, changes of names, addresses, and registrations were apparently dodges to throw police off the scent. Edwin Boyd travelled back and forth between Montreal and Toronto several times in a few weeks. He had a 10,000-mile inspection done on his car in Montreal (under the name Hunter). When he returned to the Sunnyside in Toronto, Steve and Mary left for New York.

Apparently the couple had made friends with the doorman at their Montreal hideout apartment. On January 30, they sent a postcard from Syracuse, addressed to "Eddie (Doorman)", care of their apartment building. It read:

> Hello Ed. Having a pleasant trip so far, will send you a card from New York.
>
> Vic & Mary Lenoff.

True to their word, they did send him a postcard from New York City a few days later. Its message was as enlightening as the first:

> Hello Ed. Having a wonderful time here. See you soon.
>
> Vic & Mary Lenoff.

Despite the suggestion that theirs was a pleasure trip, Suchan's real purpose was business. On February 6, they arrived in Buffalo and checked into the Statler Hotel. Suchan made a few carefully-selected contacts and arranged for some rather large purchases. Among the items contracted for were:

7.65 mm. Baretta automatic pistol
7.63 mm. Mauser automatic pistol
.45 calibre automatic Colt pistol, service type
.38 calibre Colt revolver

6.35 mm. Duo automatic pistol
.32 calibre Colt Police Positive revolver
9.00 mm. German p/38 automatic pistol

By the 10th, Suchan and Mitchell were back in Montreal. He made several long-distance calls during the next few days: two to Anna, one to his mother in Toronto, and one to Buffalo. The Buffalo call was to a man he had met in a Fort Erie speakeasy. The message was simple: the package hadn't come, and where was it? The package eventually arrived and in it was a small arsenal.

The 14th, Valentine's Day, was Suchan's birthday. In a rush of sentiment, he sent a telegram to Anna: "Many happy returns of the day to you and our little one. Val." Later he talked to her on the phone again.

Throughout their entire relationship, Anna Bosnich claims, she did not know Val by any of his aliases. She claimed to believe he was working as a tax consultant, and indeed, Suchan did put up such a pretense. He had at one time applied for a job with the Capital Tax Service in Toronto, and had been accepted. Although he had never actually worked for the company, he carried their card around in a briefcase.

However, it seems certain that Anna knew all was not on the square. On February 16, a long distance phone call was made from her Toronto number to Suchan's Montreal apartment, the caller asking for "Victor", Suchan's alias in Montreal. The following day, Suchan visited Anna in Toronto.

Suchan's increasing affection for Anna and their infant son seemed to have a negative effect on Mary Mitchell. She became jealous and determined to do something about his visits to Anna, during which he would occasionally stay away overnight.

Mitchell had been an active member of the Boyd Gang for some time, doing various chores for them both as favours, and for money. She had booked motel rooms and paid for them so that Boyd would not be seen by motel staff. When Robert Boyd rented the garage, it was Mary who drove Edwin Boyd's Nash sedan and parked it there. She had even had a part in the last holdup.

Mary Mitchell had played many different roles in the past few years: model, hat check girl in a tavern, dance instructor at a dancing school, and was also known in various circles as a "party girl". The room clerk of the Sunnyside Motel recalls: "I first got to know Mary Mitchell when she came and asked me for a room at the motel. She had been on a party with some other fellows, and as she seemed to be known around the motel, I gave her the room."

However, after she became associated with the Boyd Gang, she took on a new task. Over a period of several months, Mary Mitchell periodically dropped in to the police station to see Sergeant of Detectives Edmund "The Chinaman" Tong. The rôle she played was that of informer, but her real purpose was to gain information that could be useful to the gang.

Since she had an inside line to certain kinds of information, both through her brother Sam Stone (still in Kingston Penitentiary), and through her half-brother, Leonard Jackson, it is quite possible that she did give some useful information to Tong and his partner, Detective Sergeant Roy Perry. Or, she may have been priming the pump just to see what they knew. Whose side was she on? Or was she playing a different game of her own?

Edwin Boyd later told Sergeant Payne that he was beginning to smell a rat. Every time he would be driving in Toronto with Mary Mitchell, she would duck down and say, "Oh, there's Tong!" as if she were afraid to have Tong see her with Boyd. Boyd thought it odd that she was always spotting the detective.

The gang paid Mitchell extra for these chores, besides what she got from Suchan. Possibly the police paid her for information, too. Both the police and the Boyd Gang were soon to rue the day that they put their faith in Mary Mitchell.

There is some indication that Suchan was taking steps towards breaking off his relationship with Mitchell around the middle or end of February. His phone calls to Anna were more frequent and he visited her several times. His love for his newborn son was undoubtedly influencing him, though he still lingered on with Mary Mitchell.

In Montreal, Suchan and Mitchell lived quietly in their Côte des Neiges apartment, coming and going as Vic and Mary Lenoff. The doorman, to whom they had sent the postcards, was one of their few friends. On several occasions Suchan invited him to his apartment and played the violin for him. The doorman remembers: "I have also seen him [Suchan] in the apartment practicing with an air pistol, by shooting at pictures on magazine covers."

Suchan loved living well and eating well. Dorreen Boyd remembers: "One time in Montreal . . . Steve Suchan took the three of us to dinner at Ruby's [Ruby Foo's]. The bill was $47.00! Suchan always kept himself well. He had ten suits, each worth $150—and he drove a $4,000 car. Money to Suchan was something to be used."

By the middle of February, he was almost completely broke. He had robbed a few banks and his description was known to the police, but he was still completely unknown by name. Yet Suchan could not go back to legitimate work. He was a long way from the boy who had been the elevator operator in the King Edward Hotel. He could no longer bring himself to scramble for work as a professional musician, as he had once done briefly after leaving the King Eddy. And he certainly didn't feel capable of pulling a bank job without Boyd.

But he needed money desperately. The apartment was a luxury and he began to think about breaking his lease. Going to his parents for money would have been a disgrace. There was only one person to whom he could turn.

When Anna Bosnich received his letter, she flew into a rage. The nerve of that man. After all he'd put her through, he had the gall to ask her for money. Let him find his $200 somewhere else. In disgust, she tore the letter into little pieces and threw them away.

But that wasn't the end. Steve once again picked up the phone and dialled long distance. Anna answered.

On February 26, she wrote a cheque for $200 to her mother. Still not well after the baby's birth, she asked her mother to cash the cheque and purchase a money order. The money order was made out to Victor J. Lenoff of Côte des Neiges, Montreal.

While Suchan sweated through this temporary setback in Montreal, his father, Sam Kozak, was still in Florida seeking a cure for an ailing heart, courtesy of Edwin Boyd and Willie Jackson.

On February 22, Kozak sent a letter in Slovak to his wife, Charlotte. The translation reads:

> Well, greetings from St. Petersburg, Florida, from your husband. I am sending greetings also to my boy Edward [Suchan's younger brother]. Are you well? I am sending my greetings also to my boy Valentine and to his friends. At the present time I am well, I feel better, but nobody will help my heart. I feel sad when I see families with children, playing on the sand.

I am sending three pictures and write me a few lines. If you don't have any time to write, write whether Edward is healthy. I will be here for three more weeks, so be well, and I will come to see you in a few weeks.

Leonard and Ann Jackson finally returned from their western honeymoon the first week of February. They were down to their last few dollars and took a single room on Bishop Street for a week. Driving around in their Oldsmobile that week, they sought accommodations in which they could do their own cooking. They finally found a basement apartment on Lincoln Avenue at $12 per week, and began to pack their bags to move.

Ann went to put some clothes into her suitcase. When she attempted to lift it, she discovered it was very heavy. Curious, she tried to open it. Leonard was busy elsewhere in the room.

"Lennie, my suitcase is locked." She tugged at the clasps. "I know," replied Jackson, "I have some stuff in it."

Ann remembered that throughout their western tour Leonard had carried the same long-barrelled revolver she had noticed the first night of his escape. She hefted her suitcase again. "I was immediately suspicious," she remembers, "that it was guns of some kind. How they arrived at the apartment or when, I did not know."

When Ann and Leonard set up housekeeping in their new apartment they were anxious to appear as a normal, typical young couple. They told the janitor, Mr. Côté, that Leonard was a salesman. In order to keep up the ruse, Lennie would leave the apartment every day at ten and return around five-thirty or six p.m. Ann was left to her own devices during the day, which didn't always please her:

> I did question him as to what he did while he was away in the day time, but he accused me of nagging him, and I did not question him further. We had no visitors at the apartment, and we did not leave Montreal during this time.

The janitor's wife remembers hearing the Jacksons fighting, and at one point was sure Ann had been hit. Mrs. Côté went to their apartment and warned them they would be evicted if they didn't settle down. "Jackson was very nice about it," she recalled. "He agreed to be quiet, and the whole thing blew over."

Ann may have been cheered by the discovery that she was pregnant, but was not entirely happy about Lennie's habits.

He continued to carry his gun with him when he went out, with the exception of when he went to get a haircut, because he would have to take his coat off and someone might see the gun.

Jackson had now been out of prison for nearly four months and there were no signs that the police were even close to finding him. He felt secure enough to venture out into the streets, but not safe enough to be there without his gun. Not long after he arrived in Montreal, he made contact with his sister Mary, who was still living with Suchan. "Guess who's back in town," Mary said to Steve. "I give up, who?" "Lennie." Suchan was delighted. Jackson, too, was glad to have a friend in town. It was about this time that Suchan and Mary Mitchell parted company and Mary returned to Toronto. Whether it was jealousy or their straightened circumstances that precipitated the break, when he went over to the Jackson's for supper on March 1, Steve went alone.

Dinner was not elegant; Ann even had to ask Steve to bring his own plate and cutlery. But it was a happy reunion.

When the meal was over, Suchan suggested that Ann and Lennie might like to see his apartment. They all hopped into Suchan's big car and drove over to Côte des Neiges. Ann Jackson remembers Suchan's quarters:

> The apartment was sparsely furnished, with no curtains or pictures, and it appeared to me as if he was living alone. We sat and discussed the apartment, and he said he couldn't afford to keep it any longer, and he was going to move.

Lennie and Ann walked the short two blocks home. It was the last time Ann saw Steve Suchan in Montreal. Two days later, Suchan packed up the remainder of his belongings and took the train to Toronto. Around midnight, he knocked at Anna Bosnich's door. She was expecting him.

When he arrived at her house, Anna was ready to unleash all the resentment she'd been harbouring for months. He hung out in Montreal, never told her what he was doing, took her for granted, dropping in whenever it suited him, he fooled around with other women, especially Mary Mitchell, and worst of all, instead of helping to support his son, Suchan had asked *her* for money. They stayed up most of the night arguing.

Eventually they slept. Suchan felt incredibly weary. The train ride from Montreal had been bad enough, but then to spend half the night fighting with Anna was exhausting. When the phone rang at six a.m., Steve struggled to consciousness. He stumbled into the hallway and picked up the receiver.

"Hello?"

"Steve?"

"Yeah?"

"Lennie. I'm in Oshawa."

Jackson was at the C.P.R. station, having taken a later train from Montreal. It wouldn't be safe to appear at Union Station in Toronto. That would be like walking into the cop shop and giving yourself up. There was always a cop at the station. There were probably even pictures of the fugitives plastered all over the walls.

"Do you think you could come and pick me up, Steve?"

"Jesus, Lennie, it's only six o'clock!"

"I know, but what am I gonna do?"

Suchan sighed. He'd catch up on his sleep later. Anna was half awake now too. Suchan asked for the use of her car. She gave him the keys.

Suchan and Lennie returned to Anna's house about 9:30. With relief, Suchan headed for bed again and slept till 2:30 that afternoon. Jackson, depositing his bags in the back room, slept for an hour, then got up to talk with Anna for a while.

A couple of miles across the city, Edwin Boyd was busy. He had decided to pull a job without the others.

Boyd had stolen a car and hidden it in a rented garage. He had been expecting Suchan and Jackson, but again they had failed to show up when he was ready to pull the job. Boyd wasn't about to wait around. He found two other men.

Boyd's method of selecting accomplices for this job was, typically, through his underworld connections. He'd spent a good deal of time with Willie Jackson, but Willie was unavailable. Willie's brother Joseph, however, was on the outside, as was Willie's brother-in-law, Allister Gibson, who had a record but had been "straight" for a number of years.

"I was propositioned to make some easy money," Joseph Jackson later told Sergeant Payne. "I met a couple of fellows, and we talked it over, and we decided to rob the bank at College and Manning. I went there on the promise that nobody would be hurt." Joseph talked Allister Gibson into joining them. Said Gibson:

> I thought it over and decided to go into it to see if I couldn't make a better life for my wife and family, as I was sick of living in the hole I was in. I guess I didn't realize what I was getting into ... My job was to jump the counter in the bank and clean out the money in the middle tills. I did jump the counter and waved my gun and got the bank employees to face the wall, but I was too scared to touch the money.

Boyd was disgusted with this novice bank robber. "You didn't do a damn thing!" shouted Boyd. Boyd was paying the men a set fee for the job rather than splitting the take with them. He saw no reason to give Gibson anything, but told Joe he could give him something from his cut. Joe gave Gibson $1,000.

"I spent three hundred of it on a Studebaker car," Gibson later told Sergeant Payne. "About two hundred I gave away. I took a trip to the United States, and spent the rest on clothes for my boy.... I'm glad it's off my mind and it will never happen again."

Joe Jackson had $2,000 left. He spent most of his share on two cars, a new motor for one of the cars, then a panel truck. He later sold the vehicles at a loss.

The take from the bank was about $24,000. Boyd paid out $3,000. "The unequal division of money," Boyd told Payne, "was due to the fact that we intended to invest the large portion of it in a rooming house. The profits or income was to be split up between us." Boyd had already looked at an apartment for sale. It was $80,000 with a down payment of $20,000. "It was the ideal thing for people on the run," says Boyd. But he never got around to finalizing the deal.

By one p.m. on March 4, the robbery was long over. The stolen car had been returned to the garage where Boyd was hiding it. Joe Jackson had been paid. Gibson remembers: "I took the street car to High Park and stayed there about two hours, and I hid my gun there, but I went back later and got it again. Then I went home."

On Wright Avenue, Anna Bosnich was busy with the baby. Betty Huluk, who roomed with Anna and her mother, came home from her job at the grocery store around the corner. Betty had once dated

Suchan, in fact had been his date the night he met Anna.

When she came home that day, Betty brought a newspaper and handed it to Anna Bosnich. Anna, who was busy, tossed the paper in to Steve and Lennie without glancing at it.

Anna heard the two men talking between themselves: "Well, that is news!" and the newspaper crackled as Lennie and Steve devoured every word of the headline article. Anna paid little attention.

Anna's mother didn't like these two men friends of her daughter's. She told Anna she would not prepare their meals—they would have to fend for themselves.

About 6:30 p.m., Steve and Lennie went out to eat. They were away about two hours. Apparently Lennie had come to Toronto to see his sister Mary. Their brother Sam Stone was due to be released from Kingston Penitentiary in a few weeks and Lennie wanted to arrange a meeting with him.

It seems that Suchan and Jackson had put out of their minds a bizarre event which had occurred several weeks earlier. The consequences of this event would, within forty-eight hours, cause Steve Suchan to skyrocket from obscurity to the front pages of the nation's biggest newspapers, and Leonard Jackson to be transformed from a folk-hero bank robber to "the most vicious criminal since Red Ryan".*

Around the first of February, Mary Mitchell had visited Edmund Tong. The police version of the story is that Mitchell told Tong and his partner, Roy Perry, that a group of thugs were using a certain car to run stolen merchandise to Montreal. The car was a 1951 black Monarch sedan, licence number 418-A-2. A quick check revealed that the car was registered to Anna Bosnich at a Wright Avenue address. Sergeant Tong thanked Mary for the information and she left his office.

According to police, Mitchell then went to Lennie and Steve and claimed that the police had extracted this information from her through torture. She pulled down the front of her blouse and

---

*In 1923, bank robber Norman "Red" Ryan escaped from Kingston Penitentiary, was recaptured and sentenced to twenty-five years. He was paroled after eleven years when he convinced authorities that he had "got religion". Ten months later, in the act of robbing a Sarnia liquor store, Ryan shot and killed a policeman and was fatally wounded himself.

revealed several ugly red sores on her breasts, purportedly caused by cigarette butts.

"Mary!" gasped Suchan. "Who did this?"

"Tong," was the quick response. "I had to tell them something. So I guess you better keep away from Wright Avenue for a while. They're sure to be watching her."

Sergeant Adolphus Payne, in retrospect, feels sure that Mitchell inflicted the burns on herself. "Every time I saw her come out from Tong's office, she was smiling. I didn't see her every time she came out of there, naturally, but Tong would never have burned her."

However, regardless of Tong's personal behaviour, there were members of the police force who had a reputation for mistreating women, especially prostitutes and call-girls, who were especially vulnerable. An ex-con remembers:

> Now I knew a broad who was a hustler, who this detective picked up – and I've no reason to doubt the girl's word – took down to Cherry Beach, took her purse off her, took her money, slapped her in the mouth, and said to her, "Get the heck out, walk your way back." Not only once, but two different broads, and not together, told me the same thing. This was 1951, '52.

If there was even a possibility that such a rumour were true, no doubt Suchan and Jackson would have believed Mary Mitchell's story. Payne thinks Mitchell poisoned their minds against Tong. His analysis: "Mary Mitchell was a wicked woman." Did she love Suchan? Payne insists, "She loved the money he spent on her."

Perhaps Mary Mitchell intended to incriminate Anna Bosnich, or perhaps she just wanted to keep Suchan away from her. The result of her game, in any case, was far more devastating than she could possibly have predicted.

12

While Lennie and Steve were out for supper, Anna noticed some boxes that Steve had unpacked in her bedroom. One was a metal target, and another, an unopened box which had "Air Pistols" written on the side. She asked Steve about them as soon as he returned. "Oh, that's just a set I got for Christmas," he said, and left them on her dresser.

Lennie was made comfortable in the back room, and Suchan spent the night with Anna. The next day, she was up before either of them, feeding the baby and bustling about doing household chores. She didn't really notice when the two men got up, but they were in and out of the house all day, going out to eat or to the Kozak's.

After lunch, Anna heard some unusual sounds from the basement, as if someone were hitting a hammer against the wall. Since the only entry to the basement was from the ouside, she ignored the noise. Later, she saw Steve and Len coming through the hall from outside, air pistols in their hands. The sight of the pistols upset her, and she spoke to Steve.

"Are they dangerous?"

"No. Look," said Steve. "You can use darts, and you can use pellets with it. It's not dangerous."

"Well, what are you doing with them?"

"We're just trying them out."

"Well," said Anna, "as long as they aren't harmful — I wouldn't want them around the house where the little girl [her school-age daughter] could get at them."

Suchan reassured her, and Anna thought no more about it. She didn't bother to look in the basement.

About four years earlier, Anna had had a job making wigs for displays. When she left the job, she stored in her basement a plaster head and torso. The head had several nailholes in the skull where a skull-cap had been attached. When Steve Suchan and Leonard Jackson came up from the basement, not only the skull but the face and torso of the dummy were riddled with holes. Obviously one of them was a pretty good shot: there were four holes in the head—at the base of the nose, at th end of the right eyebrow, the end of the left eyebrow and the middle of the left eyebrow. One hole pierced the heart area.

One thing which Anna did notice was a textbook on pistols and revolvers by J.S. Hatcher. Suchan had brought it with him to Wright Avenue and left it on Anna's dresser. On page 12 was a reference to the Webley air pistol, the weapon Suchan used, claiming it was "not a firearm, but excellent for pistol practice". Apparently Suchan would sometimes drive out to a gravel pit outside Toronto and practice shooting at trees and other objects.

Suchan and Jackson made another visit that day. They stopped in to see Edwin and Dorreen Boyd.

"Well, I'm here," said Suchan.

"What's that supposed to mean?" demanded Boyd.

"I heard the news. You guys knocked off that bank. Geez, I'm short of money."

Dorreen would have none of this. "He thinks he's going to get some of your money," she said to Edwin. Then she turned to Suchan, "You're not getting any of it."

"I don't want any of it," protested Suchan. "You guys held up the bank. It's yours."

"Well I hope you remember that," replied Dorreen.

Boyd and Dorreen were now living in a rooming house on Spadina Road. The children had been farmed out to a boarding school. Dorreen had left the Pickering house to escape neighbourhood gossip. Everyone knew about Ed, and although they were kind to her, the children suffered. "If anything happened in the neighbourhood," she said, "no matter who did it, the children would be to blame because of Ed." She put the house up for sale.

The Pickering house was still unfinished, a grim little one-storey cottage made of grey cement blocks. Although she and Edwin had spent many hours working to make it fit to live in, it was still unpainted, the floor and plywood partitions between the four rooms unfinished, the yard still mud and crabgrass. But at least it had been a home.

Now she and Ed were holed up in one room of a rooming house, with $21,000 in cash in a leather briefcase by their bed, ready to try the straight life for a while. Suchan and Jackson would soon change all that.

That Wednesday night Arthur Maloney, a vigorous young Toronto lawyer with a growing professional reputation, dined at the Metropole. As he was finishing his meal, Sergeants Tong and Perry came into the restaurant and joined him for coffee. They talked for a while, then the policemen left. Maloney remembers: "They said they were going to pick up some thugs."

Sergeant Payne, relaxing at home, thought of the job he had to do the next day. It was his day off, and he had been promising his wife he would install the venetian blinds. He would try to get at it right after breakfast.

Edwin Boyd, also relaxing at home, was thinking ahead to a future that might not be so rosy. It might not be a bad idea to stash some money away someplace. Dorreen had a large box of Tampax, and Boyd started to pull some of the tampons apart. He rolled up several wads of hundred dollar bills, stuffed them into the cardboard tubes, and put the original stuffing back in the ends of the tubes. Then he put all the tampons back in the box.

On the morning of Thursday, March 6, 1952, Anna Bosnich drove to Fern Avenue School. Her daughter had been late on several occasions and Anna was determined to correct the situation. Suchan and Jackson lounged about the house for a few hours. When Anna returned, Steve asked to borrow her car for a while. Anna was reluctant to let him have it—she thought he was responsible for some recent damage done to one wheel—but she hunted up her spare keys and let him go.

The day progressed normally for Anna, Suchan and Jackson coming and going, her daughter arriving home for lunch at noon. Betty Huluk, the roomer, who also arrived for lunch, noticed Suchan and Jackson leaving the house shortly after noon. She didn't notice that each of the men carried a heavy briefcase, or that they got into Anna's Monarch and drove off, heading west on Wright Avenue.

Toronto Police car D-5 (the fifth detective car) was travelling north on Roncesvalles and had just passed Fern Avenue. Sergeant Roy Perry was at the wheel with Edmund Tong in the passenger seat. As Perry recalled, they had been looking for a certain black Monarch for some time and had often seen it parked on Wright Avenue. They knew it was registered to Anna Bosnich, but were more interested in who else might be driving it. Tong had been talking to some of his contacts, but Perry didn't know what, if anything, he'd found out.

The car ahead of them was creeping along, but Tong and Perry, always on the alert, spotted a black sedan turning off Wright Avenue, north of Roncesvalles. They could make out two figures in the car but were too far away to read the licence plate. Perry stepped on the accelerator.

Pulling out from behind the slow-moving vehicle, the two officers followed the Monarch for several blocks. In early March the roads were somewhat treacherous, and caution was required to navigate the icy ruts on side streets. The Monarch was pulling away from them.

Following about a block behind, Perry and Tong finally came to Dundas Street and turned east to cross the bridge over the railway tracks. As they approached the intersection of Dundas and College, Perry finally was able to read the licence number of the Monarch. It was 418-A-2.

As both vehicles proceeded east on College Street, the traffic light turned red against them at Landsdowne. Perry pulled up nearly beside the Monarch, which had stopped for the light. Sergeant Tong rolled down his window.

"Pull over to the curb, boys," said Tong opening the police car door. The Monarch slowly wheeled over to the side. Traffic moved forward around the two cars as the lights changed to green again. Tong began to walk toward the Monarch. Closest to him was Steve Suchan at the wheel.

Did Tong catch a glimpse of Lennie Jackson in the passenger seat? For a split second he may have realized that he should have approached with revolver drawn, or first radioed for help. In any case, he appeared to hesitate a moment, as if to turn away.

Suchan was terrified. He had a wanted man in his car and had harboured Boyd, the RCMP's tenth most-wanted criminal, to say nothing of his own criminal activities. There would be a scandal. His family would be involved. Blind panic seized him. He picked up his .455 Smith and Wesson and fired through the open window.

The slug tore through the soft flesh of Tong's left breast, ripping through his lung. Its path was almost horizontal, and the tissue barely slowed it down. Passing through the spinal cavity, the bullet severed the spinal cord, finally coming to rest under Tong's right shoulder blade.

With a half-twist of his body, Tong turned to look toward Perry, then fell in a crumpled heap on the roadway between the cars.

Almost with the first shot Jackson leapt out of the car. Grabbing his .32-20, he took aim over the rear of the Monarch. Steve was in the process of emptying his weapon's bullets into the hood of the police car.

Perry was still in the car. When he saw Tong fall, he lunged for the emergency brake. Immediately he saw a flash of fire from the front seat of the Monarch. A bullet smashed through the windshield. Yanking desperately on the door handle, Perry saw the driver raising his arm to fire again.

Instinctively, Perry threw up his arm to protect his head. Fire-flashes burst from the driver's seat and from the rear of the car. A sharp sting burned his arm and it went totally numb. He blacked out.

The light had turned red in front of him, but Suchan rammed the shift lever into first and started to pull away while Lennie ran alongside and leapt in.

"Christ," Lennie said, "that was a cruiser. Somebody's been hit! Let's get out of here."

Suchan gunned the black Monarch through the red light and drove east on College Street, frantically looking for a side-street where they could ditch the car. On Sheridan Avenue, a one-way street, he wheeled right and cruised slowly two blocks south. Luck was with him. After crossing Dundas, he spotted a taxi parked waiting for a fare. He stopped, let Jackson out, then drove ahead a hundred yards and pulled in to the left-hand curb.

Across the street Mrs. Pauline Penney was looking out her window. When the Monarch pulled in and stopped across the street, she watched the driver. She was curious because the car had been moving so slowly down the block. The man appeared to be very nervous. First he backed out of the car, then reached in and picked up something from the seat, pocketing it before she could see what it was. He stood for a moment, looking up and down the street, clutching his coat pocket. Finally, he pulled up his collar and walked away in the direction he had come.

Mrs. Penney withdrew from the window to tend to her baby. When she returned a few minutes later, the man had disappeared. Although she had only seen his face in profile she had the feeling she had seen him before.

The scene at College Street and Lansdowne Avenue was charged with excitement. A passerby ran to Sergeant Perry and shook him gently. It was enough to bring him to consciousness. He reached for his two-way radio. "This is Car D-5, College and Lansdowne. We've been shot," he said into the microphone.

Laura Price, who had pulled up behind the police car and had seen Tong fall, leapt out of her car and rushed forward to render assistance. As she ran to the injured detective, she noticed the passenger in the escaping car looking back. She spoke to Tong, and he tried to tell her something, forming his words with great effort.

At that point, William Fawcett, who had braked his truck to a stop just behind Mrs. Price's car, also jumped out of his vehicle and ran over to Tong. Tong's overcoat pocket bulged out a bit. Fawcett noticed Tong's service revolver inside, unholstered. Obviously Tong was prepared to use the gun but had never had a chance to draw it from his pocket.

Behind Fawcett, Detective Robert Miller and his partner pulled up in their cruiser. Miller jumped out and ran over to Perry who was slumped over the wheel of the bullet-riddled police car.

"I'm okay," Perry said. "See about Eddie."

Miller rushed over to Tong who was facing him, lying on his left side. Tong's right hand was near his face. Weakly, he motioned for Miller to stoop down beside him.

Fighting to maintain consciousness, Tong whispered hoarsely, "It was Steve Suchan, 190 Wright Avenue. Get over there right away." Then his eyes closed and his hand dropped loosely to the pavement.

After passing on this information to other police officers who were now converging on the scene in numbers, Miller radioed the dispatcher to make sure the ambulance was on its way.

It was 1:25 p.m. Edmund Tong was still lying wounded in the road, and the shooting site was swarming with detectives, police officers, and onlookers. One of the officers wrapped a blanket around Perry and drove him to the emergency ward of St. Joseph's Hospital. He took a description of the two men from Perry and relayed it to the dispatcher.

You can feel invisible in a big city, as though your actions generally go unnoticed. The feeling is largely illusory. Mrs. Minnie McKercher, who lived opposite the Kozak home, watched a taxi come north, turn around in a blind street and pull up at the side entrance. She recognized Suchan as he got out of the taxi and headed for the side door. A moment later she observed Lennie Jackson get out and also proceed into the house.

At the beginning of that week, Mrs. Kozak had hired a couple of painters. One of them, William Fedezyszyn, was standing on a sawhorse inside the kitchen near the side door. When Suchan barged into the kitchen, the door struck the sawhorse and slid it sideways several inches. Fedezyszyn, paint can in one hand, was forced to jump. Suchan hurried into the hallway without comment.

Fedezyszyn had no sooner resumed his stand on the sawhorse and begun painting again than the performance was repeated. Lennie Jackson shoved the door open, rocking the sawhorse precariously as Fedezyszyn saved his neck a second time by jumping to the floor.

Suchan and Jackson ignored the disgruntled painter as they searched wildly for a means of escape. Suchan knew that the police would find Anna's car in a matter of minutes — possibly they had already found it. They would grill her, search her home . . . ! There was a slim chance that he could throw them off the track. He grabbed the phone and dialled.

Anna knew something was wrong the minute she heard his hushed and guarded tone. He told her to call the police immediately and report her car stolen. She pressed him for an explanation but he insisted she would be better off if she didn't know. Then he hung up.

Suchan changed his coat, picked up his leather briefcase containing ammunition and weapons. He went to the front door and checked the street. Lennie exited by the side door. The cab was waiting near the curb, its motor idling. From across the street, Mrs. McKercher watched the two fugitives get into the back seat of the taxi, which then turned left onto Sorauren and headed south toward Queen Street.

Anna Bosnich tried twice to dial the number of the police. Her trembling fingers refused to cooperate and she called Betty Huluk for help. Betty dialled the number for her and handed over the receiver.

As the officer took down the details Anna was giving him, Sergeant Fred Raymer, in response to a police radio bulletin, was patrolling the vicinity of the shooting. At 1:31 p.m. he headed south on Sheridan, and at 1:33 spotted the black Monarch and radioed the dispatcher.

At this moment, the ambulance carrying Detective Tong was speeding away from the scene, its siren wailing and red light flashing. It reached the Toronto General Hospital at 1:46 p.m., just as the police dispatcher was broadcasting the following bulletin to all units:

DESCRIPTION OF TWO MEN WANTED RE SHOOTING

NO. 1: 35, 5'10", SLIM BUILD BLACK MOUSTACHE, WEARING BLUE TOPCOAT, GREY FEDORA, HORN RIMMED GLASSES, JEWISH APPEARANCE.

NO. 2: 35–38, HEAVY BUILD, FULL FACE, WEARING DARK BEIGE OVERCOAT, DARK FEDORA. BOTH MEN ARMED WITH AUTOMATIC PISTOLS.

The descriptions were fairly accurate except for one detail: Suchan was twenty-four years old, not thirty-five to thirty-eight. Apparently police had not yet checked their records for the name Tong had struggled so hard to give them, though officers were methodically searching Criminal Identification Branch files, and were swiftly following up the address Tong had passed on to Detective Miller.

Anna Bosnich barely had time to hang up the phone when police officers appeared at the door, began questioning her and her roomer, and initiated a search of the house.

Several miles away, Suchan and Jackson were carrying out a program of evasive action. Leaving the taxi, they boarded a westbound streetcar which took them to the end of the line, then caught a bus to Port Credit. At 2:35 they hired a cab to drive them to Oakville where they planned to catch an eastbound train for Montreal. But the cabbie was not familiar with Oakville, missed the turnoff to the station, and arrived just as the train sped by.

By the time they realized they were stranded, the taxi driver was gone. Suchan and Jackson picked up their briefcases and walked away from the station.

A few blocks away, taxi-driver William Bowles cruised east on Spruce Street. He was about three blocks from the station when he heard a whistle. Two men approached and flagged him down.

"How much to take us to Bronte?"

"Oh, that'd be $1.25."

"You got yourself a fare."

Suchan and Jackson got in the cab. Bowles asked where they wanted to go in Bronte. The two men decided the hotel would be fine. Bowles shook his head. There was no hotel in Bronte.

Well then, the bus station would do. The pair seemed to feel that an explanation was in order. They told the cabbie they had missed their connections. Somewhat later they said they had had trouble with their car. Bowles didn't care. A fare was a fare. He dropped them at the station in Bronte. Suchan paid the $1.25.

At 3:30 p.m., Sydney Plummer was having coffee in the combination grocery store, lunch room and bus ticket office in Bronte. Next door was his taxi office. A man rapped on the window, and Plummer opened the door.

"What's the cab fare to Burlington?"

"Two dollars, sir."

Suchan accompanied Plummer to his taxi. Jackson stood waiting beside the car and opened the door for Suchan. The pair got in.

In Toronto, the news had hit the radio. Sergeant Payne stopped in mid-air. He was in the midst of putting up the venetian blinds when the announcer broadcast a sketchy account of the shooting of Detectives Tong and Perry. The news was stunning. Payne picked up the telephone and called his partner, Ken Craven. They debated whether it could have been Boyd. The radio had not yet mentioned the name Steve Suchan, but police had pulled Suchan's "rap sheet"—his criminal record—and were preparing to broadcast it.

In Burlington, Suchan and Jackson caught yet another cab. The owner of the DeLuxe Taxi Company made a point of checking all long-distance fares personally. His brother-in-law had brought in the two passengers who wanted to go to the Royal Connaught Hotel in Hamilton. Before giving permission, the owner went out to the cab and took a good look at the passengers. Deciding they would be good for the fare he gave the okay, but the faces were imprinted in his memory.

Less than an hour later, the police air waves were crackling with bulletins:

MAN WANTED. STEVE SUCHAN, AGE 24 YEARS, 6'1½", MED. BUILD, DARK BROWN HAIR, BROWN EYES, CZECHOSLOVAKIAN, WANTED RE SHOOTING OF THE POLICE OFFICERS TODAY.

A few minutes later, another bulletin was issued:

BLOOD DONORS WANTED. DETECTIVE

DEPARTMENT. MARCH 6/52.
BLOOD DONORS WANTED FOR SGT OF DET'S TONG,
BLOOD TYPE "O" POSITIVE. THERE WILL BE A NURSE
ON DUTY AT 6 P.M. TODAY AT TORONTO GENERAL
HOSPITAL. AUTH; INSPECTOR NIMMO.

A correction was later issued amending Suchan's height to 5'11", and all detectives were urged to watch for the gunmen.

Edwin and Dorreen Boyd were at home on Spadina Road. Neither had listened to the radio or seen a newspaper. They were waiting for dark when they would go out to a movie. It was one of the few diversions they felt they could risk, and neither of them enjoyed being cooped up in the rooming house.

In Hamilton, Suchan and Jackson entered the Royal Connaught Hotel. Leonard thought of Ann, alone in Montreal, worrying about where he was. He wondered if she had heard the news on the radio, and if she knew that his friend Val was the man known to the police as Steve Suchan. It was still broad daylight and the pair were jittery. There seemed to be police cars around every corner. They had to get out of sight.

From a message booth in the hotel, Jackson sent a telegram to Ann: "Darling, will be in later than expected. Love, Fred." Then he and Suchan scuttled across the street to a movie theatre. They stayed until dark.

There is no record of what movie they watched that afternoon, but neither Suchan nor Jackson were concentrating on it. They had only one thought in mind: what if Tong should die? The charge would be murder.

In Toronto, Edwin and Dorreen Boyd were also at the movies. The picture was "Another Man's Poison", and it provided them with the last few hours of relative pleasure they were to have for many months. As they walked out of the theatre, Edwin spotted the headline in the *Telegram*: "Gunmen Hunted by 1,000 Officers". A name leapt at him from the page: Edwin Boyd. The police believed that Suchan and Jackson had been on their way to a rendezvous with Boyd when the shooting occured. Boyd fished out a nickel and bought a paper. He and Dorreen hurried home.

Early the next morning they bought enough groceries to last a week, then went home and closed the door. They didn't emerge for seven days. All that they knew that week they learned from the newspapers or radio, and it was disturbing news indeed.

In Hamilton, the movie over, Leonard Jackson and Steve Suchan had a plan. At the first opportunity, and with the ease of much practice, they stole a car. Until then they had been travelling further and further from both Toronto and Montreal. Now they would start the long journey back under cover of night.

The Toronto Police had already investigated and dismissed several possibilities, the latest being that Suchan was staying at some hotel in Toronto with a woman and might be registered under one of several aliases. Shortly after, all divisional P.C.'s on day duty were sent home, including all day detectives in numbers 4, 8, and 10 divisions who had offered to work overtime on the case. For a time the city slept, and Suchan and Jackson sped past Toronto in fear, but in relative safety.

In Montreal, Ann Jackson was nervous and preoccupied. She had heard on the radio about the shooting and was worried that Leonard might be implicated. She had not yet seen a newspaper which would have confirmed her suspicions, but she had no idea where he was or why he hadn't come back. She slept fitfully.

Early the next morning, Friday, March 7, Mme. Côté, the caretaker's wife, heard the front doorbell of the apartment building ring. It was her duty to answer the door and take charge of any mail or parcels delivered for the occupants, but when she arrived at the door, Ann Jackson (whom she knew as Mrs. Wilson) was there receiving a telegram from a messenger. Mme. Côté had noticed Mrs. Wilson's nervousness the night before, and now observed that she went out shortly after receiving the telegram.

Ann stayed out shopping until about 5:30 p.m. When she arrived back at the apartment, Leonard was there waiting for her. Relieved to see him safely home, she noticed immediately that he had shaved off his moustache. Mme. Côté, who had also noted his arrival, was curious about his moustache and the fact that he was now without his eyeglasses as well. However, for the time being she kept her thoughts to herself.

Ann Jackson was also keeping some thoughts to herself, although with difficulty. By the time she saw Leonard, she had seen his and Suchan's names given in the newspapers as the men who had done the shooting. She decided not to take the paper home with her, but couldn't resist telling Leonard that she had heard about the shooting.

She thought he might have heard on the radio whether Tong had died.

"No, the radio says he's still alive."

"Well," said Ann, "that's good, because you know it would be murder if Tong died."

Her husband made no reply.

Ann Jackson remembers the evening of March 7:

> Later at 6 p.m., we heard the news on the radio, and the name of my husband and Steve Suchan were mentioned as being responsible for the shooting. My husband said, "Well, he should never have approached them."
> I took this to mean perhaps the man in the car Tong had stopped, but not specifically an admission from my husband that he was one of the men.

She remembered seeing the Wright Avenue address in the paper, and the fact that the car used in the shooting belong to Anna Bosnich. She began to piece things together and figure that Steve Suchan was, in fact, their friend Val.

> I did not mention this to my husband, and we did not discuss the matter further.

In Toronto, police had staked out the Kozak house and officer Lloyd Anderson spent a nervous night there, waiting to see if Suchan would show up.

Long before Suchan and Jackson left Hamilton, Anna Bosnich had been picked up. She was taken to Cowan Avenue Police Station where she submitted to a gruelling ten-hour questioning. The police were dogged and persistent, probing, backtracking, tracing events and connections.

Her stolen car story was easily broken down, and police soon had a great deal of additional information on Jackson and Suchan. At eleven p.m., Anna Bosnich was removed to headquarters, and then taken to the Belmont Street cells for the night. She was held as a material witness.

Police searched her house and confiscated, among other items: twenty-two .455 cartridges wrapped in a handkerchief found hanging on the sunporch door handle, two air pistols found under the stove, an overcoat bearing a label with Jackson's name written on it, two books on firearms, and a receipt for a money order sent to Victor J. Lenoff in Montreal.

Also questioned were Betty Huluk and a sister of Leonard Jackson's, Jane Blahut, who had been apprehended at the Kozak home where she had evidently gone to see Leonard. The newspapers made much of the fact that all three women who were questioned by police were well-dressed. Careful not to state that the women were "kept" by the gangsters, the newspapers took pains to imply it. "Mrs. Blahut wore a smart fur coat and rhinestone earrings. Mrs. Bosnich wore a black coat trimmed with white fur and carried white gloves, while Miss Huluk appeared in a well cut fur coat. Bail was set at $1,000 each."

By 5:53 p.m. on March 7, police had a bulletin sent out to their detectives:

AUTO WANTED. 324-385 (QUEBEC). 51 CHRYSLER SEDAN, DARK COLOUR. REGISTERED TO VICTOR LENOFF, MONTREAL. WANTED FOR INVESTIGATION OF OCCUPANTS RE SHOOTING OF POLICE OFFICERS.

At 7:55 p.m. an addition was made to the bulletin:

IF THIS CAR IS LOCATED, GET IN TOUCH WITH DETECTIVE HEADQUARTERS IMMEDIATELY, AND IF SEEN OCCUPIED, EXTREME CARE IS TO BE TAKEN. ONE OF THE OCCUPANTS IS BELIEVED TO BE STEVE SUCHAN, OUR C.I.B. 323/50 WANTED RE SHOOTING.

The C.I.B. referred to Suchan's Criminal Investigation Bureau number, where police found their description of him under his only previous conviction, for fraud.

Sergeant Tong's condition was the one news item that both sides were following intensively. It was crucial to everyone that Tong should live. Thursday night, six hours after the shooting, he hovered between life and death. After conversing with doctors, a police officer was seen shaking his head in despair. Transfusion after transfusion was pumped into Tong. An hour later, his blood pressure shot up. By midnight he was semi-conscious.

Inspector Alex McCathie whispered to Tong's nurse as they stood beside the injured man's bed. Recognizing the voice, Tong struggled to consciousness.

"Hello, Mac," he gasped. McCathie turned in time to see him wince with pain.

Inspector John Nimmo hovered nearby. He bent close to Tong as he watched the big, athletic chest laboriously rise and fall.

"Eddie," whispered Nimmo, "who did this to you?"

The answer was slow in coming, as Tong fought for consciousness. A murmer came from his lips, and Nimmo bent low to hear the name, "Steve Suchan." Gently, Inspector Nimmo held Eddie Tong's head up on the pillow as he showed him a fistful of pictures.

"That's him," he whispered, and fell back on the pillow. Nimmo looked at the picture his friend had recognized. It was Steve Suchan.

Doctors decreed that Tong was too weak for an operation. The single bullet still lodged where it had come to rest under his shoulder blade.

Sergeant Perry insisted on being moved from St. Joseph's Hospital to the General, so that he could be near his friend and partner, Eddie "The Chinaman" Tong. Dr. Tovee, the police surgeon, had already removed two pieces of lead from the sergeant's badly fractured arm, and Perry was reported doing well.

Drugged and heavy with sleep, Tong asked for and was given oxygen to ease his breathing. His condition was reported as "fair" to those who inquired. He was not told what all of Toronto knew—that if he recovered, he would probably never walk again. He would be paralyzed below the waist.

By Friday morning, Tong was feeling a little better. A nurse was about to give him an injection when Mrs. Tong appeared in the doorway. As the nurse tried to hustle his wife out of the room, Tong's voice came loud and clear from the bed:

"Hi Ev, come on in!" and he mustered a weak smile.

"How are you, Ed?" she asked.

"I'm fine, and so are all the hoodlums!"

The Tongs had recently bought a new house, and today was to be a special day for the family.

"When are you going to get better so we can celebrate Raymond's birthday?" asked his wife. "He's thirteen today, you know."

"Yes, I know he is. I remembered that. We'll have his party yet."

Tears welled in Ev Tong's eyes. She tried to control her voice as she replied, "We'll get another cake, too."

Edmund Tong wearily closed his eyes, but continued to talk to his wife.

"How are you getting on? I worried about you being there alone."

"I was all right. I had a girlfriend of yours with me."

"Oh did you? Who was she?"

"Alex Gibb of the *Star*," answered Mrs. Tong.

The "girlfriend" was a reporter, Alexandrine Gibb, who had been covering the Boyd Gang's exploits from the beginning. She had many contacts on the police force and had known Tong for some time. She specialized in the so-called "woman's point of view", writing stories on the women involved with the gang — the wives, girlfriends and lovers. Tong was glad that she was with his wife.

"Good for her," he said. "That's fine." He gave another smile, and closed his eyes again. The nurse whispered that he was going to sleep now.

"Yes," whispered Eddie Tong, "I am awfully tired."

13

When Steve Suchan entered his apartment on Friday afternoon, the rooms appeared quiet, safe. The sun streamed in, and everything was just as he had left it. But the very normalcy of the scene was a mockery to Suchan, for whom everything had changed. He didn't understand what had caused him to shoot down a police detective in the street. It had all happened so quickly. He felt divorced from the act, as though it were the product of panic, reflex, of half-formed intent.

Of the four gang members Suchan was the best educated, the most artistic, had the shortest criminal record, and was the youngest and most impressionable. Perhaps, under Jackson's influence, he had begun to see himself as a tough guy who would shoot his way out of a jam. Perhaps this self-image took over when he found himself in a tight spot.

Had he recognized Tong before he fired? Did he harbour a grudge against him because of Mary Mithcell's story that Tong had tortured her? Perhaps he did.

The influence of other people was an important factor in shaping Suchan's behaviour, but perhaps there was an even greater influence. Suchan's youthful sense of himself had been formed by his close relationship with his violin. It had been like a talisman, a magic object which, failing him, he had traded for another. Whether or not he was aware of it, a powerful force began to operate in his life the moment he chose to serve the magic of the weapon.

Edwin Boyd put it another way. "Suchan loved guns," said Boyd. End of philosophy. Boyd remembered Suchan practicing shooting, aiming at whatever crossed his path, even while they were driving down the highway. Once Suchan pointed his gun at Boyd in jest. Boyd, who through his army training had developed a great respect for weapons, was furious with Suchan.

Since the summer of 1949, Suchan had become more and more accustomed to owning weapons, carrying them on his person and firing them whenever he could find an abandoned gravel pit or a remote sideroad.

A gunsmith in Toronto's east end sold him large quantities of ammunition. On one shopping spree in November 1951, Suchan bought 300 rounds of nine-millimetre ammunition clips and two shoulder holsters. On other occasions he was in the habit of ordering several boxes of shells at a time.

When Suchan couldn't practice with one of his several handguns, he would sharpen up his aim indoors with an air pistol.

Possibly he had indulged in a romantic fantasy of himself involved in a movie-style gun battle with police. Possibly he applied the same kind of perfectionism to his revolver as he had formerly applied to his violin. After all, the revolver had provided him with rewards that his violin had failed to provide—money, an expensive car, status, and plenty of leisure time.

In any case, unlike Boyd's ingrained reluctance to fire his weapon, a tremendous psychological pressure had been building in Suchan to use his handgun for the purpose for which it was intended.

One of the ironies of the present situation was that two and a half years of practice in developing his marksmanship had culminated in an event that rendered all the practice superfluous. He had snapped off a shot at a man who was less than three feet away. Any trigger-happy thug with brains enough to point could have hit a target from that distance.

But Suchan had too much on his mind at the moment to engage in such speculations.

Once inside his Montreal apartment, he removed from his briefcase a .30 calibre Mauser automatic pistol with ten rounds of ammunition in it. He took out two extra clips for the Mauser, each loaded with ten rounds. He slid the clips into his pocket along with his billfold. The pistol he seated in a small holster which fit snugly against his right side, retained by his belt.

Then he fished out two seven-round clips for a .45 Colt automatic and stuffed them into his rear pocket. The Colt he inserted under his belt in front. His favourite weapon, the .455 revolver with which he had shot Tong and Perry, he slid into its holster on the left side of his belt.

Suchan was a walking arsenal. In addition to the three handguns, he was now carrying on his person a total of forty-seven rounds of ammunition.

Thus prepared to live out his role of the heavy gangster, Suchan changed his topcoat and went out to try to raise some quick money by selling his 1951 Chrysler.

Suchan had no way of knowing that when Anna had wired him the $200 two weeks earlier, she had kept the telegraph receipt. This document, bearing the name Victor J. Lenoff and Suchan's Côte des Neiges address in Montreal, was now in the hands of Inspector McCathie, the canny Scot who headed the Detective Division of the Toronto Police Force.

McCathie had already alerted Montreal police, and at six p.m., while Suchan was searching for a used car dealer, seven Montreal detectives descended upon the Croydon Apartments on Côte des Neiges. There they questioned nineteen-year-old Claude Legault, one of the staff. Legault had a key to Suchan's apartment, and Montreal police thought they could use him to get Suchan out in the open.

"All right," one of the officers said, "come upstairs and open the door."

"Oh, no, I'm too scared to do that. You can do it yourself—here's my key."

Taking Legault with them, the seven officers went to apartment 330 and opened it. After they had satisfied themselves that it was empty, they instituted a search. In a closet near the door, they discovered the tan-coloured briefcase containing various types of ammunition, a couple of holsters, a "Duo" 6.35mm automatic pistol, and the six spent casings from fired cartridges. Also in the apartment was Suchan's beautiful new $600 violin.

The officer in charge, Detective Captain Langpré, detailed four of the officers to stake out the apartment while he and the other would take Legault and search for Suchan's car. As he was leaving, he stopped near the door. "Was the bathroom light on?" he asked.

A couple of the officers shrugged their shoulders. They couldn't remember. "I know the living room lights and the bedroom lights were on," said Sergeant Albert Dauphin.

"Well, never mind," said Langpré. "If we come back we'll knock five times, slowly."

When Langpré closed the door behind him, the four remaining officers laid plans to prepare for the return of Suchan and any of the gang members who might be with him. Sergeant Dauphin and his partner waited in the darkened kitchenette off the living room, while the two other detectives hid in the bedroom down the hall. It was ten after six, suppertime. The four police officers weren't hungry.

Suchan had finally struck a bargain with an automobile dealer. While the manager wrote out a check for $1,800, Suchan cleaned out the Chrysler. He was glad to get rid of it. It wouldn't be too long before the police had a make on it. Later when things cooled off, he'd buy another — maybe even a better one. He opened the trunk and removed a suitcase. He decided to leave it at the dealer's and pick it up later.

By 8:20 Sergeant Dauphin had settled into the oppressive tedium of the stakeout. He walked quietly around the cramped kitchenette to stretch his legs. One of the qualities a good cop needs, he thought, is a high tolerance for boredom. The four of them could spend their whole shift here, not daring to interrupt the silence for more than a few whispered phrases, unable to relax, probably stuck without a coffee break. Sure, there was always the risk of getting shot, but as the hours wore on you almost wished something would happen, just to break the suspense.

Three floors below his darkened apartment, Steve Suchan sauntered into the restaurant on the lower level of the Croydon. He sat down at his usual table and looked at the menu.

Maurice, the waiter, who recognized him as a good tipper, came over. "Yes, sir. What would you like tonight?"

"I don't know. . . . What's good?"

"The lobster is very nice."

Suchan looked up. "Oh, yes," he said, "today's Friday. I'll take the lobster."

At 9:32 Suchan finished his meal, left a fifty-cent tip for the waiter, and paid his bill. He stuffed the change into his shirt pocket and went upstairs.

Inside apartment 330 Sergeant Dauphin was alerted by the sound of a key scraping in the lock. He knew it couldn't be Langpré returning. There was no knock.

Dauphin unholstered his service revolver, peeked out of the kitchenette door, and waited for whoever had entered to step out of the entry-alcove into the lighted hallway. The man took five steps into the apartment, and Dauphin could see that he fitted the description and the photo that been circulated to his team earlier.

Suchan turned his back to the kitchenette, puzzled about a suitcase that was standing in the hall. He was sure he had left it in the closet. But sometimes the janitor went into his apartment—perhaps he had left it there. A slight noise behind Suchan caused him to wheel around. He spotted movement and grabbed for the big .455 revolver in his belt.

As his fingers closed around the heavy handle, two features of the image before him registered sharply: a man's forehead, and the barrel of a handgun. Before he could level the .455, a slug hit him in the chest just below the heart. He felt a sharp stinging pain.

In rapid succession, he took two more .38 slugs, the first in the left hand, the second lower down in the middle of the torso. The impact of the shots jerked his body around and sent him crashing to the floor on his right side. He still clutched his revolver and weakly tried to raise it. Dauphin kicked the handgun away, and another officer retrieved it.

As Dauphin and his fellow officers rolled Suchan over and disarmed him, Suchan continued to play his tough-gangster role.

"Why didn't you give it to me in the head?" he said to Dauphin. "Why didn't you finish me?"

"You punk – you won't shoot any more cops."

"Aaah, you creeps can't shoot," Suchan retorted as Sergeant Côté, Dauphin's partner, bent over him.

"As far as we're concerned, " Côté said evenly, "we're anxious to have you alive."

Suchan looked up at Côté belligerantly. "Gimme one in the head," he challenged. "Nobody'll know the difference."

Côté exchanged a look with Dauphin. It wasn't the sort of reaction they expected from a man who had just been shot three times. For a few moments nobody spoke. One of the detectives was already dialling for an ambulance, another was collecting the articles in Suchan's pockets. Suchan spoke again. "How did you find us?" he asked.

Despite his pain and the seriousness of his situation, Suchan could still engage in what might seem idle curiosity. In doing so, he revealed something about himself. Apparently he conceived of his life as a game between him and the police. His pride depended upon outwitting them, and at this moment he knew he had failed. He needed to know the circumstances so that he could rationalize his failure. There was always the chance that he could chalk up his capture to blind luck on the part of the cops, betrayal by some trusted friend, or the stupidity of an associate.

Policemen sense the criminal's need to know how he has been caught. But Dauphin and his fellow officers, feeling hostile toward Suchan, refused to tell him anything. They went about their business of collecting evidence while they waited for the ambulance.

After Suchan arrived at Queen Elizabeth Hospital, he was manacled by the ankles to a bed and wheeled into surgery where a laparotomy (incision and opening of the lower abdomen) was performed. A section of his bowel was repaired, and a slug was removed from his abdomen. Surgeons also removed a slug from the left side of his chest. It had passed through tissue an inch from the heart.

In preparing Suchan for the operation, doctors had accidentally made an interesting discovery. In the right lower quarter of Suchan's chest, the X-ray plate revealed the presence of a slug. The bullet was apparently an old one, and the coinciding wound was completely healed.

Where and when did Suchan pick up this slug? During Leonard Jackson's first Bradford bank robbery in July 1951, Constable Wilson had pumped four shots into the getaway vehicle. Wilson later thought he had hit one of the robbers. It seems likely that he hit Suchan. Edwin Boyd remembers that Suchan would sometimes entertain people by letting them feel the hard lump under his skin, rolling it around between their fingers.

Toronto newspapers had a heyday with Suchan's capture. "Suchan Mowed Down in Montreal Suite, Bullet Only Inch from Heart," explained the *Star*, with large pictures of Suchan manacled to his bed, and a head-and-shoulders cut of Sergeant Dauphin.

But the story that caught the hearts and emotions of Torontonians was the report on Sergeant Tong. "Tong 'Very Low', Emerges from Coma after Stroke" said the headline. Inspector Nimmo had spent twelve hours with Tong. Early that morning, Mrs. Tong had been called to the hospital.

One of the *Telegram*'s stories began with a grabber: "Steve Suchan had a big lobster dinner—as well as two loaded .45's under his belt— when he walked into a police ambush in his posh apartment last night."

The *Telegram* also interviewed the restaurant cashier, "shapely Cecile", as they unblushingly described her. She said that she had sold cigarettes to Edwin Boyd the week before. "I knew it was him... as soon as I saw his picture in the paper today. I just about died. If I had known it was him, I wouldn't have served him."

"Shapely Cecile" 's report was followed by Maurice, the waiter's, who claimed to have taken two detectives up to the apartment and seen a heap of large bills on the table. "I don't know how much it was ... but it must have been plenty. There were many 20's and 50's."

Another bit of gossip, if true, sheds some light on the way Suchan's mind was operating prior to his confrontation with Tong. The previous week, Robert, the young dishwasher at the Croydon, had delivered some cigarettes to apartment 330. When Suchan opened the door, Robert saw a number of guns lying around the room. Suchan reportedly said to him, "Do you want to shoot someone? Try one of these." Robert didn't want to touch any of the guns and left immediately.

The *Telegram* zeroed in on the important clue which had led police to Suchan — the telegraph receipt in Anna Bosnich's purse. Moreover, the *Tely* served up some juicy tidbits that the *Star* failed to collect or did not choose to print. But on balance, the *Star* exploited the story more effectively than the *Telegram,* and won this round in the battle for readership that was to continue for another twenty years.

The world of journalism was changing subtly. Readers were becoming more sophisticated and less willing to tolerate newspapers who sacrificed credibility to flamboyance. Eventually "shapely Ceciles" would no longer appear in print, spurious titillation would be kept to a minimum, and editors would avoid purple prose like this sample from the *Telegram*:

> Tong's eyes are shut tight. He breathes with difficulty: his breathing sounding almost like groans, strikes terror into the heart of his wife.

But in 1952, such phrases sold newspapers, and the two big Toronto dailies were locked in a circulation war. Crime stories broke fast and boosted circulation. Coverage had to be rapid and heavy.

Journalists had little time to reflect upon the fact that in the process of "getting the story" they were gradually creating a myth. Edwin Boyd read about it in his room on Spadina Road. Leonard Jackson, holed up in his Montreal apartment, saw the pages and pages of newspaper coverage. Even Willie Jackson followed the news in his cell in the Kingston Penitentiary.

None of them realized that the myth being created by the press was the phenomenon known as "The Boyd Gang".

14

During the week following the Tong shooting, Leonard and Ann Jackson had kept to their little Lincoln Avenue apartment, not once venturing out. The newspapers had published pictures of Leonard from police files, along with retouched pictures showing him wearing glasses and a moustache. The Jacksons were terrified that someone on the street or in the building might recognize him. When Mme. Côté enquiried about "Mr. Wilson", Ann replied that he was ill and confined to his room.

The afternoon of Saturday, March 8, Ann and Leonard learned of Suchan's capture over the radio. Ann started to cry. By now she knew everything, and feared that the police might come for her husband at any minute.

Leonard, too, became despondent. "Poor Val. He's only a kid!" They had to get out of the apartment for a while, so they took a drive and then went to a movie, returning only after dark.

That evening they discussed their desperate situation. They were all but out of money. Even the twelve-dollar rent was going to be hard to come up with. Leonard's suggestion was that they sell the car, and Ann would take the money and go away. Now that she was pregnant, Len worried about her.

"Do you think you would have a better chance on your own?" asked Ann.

"Well, as far as I can see, there's not much chance either way."

"Then I'm going to stay with you. I love you, Len."

"Well, we're still going to have to get some money somehow."

They decided to sell the car, and Ann went to see their old friend, the taxi driver. He agreed to come to the apartment on Monday morning and talk to Leonard about selling the car for them.

Earlier that afternoon, Sergeant of Detectives William Thompson and Detective Jack Gillespie of the Toronto Police Force flew to Montreal, carrying with them two envelopes given them by Inspector Nimmo. In the envelopes were discharged bullets and pieces of bullets taken from police car D-5 and from Sergeant Perry's arm. These envelopes along with articles seized from Suchan's apartment were forwarded to the RCMP Crime Detection Laboratory in Ottawa. Gillespie and Thompson introduced themselves to the Montreal Police, who were expecting them.

In the Lincoln Avenue apartment building, Ann Jackson consulted a neighbour about what to do for Leonard's upset stomach. The woman, Mme. Dumontier, gave her some powder which "Mr. Wilson" was to take when he felt he was going to be sick. Ann thanked her cordially, then left.

On Monday morning, the original and retouched photos of Leonard Jackson, with and without his moustache and glasses, appeared in the Montreal newspapers. Mme. Dumontier read the article with increasing alarm. She had seen Mr. Wilson when he returned on Friday, and had noticed the absence of his eyeglasses and moustache. She looked carefully at the photographs. What should she do now? She decided to wait until her husband came home. The hours ticked by slowly.

In the apartment beneath Mme. Dumontier, the taxi driver arrived to see Ann and Leonard. After a short conversation, he agreed to try to sell their car, took the keys, and said he would come back on Wednesday.

By now Jackson had placed his long barrelled revolver, an automatic pistol, and a supply of ammunition on the floor close to the chair where he usually sat. His tension grew each time the floor creaked or a car stopped outside. Ann tried to quell her own panic as the radio droned on about the shooting, the ambush on Suchan, or the condition of Sergeant Tong.

The latest news on Tong was somewhat encouraging, but hardly enough to cause rejoicing. A police bulletin on his condition told the whole story:

Sgt. of Dets. Tong showed a slight improvement today. He drank half a glass of orange juice and said two words. Det. Sgt. Perry is recovering progressively. The doctor will inspect his arm tomorrow morning to make sure that everything is all right.

Auth: Inspector Nimmo

Further information: Please advise all of Sgt. Tong's friends that he cannot have flowers in his room.

A letter from Chief Chisholm to all detectives advised that police personnel should refrain from visiting Tong and Perry in hospital, and that daily bulletins would be issued on their condition.

At four p.m., Monday, Eugene Dumontier returned home from work. His wife showed him the pictures in the paper and informed him that Leonard Jackson, the notorious criminal, was living in the apartment right under their very feet. By 6:30 p.m., he was convinced enough to go over to number 10 police station. He didn't tell his wife where he was going.

While Dumontier was away, his wife excitedly brought the news to the caretakers. She asked Mr. Côté what he intended to do about the situation. He said he would think it over. At midnight, he went up to the Dumontiers' apartment and borrowed their newspaper.

The following morning, Tuesday, Côté went to the police with the newspaper and the information that Jackson was living in the Lincoln Apartments. He said that the retouched picture of Jackson "hit me like a ton of bricks". The second tip convinced police that this was more than another wild story, of which they were receiving dozens from helpful citizens, anxious about their safety and angling for the $12,500 reward money being offered.

By this time, Ann Jackson was aware that something was happening. Around 5:15 p.m., she noticed someone going into Côté's apartment and was seized by a feeling af alarm. She went upstairs to the front door. Mme. Côté soon came up the stairs too. But the visitor was not with her, which made Ann even more suspicious. She went back downstairs and said to Leonard, "Something's wrong." Something was indeed very wrong.

Detective Gillespie of the Toronto Police Force, selected because he knew Leonard Jackson on sight, still wasn't sure what his plan of attack would be. He had several officers from the Montreal City Police to assist him, as well as Montreal Sergeant of Detectives Leo Murray, and his own Sergeant of Detectives, William Thompson.

He had arranged for Mme. Côté to leave the basement, but Henri Côté decided to hang around and watch in case something exciting happened. He wasn't disappointed.

Ann Jackson heard someone coming quietly down the stairs. She knew that none of the regular tenants did that, so she went over to the window and looked out. There was a man standing right outside the apartment window. "They're here, Leonard," she said.

Jackson sprang to his feet, leaving his supper of baked beans and eggs. He put on his coat and fedora, and went toward the door. He turned off the apartment lights.

Jack Gillespie stood down the hall a few feet. He and Sergeant Murray were still deciding what to do. The faint click of a lock turning was like the tick of a time bomb. Gillespie's eyes were fastened on the door to apartment 15.

The lock clicked again, and the door slowly opened outward

toward Gillespie. It was open only about ten inches, so Gillespie quietly tip-toed over and grabbed the handle with his left hand. In his right hand was his .38 calibre service revolver. Leonard Jackson stood ten feet inside the door.

In the split second before the firing began, Jack Gillespie and Leonard Jackson locked eyes, and knew each other instantly. Jackson's first shot whistled inches over Gillespie's head. On the second shot, Gillespie returned fire, wounding Jackson in the abdomen. Jackson spun around, but didn't fall. Both men continued to fire in the semi-darkness. Jackson had a pistol in one hand and his long-barrelled revolver in the other. Nearby was Ann's suitcase with literally pounds of ammunition in it. On the floor beside him were two Thompson sub-machine guns.

The door was still open less than two feet. Gillespie fired again and again. Jackson kept it up at an equal pace. Then Gillespie heard a clicking sound as he kept pulling the trigger. His revolver was empty, and Jackson was still firing. His heart hammering, Gillespie jumped back behind the hinged side of the door, joining Sergeant Murray.

Montreal police and Toronto's Sergeant Thompson continued the assault, firing through the window from outside, and through the open doorway in the hall. Bullets smashed into plaster. The shattering of the china sink in the apartment could barely be heard in the midst of the fusillade. Ann Jackson screamed for her husband to stop. He pushed her to the floor and continued to fire.

"Come and get me! Come and get me!" yelled Jackson. Then a moment later, perhaps for the benefit of the French police officers, he began to curse in French, "Tabernac'! Tabernac'!"

In a moment of desperation, Leonard Jackson tried to use his wife as a shield, hoping to make a break through the cordon of policemen. Grabbing Ann around the waist, he picked her up and held her in front of him as he edged toward the door. Screaming and kicking, Ann Jackson struggled to free herself from his grasp. "I'm coming out with my wife!" shouted Jackson.

Detective Landry, in the basement hallway with another officer, knew what Jackson was up to, and wouldn't let him get away with it. "If you do, we'll shoot!" he yelled back. Hysterical, Ann Jackson wrenched herself free. "Leonard, stop shooting, stop shooting! They'll kill you!" But Jackson was almost past caring.

From outside the apartment window, detectives watched Ann Jackson try to put her arms around her husband, and pull him away from the doorway. He pushed her away and drew another gun as his ammunition ran out.

Gillespie heard the wail of police sirens as reinforcements arrived. Tear gas was on the way. All the officers were now aware of Ann Jackson's presence in the apartment, and were afraid she might be hit in the firing. She crouched pathetically under the window ledge, terrified for herself, her husband, and for their unborn baby.

Down the street, uniformed police kept the rush-hour traffic away from the shooting. The residents of the apartment building were forbidden access to the area of the gun battle. Along with tear gas, sub-machine guns and extra ammunition were on the way. The shooting had been proceeding for almost half an hour.

Gillespie, out of ammunition, was now trapped at the end of the hallway, Jackson's apartment door between him and the exit. Police were still firing in the apartment windows, but Gillespie couldn't risk trying to rush past the door. The policemen outside kept talking and shouting in French. Gillespie, unable to understand a word, wondered what was happening. Fortunately, the shooting from outside had so far prevented Jackson from getting to his sub-machine guns. "If he gets those going," thought Gillespie, "I'll look like a waffle."

Finally the tear gas arrived. Shell after shell was lobbed through the window. Many failed to break when they dropped, rendering them ineffective. But the stench was beginning to build up.

"Tabernac'!" exclaimed Jackson, firing futilely in the direction of the gas. "Leonard, please don't shoot any more," cried Ann, as the gas kept coming in. Jackson was bleeding and had lost the use of his left hand. She watched, helpless, as he reloaded and fired with his right hand alone.

"Please give me the guns, Leonard. Let me take them out to the police. I want you to be alive." Jackson seemed not to notice.

"Leonard, remember the baby," pleaded Ann.

With a start, Jackson looked at his wife. She had at last touched a nerve. For a few seconds he thought of the coming child and the hopes they had for its future.

More tear gas poured through the window. Leonard and Ann

were beginning to feel sick. In the hallway, Gillespie had tears in his eyes from the burning gas. Choking and gagging, Jackson agreed to stop, not because of the gas, but for the sake of the baby.

"Okay!" he yelled. "My wife's coming out with the guns. Don't shoot any more!" Then the words that Gillespie longed to hear, "I give up."

A gun in each hand, coughing and crying, Ann Jackson warily stepped out into the hall.

"Drop them on the floor," commanded Gillespie. She dropped the guns without a word.

"Now kick them over here." Ann obeyed.

"Okay, get over here and stand behind us."

"All right, Jackson. Come out with your hands up!"

With tears stinging his eyes, his throat choking and burning, Leonard Jackson emerged from the room. He was bleeding from the abdomen, the left arm, and both hands, and held his arms at his sides.

"Put them up, Leonard." Very slowly, almost painfully, Leonard Jackson raised his arms above his head.

He looked Gillespie right in the eye. "Hello John," he said. "I'm glad I didn't hit you."

"You're not half as glad as I am," replied Gillespie.

"Did I hit any cops?" asked Jackson.

"No."

"Jeez, that's good. I was hoping I hadn't hurt any of them."

"Have you gone insane, Leonard?" Gillespie could hardly believe what was happening.

"I don't know," came the reply. "Look after my wife, will you, John? You have her to thank, you know. I wouldn't have given up if she hadn't been in the room."

Ann Jackson was trembling. By now the police were swarming around the building and surrounding area. She didn't know where to turn. Looking at Gillespie, she asked if she could go with her husband. Leonard turned, for a moment concentrating completely on her. As guns followed his every move, he slowly put one arm around her shoulders, bent his head and kissed her gently on the lips, once, twice, three times. With the last kiss, the blood from his wounds stained her bed jacket dark red. They parted. Jackson was handcuffed, then they were led out to the street.

A detective rummaged through the bags and found a sweater for Ann Jackson. It was still very cold in mid-March, and by now it was almost dark outside. Crowds pressed nearer as the group moved toward the cruisers parked on Lincoln Avenue.

In a gesture of defiance, Jackson raised his head to the onlookers. "I know who tipped off the police," he yelled, "and Boyd will be back to get them!" The words were dramatic, and many people who heard it, including Henri Côté, fully believed Jackson's warning. They didn't know it was pure bravado, and that Jackson and Boyd had gone their separate ways since the Leaside bank robbery. Everyone who heard the threat believed totally in the unity of the Boyd Gang and all that was implied in the title.

Sergeant Thompson met the group at the front door, and he and Gillespie sat on either side of Jackson. The introductions were almost comically polite.

"Sergeant William Thompson, Leonard Jackson."

"How do you do."

"How do you do."

The cruiser pulled out into the Montreal traffic. Unable to refrain from asking, Jackson, like Suchan, had to know where they had gone wrong.

"How did you catch on to us, John?"

"A little bird told me," replied Gillespie.

"It wasn't the telegram I sent from Hamilton, was it?"

"Could be," answered Gillespie, making a mental note. At that point, he knew absolutely nothing about a telegram from Hamilton. He would have to investigate that later.

The only other conversation on the way to the hospital concerned Jackson's wounds. He tried to disregard the pain, but he was fading quickly. The sweat poured down his body, and he began to breathe heavily. Sergeant Thompson asked if Boyd were in Montreal. Jackson replied that he didn't know, and Thompson, noticing Jackson's deteriorating condition, did not press the issue.

They stopped at the nearest hospital, the Western General, where Jackson was given emergency treatment, then continued on to the Montreal General Hospital on Dorchester Street.

By now, Jackson was going into shock from loss of blood. He was given transfusions, and the following day went under general anaesthesia for removal of the bullets and treatment of his wounds.

Police were taking no chances this time. Four armed policemen guarded his hospital room. His artificial foot was removed to prevent his trying to escape. One intern noted: "They're treating him like a king, even to having a four-man bodyguard. And the hospital didn't ask this guy for any $100 deposit before they let him in."

The belief was widespread that all the members of the Boyd Gang were extremely wealthy, living off the spoils of their robberies, and wanting for nothing. In fact, when Ann and Leonard Jackson were searched, police discovered a total of $1.43 divided between them in loose change. They were literally down to their last dollar.

So far, most of the public believed that Boyd was close to the scene of the shootout between Jackson and police. Even while Jackson was being admitted to hospital, Montreal police were on their way to follow up a hot tip on Boyd's whereabouts.

Armed with tommy guns, detectives surrounded a café in the town of Lachine, a Montreal suburb, where Boyd was believed to be living. Sources indicated that he had an apartment above the café. According to the Toronto *Daily Star* of March 12, "Boyd escaped by car a few minutes before police dashed into the café. They have the license number and are now searching the district for the car."

The tip was reported to have come from Ann Jackson who was being held and charged as a material witness. However, in her official signed statement to police, there is no mention of Boyd or his whereabouts.

Shortly after the raid at Lachine, two more raids took place, also in the search for Boyd. The first was at a frame farmhouse in Proulxville, about twelve miles outside Montreal. Police were keen and anxious after the two recent gun battles, and made a dramatic entrance with all guns drawn. As the *Telegram* reported, "Mrs. George Snowden was the most surprised woman in the province of Quebec last night." Boyd was nowhere near the farmhouse, but the information was not entirely inaccurate. He was certainly known there.

"I know Boyd," explained Mrs. Snowden, "but I haven't seen him lately. I don't know where he is. I'm just here with my children.... I haven't seen my husband for a week now.... Please go away."

Police left. The next raid was at the Boulevard Hotel in LaPrairie, across the river from Montreal proper. Detective Gillespie, fresh from his ordeal with Jackson, joined Montreal police in searching the halls, corridors, rooms and beverage room, but only a handful of farmers turned up, and once more police holstered their arms.

As a lieutenant of the Quebec Provincial Police said, "You raid here, you raid there. Sometimes you score, sometimes you don't." But the newspapers made much more of these raids than did the lieutenant. The "Hunt For Boyd" article in the *Telegram* covered one-eighth of the front page and a full column on page 2.

The Toronto *Daily Star*, in heavy black print one and a half inches high, headlined the March 12 newspaper, "Boyd Flees Lachine Cafe/Evades Dragnet by Minutes." In the war for subscribers, newspapers created "news" by enlarging smalll incidents to sensational proportions. The public was being set up for Boyd's actual capture and prepared for drama, tension, excitement, and all the "colour" that reporters could inject.

The day after Suchan's capture, Montreal police sent a detective to take fingerprints at Suchan's apartment. Working with prints already on file, police found prints of Edwin Boyd and Steve Suchan. Later, they discovered that the balance of unidentified prints belonged to Dorreen Boyd and Mary Mitchell. Prints were taken from pyrex dessert bowls, a ketchup bottle, a skin lotion bottle, a Dow beer bottle, Coca-Cola bottles, and a drinking glass.

Dorreen Boyd later continued to maintain that they had had no contact with Suchan or Jackson since the killing of Tong, and one can only speculate about how long the prints were on the various items before police arrived.

After Jackson's capture, Edwin's brother Gordon told newspapers that he believed Edwin was still in Toronto. He feared the results of a meeting between Edwin and police. "They'll shoot to kill him anyway, no matter whether he tries to surrender or not," was Gordon's opinion. Gordon went on to describe Edwin's first capture:

He was in awful bad shape the last time I saw him. Police held him 12 hours before anyone else knew it. Was he beaten? Are you kidding? He was almost murdered.

Police had grabbed Gordon Boyd on his was home from work and told him they knew Edwin was in his house, and he'd better go in and tell him to throw out the guns. Gordon reported that he could hardly get into the cruiser for all the rifles in it, but the police were "plenty scared.... I never saw so many guys shivering at once in my life."

More newspaper coverage, this time by Alexandrine Gibb of the *Star,* described Jackson's mother's reaction on hearing of her son's escapades. She first learned that he was involved in crime when he was charged with the Bradford robbery:

> "He told me he didn't do that," said Lillian Jackson, "and I believed him. Even if he were guilty of robbing a bank, I could forgive him for that. But shooting at police officers is not to be forgiven. Think of their families."

Not only the families but the whole police force, indeed, all of Toronto and most of Canada, waited daily for reports of Tong and Perry's condition.

The March 12 police bulletin on Tong said that he was improved slightly:

> He can talk a little and has had a little tea. He understands that they have arrested Jackson and seems quite pleased. Perry is progressing favourably.

March 13 brought more good news:

> Sgt. Dets. Tong improved slightly today and took a little consommé. Det. Sgt. Perry is improving and stood up today.

The press had interpreted recent events in black and white terms, priming the public to anticipate an appropriate cowboy-movie ending. Obviously, the bad guys would finish last. Two of them had already been gunned down, but in accordance with the traditions of the genre, the gang leader was still at large. The *Telegram* simply and effectively fixed the images of the myth. It ran a large photo of Boyd, flanked by equally large photos of Suchan and Jackson. Bold X's crossed off the faces of Suchan and Jackson. In large letters above Boyd's picture was the caption: HUNTED.

Tong and Perry were progressing, and Boyd's capture seemed imminent. There would be another dramatic gun battle and the story would be over. But the actual resolution was quite different. As subsequent events unfolded, the lives of all the participants in the Boyd Gang saga were affected in ways that were not at all what everyone had expected.

15

So powerful was the image of the gang as a cohesive group of "pals" that police concentrated the search for Boyd in and around Montreal. But "Dolph" Payne, with his uncanny sense of deduction, believed that Boyd was in Toronto. Unlike Tong, Payne did not depend upon informants. He was instead an adroit puzzle-solver who relied on detailed investigation and clever manoeuvering.

Payne was a formidable adversary who, in his field, had an even more impressive record of achievement than Boyd had in his. As a rookie in the early thirties, he began his career inauspiciously enough by collaring pickpockets on the Toronto Island ferries. But while he was pounding a beat, Payne discovered that he had a natural gift which, properly used, would be invaluable in police work — a startlingly retentive memory. When he later moved to the auto squad, he had developed this power to the point that he could recite the licence numbers of up to 400 stolen cars.

Since stolen cars are as necessary to criminals as firearms, Payne's investigative powers led him into almost all areas of police work.

He did not, however, rely solely on this enviable mental asset. He enjoyed the challenge of police work and applied himself with unvarying effort to all areas of the job. He was once given the nickname "Trigger" after he forced a fleeing auto off the road with a single shot. And he had trained himself in patient, dogged, painstaking investigative procedures.

Payne had an uncanny ability to understand the thought processes of the criminal he was hunting. He could "get inside the head" of his quarry, and anticipate his actions. This ability, more than any other, made him a threat to Boyd.

Harold Jukes, who was then a young police constable, had the greatest respect for Dolph Payne. "If I had ever done anything wrong," says Jukes, "I wouldn't want Payne to be the guy after me." Payne looked like a big old farmer. "Some people would think he wasn't the brightest," says Jukes, "but his brain was working twenty-four hours a day."

Time meant nothing to Payne. He would keep on a case until it was finished, and he would do it in his own slow, methodical fashion.

Payne now began an intensive battle of wits with Boyd – a chess game whose board was the city, and whose opposing pieces were human beings.

Aside from crackpot letters and random telephone tips which led nowhere, there were few leads to the whereabouts of Canada's "Master Fugitive". Since the Boyd children were in boarding school and Dorreen had left Pickering telling neighbours she was going back to England, the Boyd family had literally dropped out of sight.

Boyd's younger brother, Robert, worked for the City of Toronto. Payne decided to pick up the trail there. But when he questioned Robert's boss, he came up with nothing. Robert had quit his job on March 7, saying that he was leaving for California.

Payne decided to work from the angle he knew best—automobiles. Robert Boyd had switched the registration on his old 1949 Austin to Dorreen's name. If Robert was really planning to leave Toronto, he might try to sell the car. Payne and his partner, Ken Craven, read the classified section of the papers every evening. On Monday, March 10, they found the ad they were looking for: "49 Austin, radio, new tires and battery, best offer."

Payne dialled the phone number in the ad, disguising his voice as he spoke. Robert Boyd answered the phone. After talking briefly, Payne hung up. For some time he had been concocting a scheme for his next move, and knew the man he wanted to help pull it off, the young police constable, Harold Jukes. Jukes was the smallest man on the force, open-faced and innocent looking. He didn't look like a policeman, and that was exactly what Payne wanted.

The next day Jukes and a young woman, a police department secretary, appeared before Payne for coaching. The plan was designed to lure Dorreen out of hiding. Jukes and the secretary were to pose as man and wife. They would call Robert Boyd for an appointment to see the car and when they talked to him would use a cover story invented by Payne.

When Jukes and his "wife" presented themselves at Robert Boyd's apartment at 96 London Street, Payne hid behind a fence down the street. Detective Craven sat in a cruiser parked out of sight in a laneway. Jukes and the secretary oooh-ed and aaah-ed over the little cream coloured Austin and agreed to pay $850 for it—close to the asking price. When Robert Boyd showed them the registration for the car and they "discovered" that he was not the registered owner, their faces became very serious.

"Gee, we've just been through a very sad experience with our last car," said Jukes. "We thought it was all free and clear, and then the bailiff came and repossessed it. Our lawyer told us to make sure and have a release signed in our presence by the owner this time so we'd have some recourse."

Robert was reluctant. "Well, I don't know if I can get hold of the owner—it's my sister-in-law—but I think I can. Can you give me a phone number where I can reach you?"

Maybe this was a ploy to check him out, thought Jukes. Just to be sure, he gave his brother's phone number and he and his "wife" left.

Payne had watched his two operatives come out of the house and start down the street. Two men left the house behind the couple. When Jukes approached close enough, Payne spoke quietly to him: "Just keep on going. You're being followed. Don't go near the police station, get on a streetcar. We'll meet you later."

Jukes did as he was told and then went to his brother's to await the telephone call. About five o'clock Robert Boyd called. He would have the registered owner of the car at his apartment at seven that night. This time without his "wife", but with Payne again observing from a hiding place, Jukes returned, put a ten-dollar deposit on the car, and had a release signed by Dorreen Boyd. Again Jukes was followed and had to take a circuitous route back to the station.

For half an hour Payne stood waiting, flashlight in hand, ready to signal Craven, who had parked the cruiser a safe distance away. Suddenly, Robert Boyd and Dorreen came out of the house, got into the Austin and drove away, heading west on London Street. Payne blinked his flashlight and Craven cruised forward cautiously, his headlights off. The Austin turned north on Manning Avenue. As the police car neared the corner, Payne told Craven to stop. He got out and walked around the corner. Halfway up the block the Austin was parked, its occupants playing cat-and-mouse with anyone who might be on their tail. Again Payne waited until they had pulled away before signalling Craven.

For two hours the game went on within a three-square-mile area in the north central section of the city. Robert Boyd made three stop-and-wait manoeuvers and twenty-three turns before finally parking on Yonge Street just south of Heath. Payne stopped a block behind them on Heath Street, got out of the cruiser and walked toward them. He could see Robert and Dorreen standing around the corner under an awning, but they couldn't see him. Craven took the car into a circular driveway and parked. Suddenly, Robert and Dorreen began walking west up the street toward Payne. Payne had to think fast.

He ran between two houses separated only by a sidewalk. Robert and Dorreen stopped on the opposite side of the street directly across from him.

Payne backed up between the houses without looking behind him. In the middle of the sidewalk was a large tin garbage can. Payne backed right into it. "Made a hell of a racket," he remembers.

Robert and Dorreen looked over toward Payne, who quickly picked up the can and carried it to the back of the house, as if he were just a clumsy householder taking in his garbage can for the night.

Payne watched from across the street as Robert and Dorreen walked up the steps of 42 Heath Street, and after pausing at the door, were let in by someone. In the second-story apartment, a light went on, and Payne noticed that the curtains were slightly parted. From his position, he could not see into the room. He walked out into the middle of the street, trying to find a better vantage point.

Suddenly, Robert and Dorreen came out of the house. Payne was caught standing in the open. Quickly, he walked to a parked car, got in, and turned the motor over with the starter button. Robert and Dorreen walked past him toward Yonge Street without paying attention. Breathing a sigh of relief, Payne got out of the auto and followed, walking along the opposite side of the street.

At the corner, he almost got caught again. As he walked out into the lighted area at the intersection, he spotted them standing across the street. Again with inventive presence of mind, Payne started across Yonge Street and pretended to go into the church on the east side.

As he crossed, he could hear Dorreen say, "That's Payne." For a moment, Payne cursed himself for getting too close, but then Robert answered Dorreen, "No, that wouldn't be him. He wouldn't be going to church." The ruse had worked.

Payne slipped along a wall, doubled back and watched them until they got into their car. Then he and Craven followed them again in the cruiser. The same evasive tactics continued for an hour, until the Austin drove down a lane and stopped in the middle of it. Payne and Craven drove along the street parallel to the lane, observed Robert and Dorreen going into a garage, and then caught up with their quarry at the far end of the alley.

Finally about two a.m., Robert dropped Dorreen off at 19 Spadina Road and proceeded home. Police now had three addresses: 96 London Street, where Jukes had gone to buy the car, 42 Heath Street, where Robert and Dorreen had spent less than half an hour that evening, and the Spadina Road address where Boyd had finally left Dorreen.

Edwin Boyd could have been at any one of them, but to raid one or all three would have been to risk tipping off Boyd and losing him. Payne had to be certain. He and Craven drove back to the garage where Robert and Dorreen had stopped in the alley. They pried loose a couple of boards and looked inside. They saw a grey 1951 Nash with licence markers 68–J–76. Payne checked the markers. They were stolen.

Other officers wanted to hit the garage, but Payne said no. "We hit that garage, we'll have a bunch of guns and money — but no Boyd." Payne wanted Boyd.

Despite the obvious differences in backgrounds and in the life each had chosen to lead, Payne and Boyd had many things in common. They were both strong family men, both had keen intellects and a consistent sense of humour. But the quality they held in common that made both of them outstanding men, capable of capturing the imagination of the public, was a highly developed sense of personal style. Style is an intangible that grows as personality and experience work upon each other. Style is chemistry. It can't be bought or manufactured. It can only be allowed to prevail.

Payne's style was to play the waiting game, to amass all the evidence, to follow every lead, and not to tip his hand until he was more than thoroughly prepared. Perhaps it was ironic that Payne should be hunting a man who, like himself, possessed a combination of apparently opposing qualities: the tendency to be cautious, wary, even conservative, but at the same time to be capable of sudden, decisive and effective action in certain situations.

Payne knew he was dealing with explosive circumstances. After the shootouts in Montreal, the media had publicized the shoot-to-kill attitudes expressed by certain members of the public and police forces. In fact, Toronto police had never been given such an order, but by now Boyd must be convinced that capture meant certain death. Payne felt instinctively that Dorreen would lead him to Edwin, but that was the easy part. The hard part would be keeping himself, his fellow officers — and Boyd — alive and unhurt.

The following morning Payne began laying the groundwork for a trap which he hoped would checkmate Boyd without bloodshed. He visited the owner of 42 Heath Street — a lawyer named George Stoddart — and learned that Robert and Dorreen had passed themselves off as missionaries who wanted to rent the second floor apartment, now occupied by Stoddart himself who was leaving on vacation at the end of the week.

When Stoddart learned the true identity of his prospective tenants he immediately wanted to call off the deal. Look what police had done in Montreal. Who would guarantee that there would be no damage to his property — to say nothing of the danger to his other tenants, his neighbours, or innocent bystanders? In order to secure Stoddart's coöperation, the police department eventually had to post a bond which would pay for any damage incurred.

Payne's style was to jolly people along, to be friendly, to joke with them. He now used his persuasive powers to convince the next-door resident at 44 Heath Street, a Bell Telephone manager, to allow police to use his front room as a stakeout. Payne encouraged the manager's wife to believe that they were looking for bootleggers. She thought it was all very exciting until the radios and shotguns started coming in, at which point Payne was forced to tell her the truth.

The details under Payne's control had been carefully attended to. A key had been cut for the back door of 42 Heath and the night chain removed.

On the morning of March 14, Payne and Craven moved into 44 Heath Street and settled down to wait for Boyd. At 7:30 that evening they were still waiting. Payne picked up the telephone and called Robert Boyd. In a disguised voice he asked, "Have you got a car for sale?"

"Oh, yeah, but I think I got it sold," Robert replied. Payne then asked if he could come and see the car, and Robert Boyd said no, that he was going out in half an hour. Payne now knew that he could expect Edwin Boyd that night.

Payne waited for an hour and a half and then, at 9:10 p.m., Robert Boyd arrived in the Austin, made seven trips into the house, carrying luggage and clothing, and left. Thirty minutes later the car returned. Payne watched Robert Boyd get out and go into the house. There were several other people in the car, but he couldn't make out who they were. He watched as the lights came on in the upstairs apartment. Undoubtedly Robert was checking to see if the place was safe.

A moment later, Robert left the house, returned to the car and let a woman out. It was Dorreen Boyd. They disappeared into the house. Payne waited tensely. This was the moment he would know if his deductions were correct. Was one of the men in the car Edwin Boyd? Robert Boyd came out of the house again and walked to the street. As he did so, a man got out of the car and headed up the walk. Payne immediately recognized the square cut of the jaw, the set of the eyes. It was Edwin Boyd. Boyd came up to the door, pulled a revolver, and holding his topcoat out in front of him, kicked open the door with his foot. He entered the house.

To avoid inadvertently tipping Boyd off, all officers had been ordered to stay away from number 11 station, and to go instead to number 5 station at Belmont and Davenport. If any reporter had gone by that night, he'd have known something was up. "You never saw such a bunch of police cars in your life," said Harold Jukes. "There were between eighty and a hundred men around."

Acting Detective Lloyd Anderson and Sergeant "Barney" Loveridge had been detailed to enter the house with Payne and back him up. When they arrived at the station about ten o'clock, a sergeant of detectives issued Loveridge a shotgun and then took him out in the garden behind the station to brief him on the use of it.

Finally Inspector Nimmo called all men upstairs to the old guard room to give them their final instructions. Although the tone of the meeting was serious, Nimmo was forced to issue a ludicrous order. An officer who was present remembers Nimmo's comments this way:

Now look, boys, this comes straight from the boss. You're going into a very refined district. If all hell breaks loose up there, the chief says if there's any cursing or swearing on behalf of the members of this department, they will be charged.

One detective grumbled later, "The word was really laid down. You might have to kill some son-of-a-bitch, but be a gentleman about it."

Following the briefing, Lloyd Anderson tried on the bullet-proof vest which had been issued to him. As he struggled into it, it fell apart. "You're going in anyway," said one of his superiors.

At 44 Heath Street Payne waited, occasionally joking with the rest of his team to break the tension. Payne and Craven had also been given protective devices, a bullet-proof shield and a bullet-proof vest. To decide who should take what, Payne and Craven flipped a coin. Payne lost and Craven opted for the vest. To pass time, Craven grabbed the vest and shrugged it on backwards. Payne looked at him. "You got it on wrong." "Not me," Craven quipped. "I'm only going to get shot when I'm running."

But despite the jokes, the wait was long, and the tension kept building. Frequent calls came in asking Payne when he was going to move in, but true to his style, he waited. There were two factors supporting his judgment. First, the longer he waited, the surer he could be that the Boyds would be asleep. Secondly, there were two big flood lights shining down into the front yard from the second storey. Spotlighted in the dark, a man in the yard would be a sitting duck. Payne wanted to wait for daylight to neutralize the effect of the lights.

The basic attack plan was that Inspector McCathie would phone Boyd, inform him that he was surrounded, then Payne would move in. The call would be made at six a.m. But the case belonged to Payne and Craven. They had done the legwork and cornered Boyd, now they had to be the first men in. "Somebody had to go first," Payne remembers. "We couldn't ask anybody else, and nobody was volunteering." They had no way of knowing what they would meet inside 42 Heath. The entrances might be covered, or Boyd, well-armed and desperate, might be waiting for them. In their own minds, Payne and Craven had faced the fact that they stood a better than average chance of getting killed. Payne cautioned his team, "Don't leave us lying there dead, and him gone, too."

Suddenly, at about eight minutes to six, Payne began to move in with his men. "Holy Jesus," thought Jukes, "his watch is fast!"

Payne, who had been against the phone call idea from the beginning, had decided to do things his way. He was in charge here, it was his life that was being risked, and besides he felt he knew Boyd better than any of them. He felt certain that his way was best. He wouldn't wait for McCathie to phone Boyd.

Payne took the back door, followed by detectives Lloyd Anderson and Bernard Loveridge. Using the key they had made earlier, Payne tried to unlock the back door. As he attempted to put the key in the keyhole, his hand shook so badly the key rattled and clanged against the lock. In the stillness of the dawn on quiet Heath Street, Payne thought the noise was thunderous. He stopped for a moment, took a deep breath, and forced himself to calm down.

On his second try, Payne got the key in, opened the door, and slipped in quietly. He was over his initial fright, and now moved swiftly to the job ahead. He tiptoed to the front door to let in Ken Craven and his men. Since only Payne and Craven knew the layout of the house, the partners were separated, and each took a group of men, Payne up the back stairs, Craven up the front. Harold Jukes was stationed on the landing between the first floor and the basement, and all landings were covered in anticipation of possible hostage-taking by a desperate Boyd.

The stairway was the same width as the doors at top and bottom. There were no alcoves or passageways in which to take shelter if Boyd were waiting to gun them down. Lloyd Anderson, now a retired superintendent, remembers crawling up the stairs behind Payne. "What scared me most," he later joked, "was Barney Loveridge with that shotgun behind me!" He remembers thinking, *There's got to be a better way to make a living than this!*

Complete silence blanketed the house as the group made their way to the second floor. At the top of the stairs was a hallway that ran the full length of the apartment. Payne knew that if he stepped on the floor at the top of the stairs, it would creak. He decided to jump across the hallway. At 200 pounds, Payne was not particularly light on his feet. The little spring he gave made what he thought was a terrific racket. He felt sure Boyd would be well-alerted by now and waiting inside the bedroom door, his guns ready to fire at the first man to step inside.

Payne felt he had to hurry to the other end of the hallway. He wasn't positive which room Boyd would be in. He threw open the first door, his gun poised for action. "Boyd, it's Payne!" he called. The room was empty.

Payne rushed to the next door, Anderson and Loveridge right behind him, Craven and his men standing by. Grabbing the door handle he called once more, "Boyd, it's Payne!" and threw open the door, his gun ready. Again there seemed to be an empty room.

Without even checking the lump on the cot in the corner, Payne rushed to the next bedroom. Under the quilt on the cot, Robert Boyd stirred uneasily. Roused from sleep by the noise, he was barely awake as Payne and Craven burst into the last bedroom.

Dorreen Boyd, dressed in yellow silk Chinese pajamas, was sitting up in bed. In the twin bed beside her, Edwin Boyd was just starting to sit up.

"The police are here," said Dorreen. Boyd blinked his eyes trying to rouse himself. Beside him on the night table was a briefcase full of money. Tucked into the stacks of bills, handles up, ready for grabbing, were five loaded revolvers.

With a running leap, Payne was on top of Boyd in a second. "Not a goddamn move, Boyd, or I'll blow your head off!" ordered Payne. Dropping his bullet-proof shield and his gun, Payne whipped out his handcuffs and clamped them firmly over Boyd's wrists. Edwin Boyd, completely surprised, simply stared at his long-time adversary. He surrendered without a struggle.

"Well," Boyd finally said, "this is one way to meet you."

In the next bedroom, officers were putting the cuffs on a sleepy Robert Boyd, who didn't say a word. Later, the younger Boyd was reported variously as being "sound asleep", "pretending to be asleep" and "dead to the world", when police closed in. At any rate, he made no protest.

Before anyone had a chance to react to the situation, the telephone in Edwin and Dorreen's bedroom rang. Payne was on the phone in an instant. McCathie had a bit of a surprise at the other end of the line. "I've got him," said Payne, and all the officers broke into wide grins.

Relief flooded over the little group standing in the bedrooms and the hallways. They began to wander downstairs to tell the other officers the good news. An almost festive air prevailed, as various detectives and other officers made notes, phoned their spouses, discussed the "bloodless capture" and began to collect evidence.

Allan Lamport, besides being recently elected mayor of Toronto, was head of the Police Commission. He had insisted that he be notified as soon as Boyd was captured so that he could be "in on the collar". Police Chief John Chisholm telephoned the mayor at his Harper Avenue house in Rosedale. The *Star* quotes the mayor:

> I woke up at 5 o'clock this morning, and I couldn't get Boyd off my mind. I thought to myself the police were either arresting him or were about to. In my mind I could hear the phone ringing.
>
> I'd left instructions with the chief to call me. Then in a few minutes, the phone did ring, and it was the chief.

This fanciful bit of reporting could be attributed either to the *Star* or to the mayor, who had his own flair for attracting publicity. But when Chief Chisholm did telephone, Allan Lamport was very excited indeed.

Careful to dress in suit and tie, Mayor Lamport didn't bother to take time to shave, and all the newspapers would report him as looking "rumpled". While a car was sent to pick up the mayor, the press was notified so that they could witness the spectacle of Boyd being led out by his captors and Mayor Lamport.

Police had thrown a cordon around the block and were permitting no cars to leave or enter the area until cleared from the top. As Lamport drew up in a car, followed by a horde of reporters, policemen guarding the entry to the block stood at attention. "I'm sorry, Mr. Mayor, my orders are to let no cars in. You'll have to walk." In obedience to his superiors, the young policeman made no exceptions, even for the mayor.

Allan Lamport had no time to argue. He jumped out of the car and began running down the street, the reporters in hot pursuit. One policeman remembers him holding his hat as he ran, shouting at the world in general: "You got the son-of-a-bitch, you got the son-of-a-bitch!" At one point, he was so excited that he hopped from foot to foot as he talked to police and reporters.

All of Toronto would soon be able to share the mayor's exuberance. The reporters were snapping pictures and taking notes as fast as they could. The news would be on the stands by the time most people had their mid-morning coffee break.

Dolph Payne, ever methodical, tried not to get caught up in the excitement until his job was completed. Unlike many people present, he was not hanging around waiting for the press. He was waiting for proper tags and identification markers to be brought from headquarters, so that every piece of evidence would be properly itemized for the trial. There were to be no slip-ups on Dolph Payne's case.

Besides the briefcase full of money and the five handguns, police took possession of several pieces of new luggage, Dorreen's box of Tampax, a number of stiletto knives, 400 rounds of ammunition done up in woollen socks, and an electrick stock prod normally used for controlling cattle. The money seized, about $26,000, turned out to be mostly marked currency from the Bank of Montreal at College and Manning, the loot with which Boyd was supposed to be buying a house. Robert Boyd was relieved of $1,500, which he vigorously protested was his savings.

While detectives marked and gathered the evidence, Edwin and Dorreen Boyd were told to get dressed, but first, McCathie insisted, their clothes must be checked. Boyd was made to sit on the floor and hand McCathie his clothes. Rummaging through the pockets, McCathie came up with not guns, but fistfuls of pepper.

Boyd had thought of every possible angle. Rather than risk shooting anyone, should the occasion arise, he was prepared to throw pepper in their faces, to give himself a chance to escape. McCathie dumped out the pepper and tossed the clothes back to Boyd.

"You too," demanded the inspector of Dorreen.

"Could I please get dressed in the washroom?" she asked, undoubtedly thinking only of her modesty. According to Boyd, McCathie reported, "I've seen everything there is to see about you.

You'll get dressed here. We're all married men here." Boyd adds that Dorreen never forgave McCathie for making her get dressed in front of all the men in the room. (But Dorreen disagrees. She says police held up a blanket for her and always treated her with respect.)

Edwin Boyd, ever the dandy, put on a dapper sports coat over his grey trousers, white shirt and tie, then asked for his coat. "Just a minute," said Lloyd Anderson. Picking up the coat, Anderson searched the pockets and came up with more handfuls of pepper. The police shook their heads in mock disgust, and Edwin Boyd just shrugged.

Allan Lamport remembers that by the time he arrived there were chairs out on the lawn to accommodate all the people in the "capture party". Lamport went into the house so that he would be photographed coming out with Boyd and the police. And what a photography session it was!

The pictures were plastered all over the front pages of every major newspaper in Canada. There were Lamport, Payne and Boyd together, Lamport with all the detectives (twenty-seven visible in the picture), Robert Boyd with detectives, Dorreen Boyd with detectives and another with a police matron, pictures of the briefcase, money and guns, pictures of the house, the bedroom, the other tenants of 42 Heath Street, and even the neighbours.

There was a picture of Dolph Payne with the "Lucky Cat" draped around his neck. "We take it on all our raids with us," joked Payne. The cat was a neighbourhood stray.

The *Star* showed Inspector McCathie holding the pepper found in Boyd's clothes, an aerial view of the Heath Street district, a closeup of Mayor Lamport with his two daughters, and even pictures of Lennie Jackson and Steve Suchan, lying bandaged, convalescing in Montreal hospitals.

The *Telegram* had shots of Ken Craven in his bullet-proof vest and head-piece, and Adolphus Payne carrying his bullet-proof shield.

At one point, Boyd had greeted the mayor with, "I didn't think it would take something like this to meet your worship!" Then, as photographers closed in for the shot, "Shall I smile?" "I wouldn't if I were in your position," replied the mayor.

But no one could stop the smiles that Saturday, March 15, 1952.

Even Edwin Boyd, his fedora at a rakich tilt, gave his "jaunty" smile for every photographer in sight. Only Dorreen hid her face from the cameras, as she was led away from the house.

One interesting item that police discovered in Boyd's possession was a letter addressed to the editor, Toronto *Daily Star*. The letter was five pages long, and was apparently ready to be mailed, the stamp already affixed to the envelope. Part of it read:

> The detectives will go to any length to obtain connections. They will do their utmost with the full approval of higher officers to keep their weaknesses covered. They will use an order of "shooting to kill" rather than intelligent directed efforts so well known in Britain's Scotland Yard.
> Death has always been a friend to me and I will meet it face to face. So keep out of my way and avoid bloodshed. Death means nothing to me when I am fighting for my family.... Start looking over your shoulders. Start seeing me in every shadow. Start guarding your families, because they are your weakness. Like you, I am no longer a respecter of persons.

The letter was signed "Edwin Alonzo Boyd" in a bold hand. At the bottom, to prove the authenticity of the letter, Boyd had stamped in blue ink, five fingerprints.

From the tone of the letter, it would seem that his whole life had become an elaborate game of cops and robbers. He was telling the police that if their rules were "shoot to kill", his would be the same. Another letter, which was to be mailed from Montreal, was in a similar vein. It was meant to throw police off his track, and keep them looking in Montreal.

> Dear Leo,
> Thanks for fooling the cops. They had me taped until you gave the whistle at Lachine.
> O.K. pal, I'll be around your house within the next ten days and will slip you $150 for the favour you did me.
>   E.A. Boyd.
> My fingerprints are on this paper. This will prove I'm not kidding.

Both letters were held by police as evidence.

Some of the happiest people that Saturday morning were the wives and families of the officers involved. Everyone had expected a big shootout when Boyd was taken. Some of the officers had said nothing to their wives. Harold Jukes, who was supposed to have started his holidays that Saturday, had told his wife he was going to Peterborough to investigate a bigamy. Mrs. Jukes, then pregnant with their first child, had gone to her mother's house. When she read the story in the newspapers, she was very upset.

Twenty-four years later, Jukes says, "I haven't told her any stories since then in regards to what I've been doing." His postscript to the comment: "It's a little safer now!"

Douglas Payne, the fifteen-year-old son of Sergeant Payne, was delighted to be kidded by his schoolmates with the same nickname his father had been given, "Trigger Payne". "I know every one of them would like to have a father as keen as mine," said young Douglas, who later became an RCMP officer.

Dolph Payne was feeling fine. "I just finished Eddie's case," he said, referring to Sergeant Tong, still in critical condition in hospital. "Now I can get back to those venetian blinds!"

Mrs. Tong, interviewed again by Alexandrine Gibb, said, "My husband is avenged at last. I couldn't rest until all those men were taken in." However, her worries were not over:

> Ted [her name for her husband] was not too well yesterday. He moaned all day and it makes me afraid.

Reports said that Sergeant Tong managed a weak smile when told of Boyd's capture. The police bulletins offered little comfort:

> Sgt. Dets. Tong was a little restless and headachey today and had a slight temperature, but nothing to become unduly concerned about.
>
> Det. Sgt. Perry continues to progress.

Leonard Jackson was also progressing in hospital, and received the press several times daily. The day before Boyd's capture, he had offered to make an appeal over radio for Boyd to give himself up, but wondered if he'd be called a "stool pigeon". After being assured that he was not revealing anything that everyone didn't know, a microphone was sent for. By the time it arrived, he had changed his mind. "What do you want me to do," he demanded, "get myself in a mess?"

On Saturday, he was told of his friend Boyd's capture. "Don't call him my friend," he snapped. "He's no friend of mine." The newspapers played up the angle that Ann and Leonard Jackson were captured with only loose change in their pockets while Boyd was caught with $26,000 in his possession. This seemed to indicate that there had been a disagreement between Boyd and Jackson. Ann Jackson smiled at the news of the capture, but made no comment.

Steve Suchan, still in grave condition, was unable to receive the news or comment upon it.

Mayor Lamport called the capture of the three criminals, Suchan, Jackson and Boyd, a "tale of two cities, Toronto and Montreal". He claimed that reports from Montreal about Boyd's whereabouts were let out to the public so as not warn the wanted man that they were hot on his trail in Toronto. In the police station, Boyd remarked to Lamport that Sergeant Payne was "a courageous man", to which Lamport replied, "He certainly is, and we give him full marks."

Lamport then went on to argue that the city be allowed to confiscate part of the bank loot stolen in Toronto and recovered by Toronto police.

> It's all very well to have policemen shot up, their lives constantly endangered in these hunts, then what do we do? We hand the money back to the banks, while our men suffer in hospital. Aside from the danger to our men, there is a lot of expense involved. And the city is supposed to foot the bill for that too!

He later suggested that banks be forced to post armed guards at all branches. These suggestions did not win him many friends in banking circles, but the people of Toronto lapped it up. They were beginning to like this gutsy mayor.

On Monday morning, Lamport announced that nine of the officers involved in the Boyd-Suchan-Jackson captures would be given some sort of recognition by the city. He hadn't yet decided whether it would be a plaque or a police medal, since Toronto police were not allowed to accept monetary rewards. To be honoured were Inspectors McCathie and Nimmo, who had headed the entire operation, Sergeants of Detectives Payne, Thompson (who had been at the Jackson capture), and Tong, Detective Sergeant Roy Perry (who was improving in hospital), Detectives Jack Gillespie and Ken Craven, and the boyish-looking Constable Harold Jukes. (Said Jukes with a grin in 1975, "I haven't seen that medal yet!") But the publicity was lavish. Everyone got his picture in the papers again, and the stories were retold with relish.

Inspector Nimmo said that both Suchan and Jackson would be charged with attempted murder. "We fervently hope that this won't have to be changed to a charge of murder." Reports looked good for a while.

> March 16/52. Sgt. Dets. Tong is coming along. Today he partook of a little toast, soup and chicken which he asked for.
>
> Det. Sgt. Perry continues to progress favourably.

The bulletins of March 17 to 20 all reported that both Tong and Perry continued to progress favourably. On March 21, Perry was still improving, but the report on Tong looked bad.

> Fluid and blood have been removed from Sgt. Dets. Tong's chest, and he is breathing easier. He has also been x—rayed, the results of which will be known tomorrow. His general condition is slightly improved.

The next day's bulletin said only that Tong was a little low.

Saturday night, March 22, Mrs. Tong was called to the hospital. Her husband was very low, said Dr. Tovee, and the children could come too. The night was tense and wearing. Tong had never improved enough to undergo surgery. The bullet that struck him down was still lodged under his shoulder blade. It had missed his heart by the width of a razor blade, had severed his spinal cord paralyzing half his body. Finally, it snuffed out his life.

Police bulletin, March 23, 1952:

> Attention all divisions. Information received from Dr. Tovee at 12:30 a.m. this date that Sgt. of Dets. Ed Tong has just passed away at the Toronto General Hospital.

ESCAPE 2

16

As he was led back to the Don Jail, Boyd was no longer the jaunty, wisecracking, gentleman bandit portrayed by the press. He was a despondent and beaten man. He received little sympathy from jail officials. When he asked for something to read, the superintendent snapped, "No! You can stay here till you rot before I give you anything to read!"

Clad in beltless prison denims and cotton shirt, Boyd was led down the echoing corridors to number 8 Hospital Block, the row of four maximum security cells near the gallows room.

The guard's key turned, locking him in, and Boyd faced the door for a moment. There were two empty cells on his left, one on his right. Across the five-foot-wide corridor facing him was an outside wall with two barred windows near the top. The left end of the corridor was stone, the right an iron barrier beyond which a guard sat watching him. There was nothing to read, no radio to listen to, nobody to talk with. His only diversion was the compulsory half-hour exercise period every day.

A few days after Boyd's arrival, a workman came to "fix the plumbing" in the ceiling of his cell. Boyd was not deceived. He knew the man was installing a microphone and a speaker. Later on, someone accidently threw a switch and for a brief moment Boyd heard the superintendent talking.

When they brought his meals down to him, Boyd flushed them down the toilet. He lay on his cot and tried to devise an agreeable method of committing suicide.

Boyd rejected hanging as "a hell of a way to go". He had studied judo and knew that pressure applied to the carotid arteries on the neck would produce unconsciousness. He thought he would tie a rope around his neck while he lay in bed, insert two large pads under the rope at the right spot, and twist the rope behind his neck with a stick. He would keep twisting until he could barely breathe, then give a few fast twists and lie on the stick. The pressure would cut the blood supply to the head and he would black out.

"I'd just be lying there peacefully, sleeping, and the blankets would be up comfortably, and people walking by would look in and say, 'Quiet.' "

It was characteristic of Boyd that even in contemplating a suicide method he should think in terms of outwitting his adversaries. But before he found the means to carry out his plan, the long hours of solitude led him in a different direction. He began to meditate.

As a successful bank robber, Boyd had planned each robbery with meticulous care. He would shut his eyes and visualize every move he was going to make. Now as he lay on his cot in the Don, this mental process began to exert a subtle attraction for him.

He pictured the front of the jail, outside. Then as his concentration deepened, he saw himself walking down the front steps. He followed the roadway to Gerrard Street, then proceeded to the corner of Broadview. He looked at the houses along the way, picturing every detail. He read road signs and took in the colours.

While in this visionary state he was consciously aware of what he was doing, but in the back of his mind was the hope—almost a faith— that concentration on the vision would in some mystic way bring about the reality. He would get out, he would be freed.

But nothing happened. A month passed, and Boyd gave up his mental walks outside in order to concentrate on something more immediate, more attainable. *What do I want?*, Boyd asked himself He wanted something to read. He decided he would will the superintendent to give it to him.

Boyd closed his eyes and pictured himself walking through the barrier, down the stairs and into the superintendent's office. "I want something to read," he demanded in his thoughts. "What do you want?" the superintendent would enquire. "It doesn't matter." "Go back to your cell and I'll bring it up to you."

Boyd saw himself turning and walking back to his cell. He didn't know how he got through the barriers, but as he lay on his cot the imaginary incident became very clear to him. It was as if it had actually *happened*. The accompanying sensations felt real, compelling his belief. He didn't realize that for weeks he had been training himself in self-hypnosis and the techniques of meditation. He was now able to reach states of consciousness in which visions of great clarity and complexity occurred.

Time was passing, and Edwin Boyd was enjoying his mental excursions. He was interrupted only by the guards bringing his meals. After they'd gone, Boyd would dispose of the food down the toilet. He didn't want it. He was preoccupied by the tremendous exhilaration of his new experience. Sometimes he would go two or three days without eating or drinking. He discovered that fasting sharpened his mental powers, enabling him to visualize whatever he wished.

Three days after he began his mental trips to the superintendent's office, Boyd was lying in his cell, his eyes closed, relaxed. He heard a sound. It was the barrier opening. Boyd looked up. The superintendent was standing in the doorway of his cell. "I changed my mind," he said. "I brought you some books to read." The superintendent held out a Bible and a Rosicrucian pamphlet.

Boyd was almost too surprised to be elated. He thought to himself, *It worked faster than I thought.*

The superintendent studied Boyd a minute. "I'll come up and play chess with you every once in a while just to pass the time."

Starved for reading material, Boyd read voraciously for the next few days. He read until the sun faded completely and he had to hold the book three inches from his face. Later he wondered if this constant twilight reading in the Don hadn't ruined his eyes and caused him to become nearsighted.

But still he couldn't get his thoughts off the discovery he had made —that through some mysterious unexplained phenomenon he had been able to manipulate someone from a distance. He was sure that fasting was part of it, and that relaxed mental concentration was the other part. How it would be brought about he didn't know, but he was convinced that his new power could somehow get him out of jail.

How could he hone his ability to a sharp edge? He found a matchstick in the corner of the cell, placed it in the middle of the floor and sat down on his bed. He concentrated all his energy on making it move. He looked at it, pointed at it, stared at it. It stayed put. He lay down and slept. When he awoke, he tried again. The pattern continued. Still the match did not move, but Boyd was developing tremendous powers of concentration.

Despite the superintendent's occasional visits and the reading material he was now allowed, Boyd was bored and lonely. Dorreen was being held for questioning by police, and there was no one else who might have visited him.

The mental exercises helped, but he craved a little human conversation. Boyd was therefore delighted when Willie Jackson arrived from Kingston Penitentiary.

Willie was still serving the term for which he was imprisoned when he had first met Boyd and Lennie, but now he had been sent back to Toronto to stand trail on the new charges arising from the bank robberies he committed while on the lam. Boyd was overjoyed to see him. Willie was locked up in the cell near the door, on Boyd's right.

It wasn't long before Boyd got down to serious business. He came over close to the partition separating the two cells. "Hey, Willie," he whispered, "you want to get out of here?"

"Yeah!" Willie replied. "How'll we do it? I don't think it's possible. We're in the death cells."

"Well, don't give up hope. Just relax and let's talk about a few things. Ask the superintendent to let you have a Bible."

"What do we want a Bible for?" Willie said.

"Ask him for the Bible."

Accepting Boyd's instructions on faith, Willie asked for and received his Bible. Boyd chose a passage, and the two men began reading the same lines silently, over and over.

"Is there anything happening that's different?" asked Boyd.

"Nope," replied Willie.

"Well, just keep on reading."

To please Boyd, and to pass the time, Willie continued with this new game. Then they discussed what they had read and agreed that it had the same meaning for both of them.

"Now," said Boyd, "you read something, and I won't read it. Don't you say a word to me, but try and transmit it to me."

Willie obediently picked another passage from his Bible and began to read it silently, over and over until he knew it by heart.

"I can get about ten words," said Boyd. "Tell me if they're the right words." He repeated the words he had "received". According to Boyd, they were the same words that occurred in the text Willie had been reading, though not in sequence. He was so convinced by now of the power of his subconscious mind that he was certain he and Willie were on the same mental wavelength.

What a discovery! thought Boyd. *We can read each other's minds.*

The two prisoners experimented a bit more with their telepathic powers, then Boyd began to take Willie's religious training in hand. He explained the gospels and the words of Jesus. They debated the existence of God. Willie, whose education was minimal and religious knowledge less, was a bit hesitant at first.

Boyd knew the superintendent was listening to everything they said. With some dirt from the floor, he wrote some instructions to Willie on a scrap of paper and passed it through the bars of the cell. Their religious discussions grew more animated while Willie played the part of the convert. For the superintendent's benefit, Willie even began trying to convert the guards.

Lying in his cell listening, Boyd thought Willie was very persuasive. He knew that as long as they discussed religion the superintendent would leave them alone.

One day Boyd whispered to Willie, "I'd like to get out of here."

"Me too," came the quick response.

"What do you think about prayer?" asked Boyd. "Do you think that would be of any value?"

"Well, I'm willing to try anything."

Willie didn't care what they did as long as it was taking them in the right direction, namely, out of the Don Jail.

"I'll tell you what," said Boyd. "We'll pray — like after they put the lights out in the rest of the joint – we'll pray and ask for help to get out of here. It might work."

Boyd wasn't sure whether Willie was praying, but Willie assured him that he was. They kept it up for several nights. In the light of his recent experiences, Boyd felt that prayer was a form of sending messages and concentrating their mental powers.

"You know," Willie suddenly said one day, "I think we're going about this all wrong."

"What do you mean?"

"You know as well as I do that God isn't going to help us get out of here. We're doing the exact opposite of what he wants us to do. We're praying to the wrong person. We should be praying to God's enemy, Satan. That's the one we should be praying to. He's the one that's gonna help us to get out."

This idea bothered Boyd. He mulled it over in his mind. Finally he rationalized, *It's just as if old Satan himself had said it, because I always thought he was a real contrary cuss.*

Boyd and Willie began to pray to Satan. From then on things started to happen. First, Leonard Jackson arrived, straight off a TCA flight from Montreal, encased in casts and minus his artificial foot. He was still weak, but was in good enough shape to go back to the cells. Authorities were taking no chances with this criminal now dubbed "Tough Lennie" by the press. They put him in death row, along with his old buddies, Edwin Boyd and Willie Jackson.

About a week later, Steve Suchan appeared. He was in even worse shape than Lennie, with tubes still draining pus from a wound in his side. Now the four cells in death row were full. The Boyd Gang was complete and together again.

Boyd had no intention of asking Len or Steve to join in the prayers to Satan. He knew they would laugh and call him a crackpot. But he and Willie kept it up.

Each day, as required in the regulations, the prisoners were given a half-hour exercise period. They were taken out to the bull ring where they walked around and talked, and then taken back. While they were out, a prison official would turn their beds upside down, check the mattresses, shake the bars in the corridor windows, and look for any signs of suspicious activity.

One particularly zealous keeper tested each bar and cross bar with a hammer. He listened for the same ring each time he banged, as any tampering with the bars would have resulted in a different tone. Sometimes he would still be at it when the prisoners returned from the bull pen.

"Did you find anything?" they asked him.

"No, but don't you ever try to get away with anything, because I'll know about it."

Next, the superintendent's attitude softened. He decided to let the prisoners out of their cells for an hour each day so that they could walk up and down in the corridor and talk to each other. A guard was stationed at the end of the corridor behind a barred door and in front of a solid door that led to the rest of the jail.

In the corridor outside the cells was a table, a chess board, and some benches. This was terrific. Now the men could walk about, sit and play chess, or talk to the guard in order to relieve the monotony.

For a while, Boyd stayed in his cell even when they opened his door. He enjoyed lying on his bed, reading the Bible and exercising his mind, instead of his body. But he eventually got bored and began to go out each day with the others. Soon they were discussing in earnest the possibilities for an escape.

It was about this time that Boyd, for some reason, began to lose interest in his own escape. But since Lennie, with his many underworld connections, had been primarily responsible for the first breakout, Boyd felt he was obligated to help Lennie get out this ime.

However, no one had any concrete ideas about how to get a hacksaw blade smuggled into the jail. Suchan casually mentioned to the guard one day that he could make some money by helping them with a problem. Unfortunately, he chose the wrong person, an honest guard. The incident was reported to the superintendent, but nothing more came of it.

When Willie Jackson was due to go to court, the Boyd Gang encountered another piece of luck. A man came to visit Willie and in a roundabout manner suggested he could help him escape. "Anything you want me to do, just ask, and I'll do it," he said. Willie discussed this possibility with Boyd.

Boyd decided to test the man's intentions.

"This time when you write to your sister," Boyd told Willie, "instead of putting your letter through the regular channels, put it in your shoe. When you see him in the visiting room, ask him to deliver it to your sister."

Willie followed the plan, and soon there was a reply from his sister that she had received the letter. Willie and Boyd still weren't sure that the superintendent wasn't in on this game.

"Let's go a little further," suggested Boyd.

They had been observing the key that the guard used to lock them in their cells after their exercise period. Willie asked his visitor to get a key blank and a file, and bring it to him.

Apparently the man tried to get such a blank at a key shop. Sergeant Dolph Payne, who much later picked up the man's trail, questioned the clerk in a key shop. The clerk remembered the man had asked for a particularly large key blank. "That looks like an institution key," said the clerk. The man left and never came back.

Because this visitor of Willie's was never caught or tried for helping in the escape attempt, he cannot be named here. However, Payne was gratified years later when the man, an apparently law-abiding citizen, was arrested on other charges and left his profession in disgrace.

Willie's visitor came to the jail without a key blank, but with a shoehorn and a file. The metal shoehorn was the closest he could come to a key blank.

Now the convicts had to get the pattern of the key that fitted their cell locks. "Leave it to me," said Willie. On one shift they had a friendly old guard, an ex-policeman, who enjoyed talking with the prisoners. Willie made friends with him easily. In fact, Willie and the guard professed their liking for each other so often that Suchan was heard to complain, "Jesus, are they going to keep that up all afternoon?"

Suchan's cell was at the end of the block and he was first to be locked in each day. One day Willie grabbed the key as the guard was about to lock Suchan in his cell. Playfully, he coaxed the guard, "Let me do that, let me try it." Replied the guard, "Oh no, Willie, I'm the guard. You're the convict."

Willie laughed, "Jeez, you put things in a rotten way!" and handed back the key. What the guard didn't realize was that Willie had been squeezing the key as hard as he could in the palm of his hand. When he released it, a vivid impression of the key remained on Willie's palm.

By this time, the prisoners were allowed to have pencils for writing down scores in their card games. Willie quickly grabbed his pencil. He put his hand against the wall of his cell and transferred the marks, making a pencil pattern on the wall. The key was flat with one

Apparently Steve Suchan was not only an accomplished violinist but also a trombone player. (He eventually traded in his violin for a .455 Smith and Wesson revolver.)

Lennie Jackson on duty in England during World War II. Lennie missed active combat because of severe asthma.

Edwin Boyd (*upper right corner*) with his school soccer team, 1929.†

Anne Jackson †

Sgt. Roy Perry (*left*) and Sgt. of Detectives Edmund Tong (*right*). Tong was sometimes known as "The Chinaman", perhaps because of his name, although he was actually Welsh.*

Crowds gather at the scene where detectives Tong and Perry were shot by Boyd Gang members Suchan and Jackson, March 6, 1952. Tong was fatally wounded.**

Sgt. Roy Perry (*left*) arrives at St. Joseph's Hospital for treatment of the arm wound he sustained in the shooting.**

Police re-enactment of the position assumed by Suchan when he shot Tong, according to Perry's testimony. Suchan claimed at the trial that he never opened the car door.**

Police cruiser D-5 after the shooting.**

The house at 42 Heath Street where Boyd was captured, March 15, 1952. Police were staked out at no. 44 with Dolph Payne stationed at the downstairs front window.**

Edwin and Dorreen were asleep when Payne and fellow police officers burst in on them at six a.m.**

Some of the items confiscated at the Heath Street capture.**

Dorreen Boyd, "hatless" and wearing the red coat that prompted much comment in newspapers, in custody of detectives after the capture.†

Heath Street capture. Payne is second from left; Craven third from left; Mayor Lamport wearing white hat. **

The funeral of Edmund Tong.**

TORONTO JAIL

CORRESPONDENCE to contain family or business matters only.
PARCELS containing tobacco, food, etc., are prohibited.
NO READING MATERIAL of any kind is accepted from visitors.
VISITS AND LETTERS: Remanded Inmates are allowed to have two visits and two letters weekly. Sentenced Inmates are allowed one visit and one letter weekly. When possible, immediate Relatives or near Relatives will be given preference in visiting. No more than two visitors are permitted for each visit.
VISITING HOURS: 9.30 a.m. to 11.00 a.m. 2.00 p.m. to 4.00 p.m. daily except Saturdays, Sundays or Holidays.

CENSORED

Sunday, 29 June 1952

Dearest Francis,

I love you. Are you sure you're taking sufficient care of yourself? You look alright but I know how you like to put off health precautions until too late. I enjoyed Saturday's visit very much and you know, I think it makes my days go much better if I see and know you're o.k. I guess the best thing to do is not worry. I better write to the kids I think.

Dear R▇▇ — HOW IS MY LITTLE BOY TODAY? I HOPE YOU ARE ENJOYING YOUR HOLIDAYS. HAVE LOTS OF FUN. SAY YOUR PRAYERS, TOO. AND PRAY FOR ME.   LOVE — DADDY xxxxxx Boy D

DEAR C▇▇ — I LOVE YOU AND HOPE YOU ARE FINE. IS YOUR SORE THROAT BETTER? ARE YOU GLAD TO BE HOME FOR HOLIDAYS? DO YOU LIKE THE HOUSE? SAY A PRAYER TO GOD FOR ME.
                                    xxx x xx DADDY Boy

Hiya B▇▇, — I bet you're having fun now the holidays is on, eh? Are you being good to mom and doing her little favors. She has a hard job looking after you kids now and remember money doesn't grow on trees. Mom has to work for it. So please don't waste your time, son. Help as much as you can. See you in the comics.   Dad, xxxx

Well, Hon. so long for now. Your loving hubby   Eddie xxxxx
                                    xxxx

Inmates to use this side of paper only.

One of Edwin's many letters to Dorreen written from the Don. **

The Don Jail **

Cellblock in no. 9 corridor from which the Boyd Gang made their second escape, September 8, 1952.

**

Two window bars had to be removed to allow the gang to squeeze through. A conveniently positioned outside wall led to the street.**

Dorreen with the *Telegram*'s account of Boyd's second escape.†

September 10/52

My Dearest Eddie,

Am I asking too much of you under the circumstances to give yourself up? If to anyone to me or to the men both you and I know would give you a fair deal. I have thought this over so much in the past three days, and knowing me as your devoted wife, I'll wait for you no matter what the outcome may be. God willing we will have the privilege of growing old together. This is all I ask of you and Eddie remember always I love you dearly,

yours
Frances. Boyd. xxxx
B.C.R.D.

This letter printed in the newspapers and Dorreen's subsequent radio appeal urging Boyd to give himself up were in fact publicity stunts. Dorreen knew where Boyd was most of the time; he once spent the night with her and the children. **

The barn in North York where police recaptured the Boyd Gang, September 17, 1952.**

Lennie Jackson in North York jail cell after recapture. †

Suchan and Jackson on their way back to the Don Jail after being sentenced to hang. †

Boyd waves a spare sock at reporters on his way to Kingston Penitentiary after sentencing. On his immediate left are Joseph Jackson and Willie Jackson. †

Ten-year man Joseph Jackson (*left*) enjoys Willie "The Clown" Jackson's performance for reporters. Willie was sentenced to twenty years. At right is Allister Gibson who got eight years.†

Just sentenced to life imprisonment, Boyd bursts into laughter at sight of Willie's antics.

Photo Credits

*Toronto *Star*
**Metropolitan Toronto Police Museum
†Toronto *Telegram* courtesy Toronto *Sun* Syndicate

Chronology

September 9, 1949	Boyd robs his first bank, the Armour Heights Bank of Montreal in North York.
September 1949–March 1951	Boyd robs at least three more banks.
March–July 1951	Lennie Jackson and his gang of armed bandits rob banks in the towns of Woodbridge, Mitchell and Colbourne. Steve Suchan is also involved.
July 30, 1951	Sergeant of Detectives Edmund Tong arrests Lennie Jackson in Toronto. Jackson awaits trial in the Don Jail.
September 1, 1951	Boyd, Howard Gault and a third man rob the Dominion Bank on Sheppard Avenue.
October 16, 1951	Boyd and Gault are caught attempting to rob the Dominion Bank at Lawrence Ave. and Yonge St. Boyd is assigned to Lennie Jackson's cell block in the Don Jail.
November 4, 1951	Boyd and Lennie Jackson escape from jail with another inmate, Willie Jackson (no relation to Lennie).
November 20, 1951	The Boyd Gang pulls its first robbery at the Bank of Toronto, Dundas and Roncesvalles.
November 30, 1951	Robbery at the Leaside branch of the Royal Bank. The take, $46,000, was up till that time the largest in Toronto's history.
December 18, 1951	Willie Jackson is arrested in Montreal.
January 25, 1952	Boyd and Suchan rob the Bank of Toronto on Kingston Road.
March 4, 1952	Boyd and two new accomplices rob bank.
March 6, 1952	Sergeant Tong is shot and critically wounded by Steve Suchan.
March 7, 1952	Suchan is wounded during his capture in Montreal.
March 11, 1952	Lennie Jackson is captured in a shootout in Montreal.
March 15, 1952	Boyd is captured in Toronto.
March 23, 1952	Sergeant Tong dies.
March–April 1952	Lennie Jackson and Steve Suchan are returned to the Don Jail in Toronto.

September 8, 1952   Boyd, Lennie Jackson, Suchan and Willie Jackson break jail and escape. Huge manhunt ensues.

September 16, 1952 Boyd Gang recaptured in a deserted barn in North York.

September 29, 1952 Suchan and Lennie Jackson are sentenced to hang.

perfectly straight side, so it was merely a question of marking how far apart the notches were on one side.

Steve and Leonard still did not know that Boyd and Willie were working on a key. Each day when the men were allowed out into the corridor, one cell was left open so they could use the toilet. This was usually Suchan's cell. Without telling Suchan, Boyd and Willie transferred the pattern of the key onto Suchan's wall. Now they were ready to begin. But they had to be very quiet. The microphone was in front of Boyd's cell, but they did not know how far it could detect sounds.

Every so often, Boyd or Willie would go to the toilet, flush it, and quickly make a few marks on their shoehorn with the file, while the flushing covered the noise.

The only problem was that there was too much activity in the toilet cell. The guard grew a little suspicious. "What the hell are you guys doing?" he asked once. "I'm just flushing my dinner down," said Willie. "I don't want any more of it." Little by little, Boyd and Willie shaped their crude key. When they thought they had it about right, they tried it in the lock.

As soon as they turned it, the tin metal of the shoehorn bent. Next they tried doubling the metal in half. Now it wasn't wide enough. Finally they gave up in disgust.

Willie went to see his visitor and told him the shoehorn was useless. He had to have something better. Shortly thereafter, his visitor returned with a perfect piece of metal, just the right thickness, width and length. It was soft enough steel that it could easily be filed, and Boyd and Willie went to work on it immediately.

By now Len and Steve were in on the plan. Soon they had what they thought was an adequate key filed out. The day had arrived to test it. Steve and Len began an argument near the front barrier to distract the guard's attention. Boyd was at the open door to Suchan's cell. While the guard watched Steve and Len, Boyd shoved his home-made key into the lock. He turned it carefully, and the lug slid out beautifully.

Boyd was elated. He gave a sign to Willie, and grinning to himself, tried to unlock the lock. He turned his key. Nothing happened. He tried again and again, but the lug stayed out. Now they were in a jam. The door was open with the lug of the lock protruding from it. Boyd pulled out his key.

"What do we do now?" asked Willie.

"Nothing we *can* do," replied Boyd. "Just leave it."

It would soon be time for the prisoners to be locked in their cells again. the guard would discover the bolt sticking out. How could they explain it?

Just before lock-up time, the guard was called away. Another guard took his place temporarily and was still there to lock them in. Suchan went first.

"What the hell's this?" demanded the guard when he saw the door.

Boyd was ready for him. "Aw, you know the old guy. Sometimes he doesn't know what he's doing. He turned it the wrong way as he was taking it out."

The replacement guard did not question this explanation, and turned the bolt back again before locking each prisoner in his cell.

Some of the guards would hold the key in their hands and slip it quickly into the lock so that the prisoners could never get a good look at it. Their old friend the ex-policeman, however, didn't bother about such things. He just let his key dangle over the key ring. The next day, Boyd and Willie stared hard at the key when the guard was looking elsewhere.

There it was. They could see where they had gone wrong. Their makeshift key had all the points in all the right places, but had missed one small indentation, which obviously was the clue to why their key would lock but not unlock the cell doors.

Boyd could see that the indentation was tiny compared to the size of the key. He decided to start by filing very little. He would continue later, if necessary.

Willie, clowning as usual, took Suchan underneath the microphone when Boyd was ready to file the key. Suchan, of course, had a good ear for music, but Willie was totally off-key. The sound of their combined voices was hardly pleasing. However, they sang as loudly and as long as they could. "Down by the OLD MILLstream, where I FIRST MET you . . . "

The superintendent, who could hear the singing through the sound system, switched on his speaker. "Cut it out!" he called. "I can't hear anything." Boyd flushed the toilet as a signal that he thought he had filed enough, and Willie and Steve stopped their serenade.

It was time to test the key again. Boyd inserted it in the lock. He turned the key. The bolt slid out quietly. He turned it back again, and the bolt slid in again, just as quietly and smoothly as if it were greased.

"Wow!" whispered Suchan.

Until then, Boyd had been hiding the key under his mattress. But like the princess and the pea, Boyd began to develop psychosomatic pains in his back. He worried that the key would be found during the daily cell searches.

The toilet was sitting slightly off the floor on a wooden base. Boyd now removed a small chunk of wood from the base and discovered a hollow behind the toilet, between the base and the floor. He pushed the key and file inside the hollow and covered the spot with a little moistened dirt. It looked fine.

Now that they could get in and out of their cells, they had to go to work on the corridor window bars. The windows looked out over the courtyard. Beneath the windows ran a high brick wall which would make a convenient platform to step out on, once they got out.

Willie's friend obligingly brought a hacksaw blade. He had been promised $7,000 from the first bank job after the gang escaped, regardless of the take. Then he had been promised an additional $3,000 from the second job. He planned to use the money to set himself up in business.

None of the jail officials were suspicious of this respect-able-looking gentleman who visited Willie. Consequently, the frisking that Willie underwent after each visit was perfunctory. The hacksaw blade slipped quite easily into the waistband of Willie's prison trousers, and he took it to his cell undetected. Boyd thought the expensive blade was terrific.

The next step was to muffle the microphone. Every day the prisoners got half a loaf of bread, sliced, sent up to share among the four of them. With it would be a small paper cup full of jam. Boyd took a half dozen slices of bread and held them up against his ear. "It didn't do any good at all," said Boyd. "I could hear just as good with it as without it."

All the pillows were lumpy old things filled with pieces of mattress stuffing. They wouldn't be too efficient. But when Boyd tried Suchan's pillow against his ear, it shut out the sound completely.

"What's in this?" he asked Suchan.

"Feathers," was the reply.

"How'd you get that?"

"I got pull," said Suchan, and grinned enigmatically.

They were ready to begin the final phase of the escape plan. At 5:30 every morning, the guards assembled all the prisoners who were due to go to court that day. This took about thirty or forty minutes. Boyd and his cohorts knew they would have a half-hour minimum, every morning, when they could saw without being disturbed.

But Boyd was reluctant. "I had to drag myself to put my hand through the bars and open the door," he remembers. "I didn't want to go, but at the same time I wanted to help them to go. So I had to push myself to do it." Boyd wanted Suchan and Len Jackson to have one last chance at freedom. Without it, their future didn't look good.

Every morning Boyd got up before daybreak, listened, and waited while the guard shut the door and it was dark in the corridor. The only light they had was a twenty-five-watt bulb. Quickly and quietly, Boyd reached around through the bars and opened his cell door. Then he let each of the others out in turn.

Lennie and Steve were still quite weak from their wounds and were unable to help with the actual sawing. Their job was to take turns holding Suchan's pillow over the microphone. Boyd and Willie Jackson took turns sawing the window bars. Things were going beautifully, but they did have one worry— the one zealous keeper who insisted on checking all the bars with a hammer.

At first, Boyd thought they could cut through in one morning and get away without ever having the bars checked. But now they saw that it was going to take several days to cut the bars.

"I guess we'll have to pray about this," Boyd said to Willie. They were still praying to Satan, or as Boyd called him, "Our Father in Hell". Now they concentrated on one objective—to get rid of the guy who tested the bars.

Amazingly, their wish was granted. The keeper phoned in sick. His replacement was the friendly old ex-policeman. Things couldn't have been better.

The prisoners began to make up all their bread into sandwiches every day. They stacked these about six inches high on the radiator under the window they were working on. Under the other window was a small table. It was convenient to climb up on the table to test the bars, but in order to climb up on the radiator to test the other window, the guard would have to move all the sandwiches. Says Boyd, "He was such a nice guy that he wouldn't touch our sandwiches." After a few days, the gang felt confident that the bars would never be checked before they were ready to go.

Each day they packed the new cuts in the bar. Working a piece of soap until it was soft and pliable, they rubbed it through dirt, twisting and turning it so that the entire piece was the colour of the metal window bar. Then Boyd would rub his hands up and down the bars on the window so that they would all have the same shiny appearance.

Finally, they had one bar cut three-quarters of the way through on both top and bottom. Only a few strokes would be needed to cut it completely. They were ready to go.

Their luck had been so good until then, it seemed there had to be a hitch. There was. The day they were ready was a Saturday. There was no court for two days, which meant the solid door at the end of the cell block would be left open the entire weekend. They would have to tough it through. Every time the prisoners were marched out to walk around the bull ring, the four from death row sweated with fear that their handiwork would be discovered. Their friendly little old guard only worked weekdays, so they also had to worry about the replacement guard. But the replacement couldn't be bothered checking the bars.

Monday morning finally arrived. This was the day. As soon as the solid door closed at the end of the cell block, Boyd quickly opened the doors of the cells. Everyone knew what to do. The pillow went up to the microphone and with several good hard passes of the saw blade, the bar was cut through on both ends.

They had a blanket ready. The plan was to go out the window, walk along the top of the wall and jump down over the end. They had no idea what would be there waiting for them. They had heard all kinds of stories about a cop cruiser that sat waiting outside the wall. They would have to chance it.

"Okay," said Boyd, "let's go." Boyd was first. He climbed up on the radiator and poked his head out through the newly cut space between the bars. Freedom was already starting to feel good.

He wiggled his torso out through the opening and tried to pull his hips through. They wouldn't go. He squirmed and twisted. His hips were too big. He gave it all his strength, and still he couldn't squeeze through the hole.

They had got away on the last escape by cutting through just one bar. This time, however, they had neglected to take into account that the cross bars were much closer together. The space left by the removal of one bar was too small.

"Jeez, what's wrong?" said Boyd. "You try it, Willie." Willie was close to Boyd's size, Suchan and Len were bigger. Willie striped out of his clothes.

Boyd got some butter from their sandwich pile. Len and Steve helped him as he smeared it over Willie's naked hips. A guard walking in at that moment would have encountered a strange sight in the pre-dawn light of death row.

Willie climbed up to the window. He poked his head and shoulders through the opening. Edwin, Steve and Len grabbed his legs and tried to shove him through. His hips were too big.

"Jesus Christ, you guys! It hurts," whispered Willie. "Pull me back in."

Too much time had already elapsed. The guard could be back any minute. Boyd quickly locked up the other three men and Willie pulled on his clothes. Boyd grabbed the bar that he had so recently removed in triumph. He slapped a gob of soap on each end and hastily shoved it back in place. He stuffed the cracks with his blackened soap and ran his hand up and down the bars. His heart pounding, he grabbed his key and locked himself back in his cell.

Now one bar was held in place only by soap. It could slide out and crash to the floor. It could fall out if the guard even breathed on it, let alone banged a hammer on it. The Boyd Gang was sweating.

The next morning they began to saw on the bar adjacent to the soaped-bar. There was no other choice. They tried to step up the pace. With a nail in each end of the hacksaw blade and tape wrapped around for handles, Willie and Ed sawed as fast as they could every morning, while the guards took the other prisoners off to court. Soon it would be their turn for court, and they would have to leave at 5:30 every morning. Suchan and Jackson were also due in court the following week.

Labour Day came, and again they went through agony. There was no court on legal holidays so they couldn't saw in the morning. They had no idea how long the zealous keeper would be away from work. He could come back any day and start hammering away again on the bars.

Finally they felt they were ready. But they had to wait through another weekend. Boyd was still saying that he wasn't going with them. He would get them out safely, then go back inside and lock himself in his cell. He thought it would be a great joke on the police and jail officials if he locked up the other guys' cells too, after they had disappeared.

"Are you sure you want to do that?" asked Len. "You know you're crazy to stay. You know what's gonna happen when they find us missing? What're they going to do to you?"

"It doesn't bother me," said Boyd. "I was sleeping. I didn't know what went on."

It was September 8, 1952. This was their last chance. Len and Steve were due to go to court that day to begin the proceedings for their murder trial. They would have to start extra early in the morning.

Boyd went first to clear the way. This time he slipped easily through the hole between the bars. It was still dark outside. They stepped out onto the wall one at a time. Suchan was the biggest, and his hips were snug against the bars, but he managed to wriggle his way out.

Boyd was just about to go back inside when Suchan came back from the wall. "There's a policeman down below," said Steve.

Boyd felt the onus was on him again. He still hadn't gotten them away safely. He stepped over each of the others and slipped along the wall. The policeman was whistling and talking to himself. His shift was almost over and he was anxious to get home. But he had to stand and guard this courtyard, even when there was no one in sight anywhere.

The four men lay on top of the wall. Dawn was breaking. They could see each other's faces quite clearly. They could see the odd car passing on the street. But they couldn't make their move to the end of the wall.

"We're going to have to go back in again," whispered Boyd. "We'll have to put those bars back and lock ourselves up."

"It's to late!" Willie whispered frantically. "The guards will be coming in and opening the door, and they'll discover we're missing, and we won't be able to get back in the cells in time. You'll never get the bars back in time."

Boyd realized he was trapped. He knew he had to go with them. *Aw, what the hell*, he thought. *That's the way the cookie crumbles.* Besides, it felt great to be out of that dingy cell, breating the crisp September morning air. It really felt too good to go back.

Boyd kept his eye on the policeman below. Suddenly, the policeman wheeled around and marched over to a door across the courtyard. He knocked on the door. It opened. Somebody handed him a cup of coffee and in he went.

The Boyd Gang wasted no time. One by one they dashed to the end of the wall, dropped over the edge and started running up the Don Valley.

Even without his foot, "Tough Lennie" was the fastest. They all pushed themselves to the limit. Willie's visitor had arranged for a cache of food and guns to be left buried at a dump, but that was up near Sheppard Avenue, several miles to the north. They agreed to meet there as soon as possible.

By seven a.m., the break was discovered at the Don Jail. The Boyd Gang didn't know how soon the police would be on their trail. They followed the river as it wound its way up the valley and tried to keep under cover of trees and brush. It wasn't long before they heard the whirring of a helicopter overhead. They took shelter under some bushes. Were they visible from the air? They had no idea. They would have to wait until the helicopter passed over.

The four fugitives were soon separated as they worked their way north. Their only plan was to meet at the cache and decide what to do from there. They were trusting in Willie's friend to carry out his part of the plan. Would he let them down? Was it a trap? They didn't know, but it wouldn't be long before they found out.

MANHUNT

17

BOYD, SUCHAN, 2 JACKSONS SAW WAY OUT OF JAIL/ POLICE TOLD SHOOT TO KILL, blared the headlines of the Toronto *Star*. It was the morning of September 8, and already police from coast to coast in Canada had been put on the alert. Toronto was in an uproar.

"It's a disgrace to the city," said Mrs. Edmund Tong, wife of the late sergeant of detectives. "All criminals had to do was to sit in jail and think up ways of escaping. Why, even Jackson's sister told my husband that Leonard would get him if he were ever in a tight spot."

Other people now feared that Jackson and Boyd would "get them". In Montreal, Henri Côté and his wife asked police for protection, fearing that Jackson would come to extract revenge for turning him in. Sergeant Roy Perry, the key witness at the fatal Tong shooting, was rushed into hiding from his home in Swansea. Police feared that he would be a prime target for Suchan and Jackson, already charged with murder.

Police, jail officials, the city and the entire country tried to figure out what had gone wrong. A guard at the Don Jail had been convicted for accepting money from Steve Suchan, and there was a suspicion that he had helped the prisoners obtain a key for their escape. A mystery turned up in the investigation: four keys were found for the cell where the Boyd Gang was held, while jail records listed only two keys in existence.

Mayor Lamport, returned from a vacation at his summer cottage, blamed the jail administration, calling it "the operation of a bunch of morons". He also had another round with bankers, blaming them for leaving their "loose cash" lying around to be robbed. "Bank officials have nothing but money in their veins!" he declared, pounding his fist on the desk for emphasis.

Gordon Sinclair, in his Toronto *Star* column, reported that Dorreen Boyd had telephoned him in June offering him the chance to write her husband's story in return for half the fee. She would arrange for Sinclair to bypass the governor of the jail and see Boyd without permission. Sinclair was willing to go only through proper channels, and was eventually refused permission by Colonel Hedley Basher, deputy-minister of reform institutions. The minister himself, Major Foote, finally called Sinclair into his office, warning that Dorreen was far from the innocent victim of circumstances she presented herself to be and was in fact working closely with her husband.

Contact with Dorreen Boyd, Sinclair claimed, gave him valuable inside information that the Boyd Gang intended to rob several banks in Toronto and area in commando-style attacks. He concluded that the gang was still in the Toronto area and would bet "dollars to duck eggs" that they planned on staying there.

Sinclair was not alone in his conviction that the gang was nearby. Hot tips began to pour into police stations by the dozen. The Boyd Gang had been seen everywhere, by everyone, and police had to check on every lead.

An anonymous phone call led Sergeant Payne to interview a distant relative of Edwin Boyd. Payne's report ends: "Apparently O.K.–queer." An informant sent officers checking on a man named "Wally" around Lake Simcoe. Again nothing turned up. Gordon Sinclair received a phone call giving a telephone number where a girlfriend of Suchan's could be reached—another false tip. George Stoddart, the lawyer who had rented Boyd the Heath Street apartment, received a crank telegram from Barrie, Ontario which said simply: "Have you any rooms for rent? Book lover."

Most of these tips were unsolicited, but by evening, police had a new channel of communication with the public. September 8, 1952 was the official opening of the new CBC television station in Toronto, CBLT. Several hours before the station was scheduled to begin broadcasting, television cameras focused on police rogues-gallery photographs of Edwin Boyd, William R. Jackson, Leonard Jackson, and Steve Suchan.

"Canadian talent!" boasted a CBC official, only half in jest. The Boyd Gang had stolen the spotlight even before Prime Minister St. Laurent marked the formal commencement of broadcasting. St. Laurent's comments at the opening were prophetic:

> Because television will bring vivid images to so many homes day after day, it will become a very strong social force. This force could be harmful to the nation, or it could bring great benefit.

In any case, the force was already being felt. Response to the Boyd Gang publicity was enthusiastic with informants eager to assist in the capture.

A man reported that he overheard the following conversation in the Varsity Grill at Bloor and Spadina:

"They'll never get your friends."

"No, they'll never get them, they're in the bush."

The amateur detective followed the speaker for several blocks and took down the licence number of a car. Another citizen reported that he had seen three men helping a fourth from an automobile into a cabin at Oak Ridge, Ontario.

Police began a series of raids on well-known criminals and associates of the gang. All suspicious persons were questioned, some extensively. No one knew anything.

A police detective reported that some of Boyd's friends had attempted to purchase a cottage near Sutton, Ontario. Another detective received a phone call from a man who had known Boyd and had definitely seen him appear from behind a hotel in Cooksville, walk across the highway and get into a 1938 or 1939 coupe. The informant felt sure that the gang was holed up in the hotel. Seven police officers were despatched to the hotel to check out the information, again to no avail.

A friend of Suchan's was followed for twenty-four hours, then confronted by police. The friend thought there was a possibility that Suchan might try to contact him and agreed to notify police if he did.

Sergeant Payne and Detective Cook observed a Howard Street apartment for four hours, then rang the bell. They discovered an unlikely couple living there—Leonard Jackson's wife, Ann, and his half-brother, Sam Stone. Ann Jackson had moved out of her

Humberside apartment with her baby two weeks earlier, and Sam Stone was acting as her protector, keeping press and curious public away.

Everyone was suspect. Neighbours began to report everything overheard or seen. As the reward money mounted, anxious informants phoned in every clue they could come up with.

Address after address was checked out as information poured in to police. Raids were made in cities across Canada. Memos were sent air mail to police departments all across North America. A man was hauled off a train in Regina by a posse of armed citizens and an RCMP constable. In Edmonton, police raided a downtown hotel where four easterners had checked in. All the way to the west coast, people were on the lookout for the Boyd Gang. Ships leaving Vancouver for Australia were checked for stowaways. The FBI in Washington was notified.

But police still believed the Boyd Gang was in Toronto and concentrated their efforts in that area. The RCMP revised their "Most Wanted Criminal" list, placing Edwin Alonzo Boyd's name at the top. Within thirty-six hours after the breakout, reward money offered totalled $26,000, the highest ever in Ontario. The public was frantic in its efforts to capture the gang.

A drugstore clerk was positive she had sold hair dye to Boyd. She claimed that she could see his picture in the newspaper under the counter as she spoke to him. When she asked what colour of dye he wanted he replied, "Never mind about that," and appeared in a great hurry. The man also purchased peroxide, mentioning that his girlfriend knew how to use it. Police in Ontario and Quebec covered 200 miles of roads looking for the suspect's car, but nothing turned up.

A farmer near Whitby, Ontario sat listening to the news of the Boyd Gang breakout on the radio when he heard a squawking in his chicken yard. Grabbing his .22 rifle, he ran out in time to see a man limping away toward the fence. The farmer shot three times at the ground, but the intruder only limped away faster. Thinking it might be "Tough Lennie" Jackson, the farmer aimed higher. With a howl, the intruder hit the ground. He had been shot in the seat of his pants. Police returned the man to the nearby Ontario Hospital, from which he had escaped.

Mayor Allan Lamport, busy practicing on tractor and plough for a ploughing match with Ottawa's Mayor Charlotte Whitton, took time to comment on the breakout, in his official capacity as chairman of the Toronto Police Commission. "What fool put those four in the same cell block with club car privileges?" he demanded. "The place was so wide open they could have walked out the front door. All they wanted was a cocktail bar."

Apparently the province agreed. Premier Frost of Ontario announced the suspension of the Don Jail governor, deputy governor, and six jail guards, the entire staff on duty at the time of the breakout. An inquiry into jail administration was opened, and the Ontario Provincial Police took over duties until the matter was thoroughly investigated.

Police and public were stymied by a number of puzzling questions: Where did the convicts get the saw blades? Where did the key come from which opened the cells? What was the purpose of the wooden key, the same size as cell keys but unnotched, which was found in one of the cells? How did Leonard Jackson get away without his foot? How did the men saw through the bars without the noise being picked up by the supposedly secret microphone?

Welders already repairing the cut bars in the cell block noticed that the same bar had been repaired once before. The soft iron bars were such a joke by now that one official commented wryly: "Pretty soon they'll have nothing but weld bumps along the bars."

On Thursday, September 11, the fourth day of freedom for the Boyd Gang, Dorreen Boyd made a public appeal. She wrote a letter to her husband which was reproduced in the newspapers, along with large pictures of herself:

My Dearest Eddie,
Am I asking too much of you under the circumstances *to give yourself up?* If to anyone to me *or* to the men both you and I know would give you a fair deal. I have thought this over so much in the past three days, and knowing me as your devoted wife, I'll *wait* for you no matter what the outcome may be. God willing we will have the privilege of growing old together. This is all I ask of you and Eddie remember always I love you dearly.   Yours,
                                        Frances Boyd. X X X X
                                        B.C.R.D.

The possibility of a "secret message" hidden in the final initials drove readers crazy, until Sergeant of Detectives Adolphus Payne told them he was satisfied with Dorreen's explanation. They were the initials of the three Boyd children and Dorreen. Frances was Dorreen's second name, which she preferred, and which Edwin often called her.

One amateur sleuth was not satisfied with this explanation. He translated the initials B.C.A.D. into a code which he said revealed a telephone number. He passed this number along to police, certain that the gang would turn up if they simply dialled the number. Like so many other clues, this too led nowhere.

The following day, Dorreen Boyd took her children to radio station CKEY in Toronto and recorded an appeal to Edwin to give himself up. The children added their own poignant plea: "We miss you, daddy, please come home." The appeal was broadcast at six p.m. and repeated almost hourly throughout the night. The station was deluged with phone calls.

Half the callers were offended that the children should be involved in the affair. Some said they would never listen to CKEY again, although one of these asked the time of the next appeal broadcast. Others said they were moved to tears, and many sent good wishes to Dorreen and the children. (The appeals, of course, were just another red herring. Dorreen knew where Ed was most of the time; he spent the night with her and the children at least once.)

By Saturday, September 13, police were telling the public that a break in the case was very near. It was the sixth day of freedom for the Boyd Gang and the underworld was said to be tiring of all the police raids. "The stool pigeons are beginning to sing," said the police. Yet it seemed that the songs they were singing were familiar old tunes.

Informants called about the cottage the Jacksons had rented the previous summer or offered tips about people the police had long since checked out. Others suggested the obvious: "Watch their families."

Crank letters poured into police stations. One warned it was only a rumour, but what I understand, the Boyd gang are *Still in Toronto*, and hiding out on a *street* or *avenue* not very popular in Toronto. In a *basement house*, a *house* of *brick* or *wooden frame*, I am not sure. But in *due course* of time, they intend to flee the country. Be on the alert on the *Quebec, New Brunswick* border, and watch your *airports*. If you care you can take what I have told you as a grain of salt. Wishing you the best of luck, *A true friend of the Law*.

Some were almost incomprehensible:

Dear Sirs,
Some twenty years or more, the President of the Watch Tower Bible and Tract Society of World Organization made the statement the Heirarchy of Rome was accomplishing many exploits thro what he termed *Buck Nun Exploits of R.C.* and its followers. Judge Joseph Rutherford was considered by Church that he was a bitter enemy, and he suffered much at their hands during his earthly ministry.

Judge Rutherford died over ten years ago Jan 8, 1942, but we must own the Heirarchy of Rome is not dead but is still alive and active. This suggestion might assist to bring to justice this Canada wide terror which took place in Toronto last Monday.
                                                                       Interested.

Other writers displayed their prejudices. One, "A Citizen", warned police to watch a certain address because "these houses are owned by Italian characters, and will do anything for money".

One man was sure that Boyd had walked up to him on the street in London and spoken to him, asking directions. He had been an army buddy of Boyd's and thought that Boyd had been testing out his disguise. The letter went into great detail, quite lucidly offering to assist police in any way, but ended with the phrase, "We simply cannot have these mad dogs prowling around loose with death lurking in their every step."

Letters were sent to detectives, the police chief, the mayor, newspapers, and the attorney general. All were received seriously.

The reality was much more dismal than these concerned citizens imagined. Boyd and his friends were north of Toronto, hiding out in the woods and working their way toward an abandoned farm where they hoped to take shelter.

The first night, Lennie Jackson had disappeared. When he showed up the next day he sported a new wooden foot. Suchan also left the gang for a day, and reappeared with an armload of clothes. Most of the clothes fit Suchan, some of them fit Len, but Boyd and Willie were too small and looked ridiculous in the outfits. They still wore their prison blues.

Willie was appointed food scrounger for the gang. Boyd decided that Willie would have to be disguised if he were going into Toronto. With the razor that had been left at the cache Boyd scraped away what little there was of Willie's hair in front. Willie bemoaned his sudden baldness but was delighted when he was picked up by two different woman as he hitchhiked over to Yonge Street.

Willie brought back bread, cheese, a few staples, and some blood sausage which Boyd had never tried. Too hungry to care what he ate, he sliced off a hunk and gobbled it down. His verdict: "Delicious!"

The Boyd Gang knew they were causing a lot of excitement in Toronto, but would have been amazed—and pleased—that so many people were obligingly leading the police on all those wild goose chases.

A woman wrote to tell police that she and her mother were gifted with "second sight" and had several strong mental pictures of the Boyd Gang. There were indications that the breakout had been an inside job, assisted by an "older, grey-haired, tight-lipped man" and a younger man, "much more cagey, but not as directly to blame". The writer warned police to watch all waterways, especially a small ocean liner, and bridges, tunnels, river banks, water fronts, and marshy swamps. She also felt sure that one man was thinking of Detroit, and one man had changed his hair or head in some way.

The letters went on and on. Some were obviously pranks, some were sincere. The best prank was played on Detective Jack Gillespie, who had captured Lennie Jackson in Montreal in March. A parcel was delivered to Gillespie at the police station with a note enclosed:

> Dear John: I can still see your big fat ugly face—I need this foot badly, and I know that you will take good care of it for me. I won't be around for a few days yet, but I will eventually call for it—so take good care of it. Will be seeing you John my boy!
>
> Signed: Your ever loving gun toting pal,
> "Tough Lennie".

XXXXXX

Inside the parcel was a wooden left foot. It was years before Gillespie discovered that another detective had sent the parcel.

Police welcomed any and all ideas or clues, but nothing seemed to help. The Boyd Gang had dropped out of sight completely. Sergeant of Detectives Bill Matthews summed up the situation:

> We're just going crazy. Rumours, rumours, rumours, that's all we are getting. No leads. They're supposed to be in Maine, then Boyd pops up in Winnipeg. Jackson's supposed to be heading for Montreal. Suchan was seen at Lake Simcoe, or so somebody thinks.
> Everybody thinks they've seen them, but nobody we've talked to really has.

Toronto police came up with an idea that since Boyd was supposedly a master of disguise, the whole gang could be walking the streets unrecognized. An artist put together composites of photos and produced a funny set of pictures which were published in the Toronto *Star*. Steve Suchan was shown dressed as a female nurse, a male bus driver, and a female Toronto Transit Commission guide. Edwin Boyd was shown as a labourer (probably much the same as he looked while working on the city streets), a chauffeur, and a fireman.

Curiously, no composites were shown of William or Leonard Jackson. Perhaps police (or the newspapers) felt "Tough Lennie" would be recognizable enough without his artificial foot, even though there was speculation that he would have a new one by now. And Willie may have been neglected simply because he had less "star" quality for the newspaper-buying public.

By Monday, September 15, a week after the escape, police were forced to admit that all leads had run into dead ends. One policeman remarked that it would be difficult to get Boyd because "he knows us as well as we know him. He thinks like a policeman."

On Tuesday, Police Constable Andrew Oulette of the Scarborough Police spotted three men in a suspicious-looking 1951 black Ford northeast of Toronto. The rear licence plate had been bent up so that the number could not be seen. Oulette began to follow the car. The Ford speeded up until the chase was on at ninety-five miles per hour. Holding the steering wheel with his right hand, Oulette fired a warning shot out the window with his left. The Ford kept going. It had to be the Boyd Gang.

Oulette fired until his revolver was empty. Four shots came back in rapid succession. Two missed him by inches. Oulette lost control, crashed through the highway fence, hit a tree, and finally rammed into a brick wall. He took the main shock of the impact in the stomach. In severe pain, he grabbed his car radio and called for help.

At police headquarters, all available detectives seized machine guns, tear gas, hand grenades, and their service revolvers and raced off to Scarborough. Chief John Chisholm ordered several officers out of court cases for the day, cancelled lunch hours, sent motorcycles on patrol, and told all policemen to pay special attention to banks.

The Royal Canadian Air Force loaned police a helicopter and the whole area was searched from the sky. Roadblocks were set up and every suspicious care was checked. Police probed through barns and haystacks in the rural area. Farmers locked their houses up tight.

There was no doubt in anyone's mind. The Boyd Gang was very near. A police officer reported that Oulette had had a good look at the driver of the fleeing vehicle. "The only thing he isn't sure of," said the officer, "is whether it was Boyd or Leonard Jackson."

CAPTURE

18

By noon the Malvern area, northeast of Toronto, was swarming with police. Local residents were uneasy. Several farmers remembered that their gardens had been raided and jokes made the rounds about whether the Boyd Gang were the thieves.

Slightly south of the search area, farmer Bob Trimble had noticed a couple of tramps near a deserted neighbourhood house the day before. Since he had been appointed manager of the unoccupied farm, he was concerned about trespassers. "Maybe they're the Boyd Gang," he remarked to his brother. "Don't be silly," was the reply. But Bob Trimble was not convinced. He decided to visit the old farmhouse.

There he discovered four straw pallets and the remains of a canned pork and beans supper. The house was dirty and in a state of disrepair, an unlikely hideout for a gang that made thousands robbing banks. Still, Trimble wanted to be sure. He walked to the barn behind the house.

Inside the barn, Bob Trimble tramped on the hay. Someone had been here, all right, but nothing seemed to be missing or out of place. He walked away, but did not dismiss the incident from his mind.

Earlier, Trimble's brother-in-law had taken a relative over to the barn, looking for some stray heifers. They chatted for about half an hour, among other things discussing the flurry of activity north of them surrounding the Boyd Gang car chase. Noticing signs of recent habitation in the barn, the two men assumed that passing hoboes had slept there. Twenty-six thousand dollars in reward money slipped through their fingers that day.

By 4:30 p.m. Boyd, Suchan, and the two Jacksons felt safe enough to come out of the woods and head for the barn where they intended to spend the night. They had been sleeping out in the open, but the barn would be more comfortable. Boyd was worried about hanging around too long, and the gang discussed plans for the next day. They were all losing weight from their sparse vegetarian diet. They craved a good meal, including meat. They decided to get away from the centre of action.

The plan was to move north, get a car, and perhaps even take its driver hostage. Boyd wanted to go a certain distance with the hostage, then let him go and head off in the opposite direction with a different vehicle. Then they would walk a bit, and thus keep their tracks covered while they travelled. The four men discussed the matter as they began to settle into the barn for the evening.

They had chosen the upper floor of a banked barn, which they entered from the side of the hill. The main floor was beneath them. Suddenly, there was a noise below. They froze. Slowly and quietly Willie Jackson and Edwin Boyd crept to a crack in the floorboards. Leonard Jackson, suffering severely from asthma, refrained from so much as a sniffle. Steve Suchan fingered his P-38 automatic.

Peering through the hole, hardly daring to breathe, Boyd and Willie saw a man, almost directly below them. They watched in silent fascination as the man reached for the button on his pants. He had come to the supposedly deserted barn to masturbate, and when he finished, he wandered away again.

Although they felt secure enough, the gang was not entirely unobserved. A few hundred yards from the old barn, a crew was working on the installation of a new oil pipeline. Two of the men were twenty-year-old Evan Taylor and Elgin Rohrer, aged nineteen. They were taking a load of waste to dump in the trench when they stopped at the top of the hill near the old farmhouse. Taylor jumped out of the truck to urinate by the side of the road. Rohrer, teasing him, said, "Look at the woman over there!"

Taylor looked up and saw that it was a man, lying on the ground about twenty-five yards from the barn. The man stood up and waved something that glittered, as if to signal someone. Another man appeared from behind the barn.

The two pipeline employees continued down the hill and dumped their load. One of the men from the barn came over to them. "Hello," said Taylor. "How are you today?" replied the man. "Pretty slippery since the rain." Taylor and Rohrer watched as the man walked over to the side of the road and picked up some articles near a tree, wrapped them in a rubber raincoat, and walked back to the barn. The articles appeared to be shirts, Taylor thought to himself.

Taylor looked at Rohrer. "I've seen that face somewhere before. I bet it's that gang." Rohrer replied, "That's what struck me."

Discussing the possibility, they discovered that each had noticed some unusual details about the man. He was very pale, as though he had been out of the sunshine for a long time. The other odd thing was that he was wearing two coats. Taylor and Rohrer decided to notify the police. First, however, they would finish dumping their load.

Bob Trimble, still mulling over the clues found at the neighbouring farm, talked to his brother, John. John had heard dogs barking in the area one night and thought that tramps were raiding the local gardens. He mentioned his worries to Maurice Doyle.

Doyle was a chauffeur for Colonel Phillips on a nearby estate. He had also heard the dogs at night and was aware of the shooting that day in Scarborough. At 5:25 p.m. Doyle called the North York Police. He told the officer who answered about the tramps in the barn. "It certainly is worth an investigation," he concluded. The officer agreed, but as the next shift was due to come on shortly, he would wait for them before sending someone over.

Meanwhile, Taylor and Rohrer had asked their boss for permission to go to the local country store to make a telephone call. When they arrived at the store, the Oriole Lunch, they bought a couple of soft drinks. The elderly woman who served them mentioned that a policeman had been shot at by some men in a car that morning. Rohrer spoke up, "We saw some suspicious characters not too far from here that could be them."

"Where was this?" enquired the woman. "Not too far," replied Rohrer. He and Taylor walked outside to the telephone booth. While Taylor put in the call to police, Rohrer waited beside their truck. In a moment, the proprietor of the store came out and spoke to him. "Did you hear about the rumpus out this way? There was some fellow tried to shoot it out with police." Rohrer told him they were calling police at that moment about some tramps they had seen.

The storekeeper tried to get information from the two men about where they had seen the tramps, but Taylor and Rohrer were cool. "Not far from here," is all they would tell him.

At the North York Police Station, Detective Sergeant Maurice Richardson and Detective Bert Trotter had arrived for the six o'clock shift and had already strapped on their guns. They had been given the information from Doyle's phone call and were on their way to make a routine check of the barn.

When Taylor's call came in, the sergeant on telephone duty didn't mention it to Richardson and Trotter because he realized it was the same location they were already headed for. However, before the detectives left the station, a third call came in about tramps. This was from the owner of the Oriole Lunch. He described a different location he thought police should investigate, so the sergeant sent the two detectives to the store on their way to visit the old barn.

Richardson and Trotter left the station about 6:30 p.m. They went immediately to the Oriole Lunch. The proprietor was sweeping the floor and barely looked up. "Did you want to see the police?" asked Trotter. "Yes," was the reply. "A fellow dropped in here and said he had seen a tramp in a barn on Don Mills Road." There were dozens of barns on Don Mills Road and the man could give no more specific information, so the detectives continued on to their original mission.

Inside the barn, the gang was arranging their quarters for the night. It was Lennie's turn to keep watch, but he was not too keen. "Tough Lennie" had been reduced to a sniffling, wheezing, runny-eyed asthmatic by his exposure to grain fields and now this dusty, hay-filled barn. But the gang members felt no sense of imminent danger and lounged about in the hay.

Suchan decided to go over to the nearby orchard for more green apples. He felt safe in the fading light of the approaching dusk. He put his P-38 automatic in his pocket, but the others left their guns lying under a small pile of hay off to one side. Suchan went out through the second-level door on the hillside and wandered off to the rear of the barn.

Richardson and Trotter pulled up to the side of the road. The pipeline crew had the road blocked with bulldozers and one of the crew told them to wait while he cleared the road for them. "Never mind," said Richardson. "We'll just walk in." They parked the car and got out.

First they checked out the old house. There was nobody there, so they strolled over toward the barn.

Trotter went around to the second level entry and poked around the back. Richardson walked in the main entry, after first relieving himself against the side of the barn. In plainclothes he could have been any ordinary passerby.

Boyd and the two Jacksons heard a sound below. Thinking it might be their earlier visitor returned, Boyd stuck his head through the hole where he could view the intruder. *It's not the same guy*, thought Boyd, but he wasn't particularly worried. It was probably just some local farmer, walking around. Richardson, unaware that he was being watched, looked around the main level of the barn.

Outside, Trotter paused before opening the door that led into the second level. He peered through a crack in the door and saw three men in the dim light. He drew his revolver. Quietly pushing open the door, he stepped inside.

Remembers Boyd: "He's got us covered, and we don't even have our guns within reach. So we're just standing there, like figures in a tableau, and there's no movement, and nobody says anything. This guy's just as surprised as we are—but he's got the gun!"

"Maurice!" yelled Trotter. "Come on up here!" Then to the three men, "The first one that moves gets it." Richardson arrived in a few seconds and the two detectives herded the three men out into the farmyard.

Leonard Jackson, wheezing and coughing, doubled over several times. Boyd watched the police officers. *Jeez, he's gonna shoot him*, thought Boyd, as the detectives eyed Jackson.

"All right, take it easy," said Boyd. "The guy's got asthma. He's weak because he was hurt one time. So don't let your gun go off without thinking." "Don't worry about it," retorted Jackson, "I'm all right."

In the farmyard, the officers searched Boyd and the two Jacksons and finding no weapons, Richardson went back to the cruiser to radio for help while Trotter held his gun on them.

"What's your name?" asked Trotter. "What are you guys doing?"

Boyd spoke up, "We live in the district here. We just came in to relax and talk, maybe have a drink."

"What's your name?" the detective asked again.

Boyd thought quickly. The first thing that popped into his head was north-south-east-west. "My name is West," he said. But by now Trotter and Richardson were fairly certain who they had. And they were also certain there should have been a fourth man.

Richardson walked back into the barn to pick up the guns that he knew were in the hay. "I had the awfullest feeling," he remembers. "My hair started to go up. I was looking around for this gun, and I couldn't find it, so I said, 'To hell with it,' and I came out."

Suchan had returned from the orchard with his supply of green apples and finding his buddies gone, decided to play a little trick on them. He climbed up on a beam and pulled out his gun. When Boyd and the Jacksons returned, he intended to point his gun at them, and say, "You're dead." He waited in silence, until he saw a strange man searching around in the hay below.

By this time, three uniformed constables, Ernest Southern, Havre Lowe, and William Adams, had arrived in response to Richardson's radio call for help. "Be careful," Richardson told them. "Go back and search that barn." They went in with their guns drawn. Suchan had dropped down from his beam and was crawling over to the wall to have a look at what was going on below. Southern came in on the second level, while Lowe and Adams stayed below. "Hands up!" commanded Southern, as Suchan turned in surprise.

It was all over in a matter of seconds. Taken off guard, Suchan did not reach for his gun. Southern waved him over to the ledge and Suchan jumped down to the waiting Lowe and Adams, who had their weapons drawn.

"What's cooking?" asked Suchan, as innocently as possible.

"I guess you know what's cooking," replied Southern. "One move and I'll blow your bloody head off."

Searching their captive, the detectives discovered his P-38 automatic with the safety catch off. The three constables escorted Suchan to the police cruiser where Boyd and the Jacksons were waiting quietly.

The news of the capture had already brought several more policemen to the scene. The group of jailbreakers were handcuffed and put in cruisers to be taken to the station. As Boyd remembers, one policeman had a gun trained on them and seemed quite nervous. "For God's sake," said Boyd, "didn't you ever handle a gun before?

Quit pointing the thing at us, and act like a grownup!" After a false start occasioned by the need to change a flat tire on one of the police cars, the parade of cops and robbers threaded its way through the gathering crowd of spectators, and proceeded to the North York Police Station.

The capture had hit the airwaves, and the crowds began to gather. By the time the group of captors and captives arrived at the North York station, a few hundred local residents were already waiting to see the famous gang. Detectives and uniformed constables patrolled the vicinity with machine guns, shot guns, and their service weapons. The helicopter used in the search was sitting across Yonge Street in a field. The crowds spilled off the sidewalks and onto the streets.

Teenagers shouted in unison, "We want Boyd, we want Boyd!" but the dapper folk-hero and his cohorts were whisked inside and quickly locked up in cells.

At the Don Jail, down in the heart of the city, crowds were forming in hope that the prisoners might be brought in that evening. Zoot-suited teenage boys and their girlfriends stood watch for hours, hoping to catch a glimpse of the Boyd Gang. Not until near midnight, when they were informed that the gang would be kept overnight in North York, did the fans disperse.

In their cells in North York, the prisoners had several visitors that evening. Among the first of these were Police Chief John Chisholm and Mayor Allan Lamport. Lamport had his ritual picture taken for the newspapers, along with the detectives who had made the capture and the constables who had come along to help. Then the ebullient mayor raced off to another meeting with the comment, "They were meek as lambs when I saw them. But I don't know how long they'll stay that way!"

Toronto *Star* reporter Alexandrine Gibb was given permission to see the gang, accompanied by Inspector Archie McCathie. She was allowed to give each of the prisoners a cigarette, and was courteously received by all except Lennie Jackson. Jackson, wheezing miserably, could barely manage a smile for the reporters who badgered him. Finally McCathie sent for a doctor who gave Lennie some medication.

The prisoners seemed almost happy to be captured, now that they were safe, warm, comfortable, and most important, well fed.

McCathie had more or less taken control of the situation, even though he was a Toronto inspector and this was North York, which had at that time a separate police force. McCathie knew the prisoners, and understood the whole situation. Even though some of the local policemen treated the gang like the "most wanted" criminals they were, McCathie treated them like truant schoolboys, naughty but loveable. Sandwiches and coffee were sent for, and everyone settled in for the night.

There was much discussion, laughter and camaraderie around the jail cells that night. Willie R. Jackson, after being given an aspirin for a toothache, regaled the crowd with tales, most of them fictitious.

"In jail, I read about the great Morton," said Willie, "and decided to be a hypnotist. I had the jail librarian bring in a book on hypnotism and I got so good at it I could hypnotize the screws. I had them under my spell, every one of them. They did everything I told them. They were sawing the bars under my spell, and we were wearing their caps and punching the clocks. They couldn't get away from it!"

Willie Jackson waggled his fingers in imagined imitation of a hypnotist, and Boyd and Suchan laughed. "Better watch those fellows guarding us tonight," warned Willie, "or I'll put them under the spell too."

Leonard Jackson greeted Sergeant of Detectives William Bolton, who had been at his shoot-out in Montreal, and smiled as he handed over a grimy Toronto Transit ticket. "I guess I won't have any more use for this for a while," said Tough Lennie.

Edwin Boyd, joking with a reporter, asked him to make sure his car was gassed up. "I'll be needing it a year from now in Kingston," laughed Boyd.

Suchan chatted with his captor, P.C. Southern. Suchan claimed that he had been prepared for the police when they came in. "I could have blown your brains out," he told Southern.

"Why didn't you?" the constable asked him.

Suchan shrugged his shoulders, and looked away. "I just didn't," he said quietly, "that's all."

Down the corridor from the cells, standing upright on a table, was Leonard Jackson's artificial foot. The black shoe with the diamond-patterned sock covering the upper leather casing looked abandoned in the midst of all the activity, and Leonard Jackson forlornly peered out at it between the bars. Earlier he had wanted the police to shoot him as they took the gang captive, but now he only wanted to forget his asthma, forget his situation, and sleep like he hadn't slept for more than a week.

Police had questioned all four, separately and together, about the shooting of Constable Oulette, the event that had intensified the manhunt in the North York area. Each denied having anything to do with it, even after being assured that the officer was not wounded, only bruised from the crash.

"Why wouldn't I tell you if I knew?" Suchan asked reasonably. "I already have one murder rap against me."

Police were finally forced to conclude that the gang was telling the truth. It was merely a fortuitous coincidence that a group of rowdies had created a disturbance with a policeman within a few miles of the Boyd Gang hideout.

Dozens of people later made claims for the reward money, some of whom had only the remotest connections with the capture, some none at all.

"Dear Sir," read a letter from Alberta,

> If this letter is not address to the right person, please pass it to the right person that takes care of the reward to be given for finding the Boyd Gang. Has I am a cripple of polio in wheelchair I like to have a share of the money if possible. Then I will be able to start a small business to make some money. If possible, please help me out.

Like all others, this one got a reply, but the answer was negative.

Of the legitimate claims to the reward, John Trimble made the following statement: "You give any money to Doyle. He has a girl that has infantile paralysis and needs the money. I earn my money with my hands, and am quite content that way."

The Department of the Attorney–General of Ontario finally divided the $26,000 reward money among five men. Maurice Doyle, who had phoned in the first tip to North York Police, received $11,000. John Trimble, who had spoken to Doyle about the tramps in the barn, received $4,500. Bob Trimble, for relaying the information to his brother John was given $2,500. The two pipeline employees, Evan Taylor and Elgin Roher, each received $4,000. Although the claims were to continue to come in for the next three years, those who offered the rewards, the Province of Ontario, the City of Toronto, and The Canadian Bankers' Association, were satisfied that justice had been done.

The night of September 16, 1952, the Boyd Gang waited in North York. Their trials would begin within a week. Steve Suchan and Leonard Jackson awaited arraignment for murder. Edwin Boyd was up for eleven charges of bank robbery. William R. Jackson, with the other three men, faced new charges of escaping custody.

As the Boyd Gang languished in the ultra-modern cells of the new North York Police Station, repair crews at the Don Jail attempted to make the ancient structure escape-proof. The gang would be going back to the same four cells from which they had escaped, but this time would be confined behind new, case-hardened, saw-resistant steel bars. New locks graced the new cell doors. And Reform Institutions Minister John Foote promised that the gang would be under twenty-four-hour armed guard.

Edwin Boyd laughed when he heard they were going back to the Don. "If I'm in there another month," he said, "I'll saw my way out again!"

19

Traffic stopped as the procession wound its way to Toronto City Hall. Steve Suchan and Leonard Jackson were on their way to see Chief Justice McRuer for arraignment on the charge of murdering Sergeant Tong. Crowds tried to get a glimpse of the famous criminals, but the pair were loaded into a patrol wagon inside a garage, and whisked quickly away. As the heavily-guarded prisoners reached City Hall, fifteen policemen armed with shotguns kept spectators away from the building. This time they were taking no chances.

In a similar performance, Edwin Boyd, his brother Robert, William R. Jackson and his brother Joseph were taken before Judge Robert Forsyth. "Good morning," said Edwin Boyd to reporters and cameramen, as the procession of prisoners, handcuffed to one another and to policemen, shuffled out of the Don Jail. Allister Gibson, charged with the robbery at College and Manning, had been out on bail and failed to appear in court that morning, but there was no possibility that they were ready to start without him.

"Is your counsel present in the courtroom?" asked Crown Attorney Arthur Klein.

Replied Boyd, "I haven't heard a thing since I was caught."

"Who is your counsel?" asked Klein.

Boyd replied that Fred McMahon was representing him and Robert. Joseph Jackson had no lawyer. Kenneth Cunningham was to represent Willie Jackson.

The prisoners were taken back to the Don and efforts commenced to find the various lawyers.

The arraignment of Suchan and Jackson finished, Chief Justice McRuer left the court to go to lunch. Arthur Maloney, the young lawyer who had chatted with Tong and Perry in a restaurant the night before the fatal shooting, happened to meet McRuer. The chief justice stopped Maloney and told him that Leonard Jackson was in need of counsel. "I didn't relish the assignment," remembers Maloney, "but you don't decline an invitation from the chief justice of the High Court."

Suchan already had a lawyer. Before his escape, he had been in the Don Jail without legal counsel. His mother worked as a cleaning woman in the Canada Life Building. In the same building was the law office of John J. Robinette. One night as Robinette worked late at the office, he was surprised to see the cleaning woman come forward to speak to him. Her son was in trouble, she said, and would Mr. Robinette take his case? She was a decent woman, thought Robinette, and very upset. He went almost immediately to the jail to see Suchan.

An irony which struck Robinette later was the fact that a client of his father's, a man named McCullough, had escaped from the same cell in 1918. Of course Robinette did not realize when he met his new client that Suchan was about to take a leave of absence from his death-row cell in the Don. But the vacation did little for Suchan or the case, except to attract even more publicity.

By September 22, all the lawyers, witnesses, prisoners, and judges were finally gathered together, and the trials began. Sergeant of Detectives Adolphus Payne and his new partner, Detective Charles Cook, had spent the past six months preparing the case against Edwin Boyd and his cohorts. The trials were to have started the day the gang made their most recent escape, so the prosecution was well prepared. Crown counsel Arthur Klein had subpoenaed 147 witnesses against Boyd, a Toronto record for a criminal case.

In a separate courtroom, Maloney and Robinette tried to delay the Suchan and Jackson trial, but the judge, Chief Justice McRuer, would hear none of it. He told Robinette that an adjournment should have been requested on September 8 (the day of the escape), after the grand jury presented a true bill against his client. "At that time," said Robinette, "I wasn't sure there would be a trial."

"I'm not asking for a lengthy adjournment. I'm just asking for a short delay so I can adequately prepare a satisfactory defence." Arthur Maloney agreed with his colleague and asked if they might study the evidence which Crown witnesses were prepared to give.

McRuer was not interested. "There is no law that requires me to direct the Crown to give to the defence a statement of the Crown's evidence. I will do everything in my power to see that the accused have a fair trial. The adjournment is not allowed."

While the lengthy process of choosing a jury began on the Suchan-Jackson case, the Boyd courtroom was already jammed with spectators as the pleas were given.

Edwin Boyd, in contrast to his earlier defiance, was now meek and quiet. Initially he had pleaded not guilty on his first four charges, but now, at the suggestion of his counsel, he changed his plea to guilty.

Everyone involved in the Boyd Gang, with the exception of Suchan, Jackson and Dorreen Boyd, would be tried in the same courtroom, before the same judge, and with different juries to be chosen as each case came up. Along with Edwin Boyd were his brother Robert, charged with harbouring Edwin; Joseph Jackson and Allister Gibson, charged with armed robbery at the College and Manning bank; William R. Jackson, charged with breaking jail, escaping custody, and armed robbery; Mary Mitchell, and Suchan's parents, the Kozaks, charged with harbouring Edwin Boyd and William R. Jackson.

The first four charges against Boyd were for breaking jail, escaping custody (two offences), car theft, and the armed robbery of the Bank of Montreal at College and Manning. When he changed his plea to guilty, he became merely a spectator at the other trials. Boyd remembers:

> They always brought me into court for their cases, even if I wasn't gonna be up in court. The police brought me in for one reason — to influence the jury and the judge concerning the person who was being tried. The idea was that the very fact that I was beside them made them guilty. And it worked, no trouble at all.

Covered by machine guns, manacled together, there was no question who were the accused. The trials went on every day for three weeks, but no sentence was handed down on any case until all were heard.

The weeks dragged on. Joseph Jackson was positively identified by a bank employee because of a scar on his face, and was promptly dubbed "Scarface" by the press. Sergeant Payne testified against Robert Boyd, quoting him as saying, "I told you before that I would help Edwin if I could, and I did."

Dorreen Boyd, remanded on a charge of conspiracy, tried to raise $1,000 for her bail. She too sat in on the trials every day, and was closely watched by the press. Her scarlet coat was seen as a symbol of her defiantly independent outlook, and she was reported to be "hatless" in court, when woman were expected to cover their heads in the courtroom as well as in church. Several times she was instructed to move further away from her husband in the courtroom, and then would slip back into a closer seat as soon as an opportunity presented itself.

Boyd's sister Irene, a missionary, sat with Dorreen for several days. She was genuinely moved and distressed by her brothers' situation, but the press was often sceptical, associating her with Edwin's masquerade as a missionary when renting the Heath Street house.

While the trials continued, the world outside the courtrooms did not stand still. Bob Trimble saw a suspicious-looking person running away from the hideout barn. Within hours it burned to the ground. Police assured the public that the barn had been combed thoroughly for evidence and clues, and would have been torn down in a few weeks anyway. In New Brunswick, H.J. Flemming led the Progressive Conservatives to victory after seventeen years in opposition. In Washington, Senator Richard M. Nixon, Republican vice-presidential candidate, came under fire for receiving expense money illegally from seventy-six businessmen. After he was vindicated, General Dwight Eisenhower announced that Nixon stood higher in his esteem than ever. Rocky Marciano, with a single devastating blow, knocked out Jersey Joe Walcott in the thirteenth round, to become the world heavyweight boxing champion. But in Toronto, the news still centred on the Boyd Gang.

The jury had already returned verdicts of guilty against Joseph ("Scarface") Jackson and Allister Gibson for armed robbery, and against Robert Boyd for harbouring his brother. However, Robert was found not guilty on the charge of receiving stolen money, and police were forced to return to him the $1,500 they had confiscated at the Heath Street capture. A new jury was chosen for the next set of charges.

Edwin Boyd and William R. Jackson pleaded not guilty to the robbery at Dundas and Roncesvalles, the Leaside robbery, and to breaking jail. They pleaded guilty to escaping custody. Facing the same jury, Robert Boyd pleaded not guilty to the Leaside robbery.

But suddenly the focus of attention shifted. No longer was Edwin Boyd the star of the courtroom dramas. The Boyd Gang as an entity no longer existed. Boyd and Willie Jackson were only bank robbers, albeit wonderfully flamboyant ones. Steve Suchan and Leonard Jackson were killers, and now received top billing in the press. They had murdered a policeman, and all Toronto, and most of Canada, watched carefully to see their fate.

At the opening of their trial, Chief Justice McRuer explained to the jury why both men were charged with murder, when only one could have fired the fatal shot. The Crown's case against Suchan and Jackson would be based upon evidence that the two men had conspired together to resist legal apprehension with violence, or to carry out any other unlawful purpose by violence and if necessary to resist legal arrest by violence, and had agreed to assist each other therin. If such a conspiracy had been formed, each man would be considered a party to the actions of the other in carrying out their common purpose.

McRuer also reminded the jury that they were the sole judge of the facts; he was the sole judge of the law.

After a summary of the case presented by the Crown and the opening instructions by His Lordship, the trial began.

The testimony of the presecution in the Suchan-Jackson case was exhaustive. Anna Bosnich, regretfully but without hysterics, told the story of her association with Steve Suchan. When she talked about the bullet-riddled dummy head and torse that police had taken from her basement, the jury listened in wide-eyed fascination.

Sergeant Roy Perry, visibly distressed, took the stand against Suchan. He seemed very certain of his memory:

> The car stopped suddenly, and the door opened, and I heard a report, just as Tong approached the car. Tong made a half turn and fell to the roadway. With that I applied the foot brake and the emergency, and as I was doing so I observed the driver of this car, who by this time had made a turn and both legs were dangling over the side of the seat.

Perry admitted to having seen three photographs of Suchan in the newspapers after the shooting and before he attended police lineups. At the lineups, he had no trouble in identifying Suchan and Jackson as the men who had shot Tong and himself.

When the prosecution succeeded in entering as evidence the mangled dummy that Suchan and Jackson had used for target practice, the jury was stunned. Robinette and Maloney protested vigorously that the evidence was not relevant to the case, but Chief Justice McRuer was able to quote precedents for such evidence, and the dummies were shown to the jury. Many people were later convinced that this was the turning point of the trial. When the jury saw the bullet holes in the head and heart area, the full impact of the crime became clear to them.

The violin-maker, George Kindness, testified that he had given Suchan his .455 Smith and Wesson plus some cash in trade for Suchan's violin. The taxi drivers who took Suchan and Jackson in their frenzied escape from Toronto to Hamilton, identified the two men for the court. Jack Gillespie told the story of his shoot-out with Jackson in Montreal. In all, the prosecution presented forty-six witnesses.

The final Crown witness was Staff Sergeant William W. Sutherland, in charge of the Crime Detection Laboratory of the Royal Canadian Mounted Police in Ottawa. He testified that through his testing of the guns and bullets he had determined that the bullet which was removed from Tong's body came from the same gun that Suchan had when he was shot down in Montreal.

Robinette forced Sutherland to admit in cross-examination that it was solely a matter of the personal opinion of the individual ballistics expert whether or not the bullet came from the same gun. Sutherland added, "It is a matter of the examination of the material under consideration, plus the previous experience."

The judge, however, pursued the point further, pointing out the serious nature of the evidence, and asking whether Sutherland had come to a firm conclusion.

Sutherland: I have no real or honest doubt.
His Lordship: You have no doubt about it at all?
Sutherland: No doubt.

During the last day of Crown evidence, one of the spectators in the packed courtroom was watching the prisoners closely. His attention was suddenly diverted to Leonard Jackson's hand which was clenching and unclenching and fidgeting with something. The spectator summoned an RCMP officer. Remembering the reputation of the Boyd Gang for shootouts and escapes, the officer went into immediate action.

Without preamble or explanation, court was suddenly recessed. Suchan and Jackson were searched. The prisoner's dock and the courtroom were searched. Finding a cigarette butt, two small tacks and a piece of thread, police decided to investigate further. Searching the prisoners' cells, the officers drew a blank. The trial continued without further interruption.

The Crown concluded its testimony Friday afternoon. His Lordship decided not to sit on Saturday and apologized to the jury for keeping them over the weekend. Robinette and Maloney were relieved to have the two days for further work on their defence.

Jackson, who until this time had been forced to attend the trials without his artificial foot and wearing only socks, suddenly had his foot returned. For the first time in a week he walked without a limp, wearing shoes on both feet as he left the courtroom. He and Suchan were still sharing the death cells at the Don Jail with Boyd and Willie Jackson. Each night after the trials they recounted to each other the events of the day.

None of them thought about the fact that this might be their last weekend together. Instead, they talked about old times, about the robberies, the escape, where they went wrong, and how they would do it if they had it to do again. Edwin Boyd talked a little religion but none of them paid much attention.

Willie "The Clown" Jackson seemed the least concerned of anyone. Inspector John Nimmo had promised to give him a cigar at the end of the trials. Willie knew he was going back to Kingston regardless of the verdict; the only question was how long his sentence would be. "I don't care how much time they give me," he joked to Sergeant Payne. "Whatever it is, I'll do it standing on my head!"

But Monday morning came quickly, and with it the realization that time was running out. While Boyd and Willie Jackson went back to the same courtroom routine, Suchan and Jackson faced a new order of business. Today it was their turn. After hearing the testimony of the witnesses against them, the defence would present its version of the Tong murder case. There were only two witnesses for the defence—Steve Suchan and Leonard Jackson.

Robinette began by asking Suchan general questions about his background. Suchan told about his schooling, his first jobs, and his study of the violin. Then Robinette gently led Suchan into a discussion of his actions on the day of the shooting. Suchan described how he had been driving along and had seen a car that he thought was trying to crowd him over to the curb. Earlier he had cut off a car in traffic, forcing the driver to screech to a stop. He thought this was the same car coming to crowd him over in return.

"I had Len in the car; I got panicky, I guess," Suchan told the court. "At the time, Len was hotter than a firecracker."

His Lordship: What do you mean by that?
Suchan: He escaped jail.

Robinette: Yes?
Suchan: I didn't want to be discovered with him. I couldn't risk any investigation, because through investigation my connection with Boyd would be found out.

Robinette, attempting to cast doubt upon the Crown's contention that Suchan and Jackson had formed a common purpose, asked Suchan if he were thinking of Jackson's position when the car crowded him over to the curb.

A: No, I was not.
Q: Whose position were you thinking of?
A: I was thinking of myself.

Suchan told about how he reached for his gun and fired in the direction of the hood of the other car.

Q: What was your purpose?
A: The purpose was strictly to damage the engine of the car and get away from there.
Q: Who wanted to get away?
A: I wanted to get away.

Then, in contradiction to Perry's testimony (and in agreement with several other witnesses), Suchan told the court that he had not opened his car door to fire.

Q: At any time did you turn and sit sideways on the front seat with your legs dangling out the side?
A: No I did not. I couldn't on account of the wheel right in front of me, the steering wheel.
Q: You did not open the door?
A: No I did not.

When asked if he knew that the car at which he fired was a police cruiser, Suchan replied that he did not.

Q: When you fired the shot were you aiming at any person?
A: No, I was not. I was aiming, trying to hit the hood.

Robinette repeated the question in various ways, and each time

Suchan reiterated that he had not tried to shoot any person but merely trying to damage the car.

Until this point, Suchan had been an excellent witness, answering each question exactly the way it should be answered in accordance with his own best interests. Then Robinette asked him if he knew where Jackson was when the shooting was going on.

> Suchan: No, I didn't know where he was until I already had the car in motion, and he jumped in. I already had the car in motion. He jumped in. He said, "Christ! That was a cruiser!" He said, "Somebody has been hit. Let's get out of here!"
> His Lordship: No, no. Mr. Robinette, I do not know whether you knew that evidence was coming out or not.
> Robinette: I certainly did not know all of it, my lord.
> His Lordship: The rule applies to the defence as well as the Crown, that hearsay evidence is not admissible.
> Mr. Robinette: [to Suchan] Don't say what anybody said to you.

Suchan continued the story of how the pair had gone to Hamilton, stolen a car and driven back to Montreal. Then Robinette began detailed questioning about Suchan's capture in Montreal. He asked Suchan to indicate on his body where he had been shot, but quickly added, "I don't want you to show the actual scars."

His Lordship interrupted, "What relevance has this now?"

> Robinette: My lord, the relevance is that your Lordship admitted the evidence of the police detectives on the theory that subsequent conduct is relevant, and in my submission I am entitled to develop the whole of the subsequent conduct.

The judge allowed him to continue. The point was made that Suchan had had an opportunity to shoot at the policemen coming to recapture him, but had not. The lawyer's intent was to show the jury that Tong's shooting had been an accident, the result of a single unplanned, panicky act, whereas in subsequent episodes both in Montreal and in the barn in North York, Suchan had not fired at police.

Then Arthur Maloney, counsel for Leonard Jackson, had an opportunity to cross-examine Suchan. He asked only a few questions about what Jackson was doing as the two drove around in the car. Then they could delay no longer. It was the Crown's turn to cross-examine the witness. Detective Jack Gillespie, who had testified against Jackson, remembers Crown Attorney W.O. Gibson, Q.C. "He had a beautiful command of the English language."

At several points, Gibson simply could not force Suchan to say what he wanted him to say.

> Gibson: The immediate reason for your not wanting to get into the hands of the police was Jackson, and another reason that was not so pressing was Boyd?
> Suchan: The only reason there was pressing was Boyd.
> Q: Boyd was not in the car, was he?
> A: No.
> Q: Jackson was?
> A: Jackson was, yes.
> Q: And you knew the whole countryside were looking for him?
> A: I didn't know the whole countryside.
> Q: You knew the whole Province of Ontario were, didn't you?
> A: I didn't go as far as to think the whole Province of Ontario was looking.
> Q: Let us just reduce it then to the County of York.
> A: I knew he was wanted.

Gibson then questioned Suchan about his target practice, both at gravel pits east of Toronto and in Anna Bosnich's basement. He also asked about Leonard Jackson's eyeglasses, whether they were part of a disguise, but Suchan replied that Jackson had had them prescribed by a doctor.

On re-examination by Robinette, Suchan stressed the point that he had harboured Edwin Boyd both at his parents' home in Toronto and in Montreal at his Côte des Neiges apartment. Attempting to show that Suchan was in Boyd's debt and therefore less concerned about Jackson, Robinette asked Suchan if he had ever received any money from Boyd. Suchan replied that he had.

Gibson was quiet but forceful. He was, above all, well-prepared. He knew all the details of the case, and extracted information from Suchan that Robinette had taken care not to disclose. He forced Suchan to admit that he was constantly armed with deadly weapons, that he had been living "in sin" with Mary Mitchell. And then he tried to get Suchan to admit that he had formed a common illegal intent with Jackson. That was where Suchan shone as a witness.

Gibson tried again and again to get Suchan to say that he was assisting Lennie in escaping or avoiding legal apprehension. He spoke of the morning that Suchan picked up Lennie in Oshawa before Tong was shot.

> Gibson: And the reason he got off at Oshawa was so that he would not come into Toronto Union Station and expose himself to the police who were around there. That is obvious?
> Suchan: Whatever his reason was.
> Q: That was obviously his reason, wasn't it?
> A: It might have been.

Gibson tried another angle.

> Q: You knew he was wanted by the police?
> A: Yes, I knew he was wanted.
> Q: Why did you not tell the police to come and get him?
> A: I have never been a stool pigeon in my life.

Suchan answered all Gibson's questions as if he had a working knowledge of the law. He was a good witness for himself as well as for Jackson in refusing to admit the two had been working together in an illegal action.

When the lawyers had finished their questioning, Chief Justice McRuer asked Suchan several questions for the purpose of clarification.

> His Lordship: You are saying that, taking full responsibility that you fired the first shot that was fired.
> Suchan: Yes, I fired the first shot.
> Q: And if that shot was the shot that caused the death of Edmund Tong, it was fired by you?
> A: I didn't aim the gun.

Suchan continued to maintain that he did not know he had hit anyone. He said he was in a cramped position in the car. Robinette hastened to remind the jury that his client had already said the car door was not open.

> His Lordship: I understand he said the door was not open. There is evidence the door was open.

Robinette: There is evidence also that it was not. All I want to make clear is that the gentlemen of the jury understand, because it is a little difficult for the witness –
His Lordship: Mr. Robinette, I have asked my question. Do you think there is anything unfair about it?
Robinette: No, I just want to make it clear.
His Lordship: The jury understands.
Robinette: Thank you very much, my lord.

With that, Suchan stepped down from the stand. Both Robinette and Maloney agreed that Suchan had been a fine witness, for the most part speaking well in his own defence. But they didn't deceive themselves. They understood fully that their clients would be found guilty for the shooting of Tong. What they were hoping for was a conviction for manslaughter rather than murder. In 1952 if the verdict was murder, the sentence was death.

Maloney asked the judge for a few minutes to decide if he would call any evidence. He was given ten minutes.

Leonard Jackson was anxious to testify. He did not seem to understand that Suchan had done well. He thought Suchan had incriminated himself rather badly, and worse, that it was because of his association with Jackson. Jackson wanted to set everything straight. He didn't want Suchan to get a worse conviction than his. "That would be a fate worse than death for Jackson," said Maloney.

At 11:40 a.m., Maloney announced: "I will call the accused, Leonard Jackson."

After a brief history of Jackson's early life, army stint and work history, Maloney came to the point. He questioned Jackson about the day of the shooting, March 6, 1952. The witness described how he had started to flee when Suchan stopped the car and then heard a volley of shots. He testified that he got out his gun to protect himself.

Maloney: Did you at any time that day fire that gun?
Jackson: No, sir.

Jackson said that he saw someone lying face down on the street, but could not tell it was Sergeant Tong as his face was turned away. But he surmised that the car was a police cruiser because of the aerial in the middle. As soon as Suchan started to pull out, Jackson jumped into the car and they drove away.

Mr. Robinette declined to ask any questions and the Crown attorney began the cross-examination.

It was only a matter of minutes before Gibson had Jackson admitting all the things that Suchan had been so careful to avoid. Jackson agreed that he was looking for protection from Suchan by riding with him in Anna's car. He agreed that he stayed at Anna's house because he thought the police would not find him there.

> Gibson: And you would not have been able to stay at that house unless Suchan was there first?
> Jackson: Yes, sir.
> Q: And as the witnesses all told us (not all but several), by that time you were appearing in Toronto with glasses?
> A: Yes, sir.
> Q: And a moustache?
> A: Yes, sir.
> Q: For the purpose of disguise?
> A: Correct, sir.

When Gibson finished, Maloney asked a few more questions, then the judge again took over, clarifying points for himself and the jury. He asked Jackson what calibre of revolver he carried when he was out of custody in Toronto and Montreal. Jackson replied that it was a 32-20.

> His Lordship: That is a revolver that will cause death?
> Jackson: Yes, sir.
> Q: No doubt about that?
> A: That is right, sir.
> Q: What was your purpose in arming yourself with a loaded revolver?
> A: To aid me in attempting to flee if I was apprehended.
> Q: That you would fire it to assist you in attempting to flee if you were apprehended — was that the purpose?
> A: Not to kill, sir.
> Q: I am saying to fire it?
> A: Yes, sir.

Maloney was surprised by Jackson's statements. "I wouldn't have called him as a witness," he remembers, "had I known he was going to say what he said. It was different from what I had reason to believe he was going to say."

The court adjourned for lunch. At 1:48 p.m., J.J. Robinette began his address to the jury.

Robinette spoke for thirty-five minutes. His voice and manner were confident. He stood well back from the jury and spoke in what the *Telegram* called a "ringing voice".

Robinette insisted that Suchan had had no intention of killing, maiming, or injuring anyone. Suchan was only interested in helping himself, not Jackson, said Robinette, and thus there was no "common intent".

Finally, he spoke of Suchan lying wounded on the floor of his Montreal apartment. "Something intervened," said Robinette. "He could have died there, but he didn't." His suggestion was that some greater force had intended that Suchan should live. The jury listened to every word with rapt attention.

Robinette pointed out that the jury could find Suchan not guilty of murder, but guilty of manslaughter. "If, after all the evidence, you are not certain, you must find him guilty of the lesser charge."

At 2:20 p.m. Arthur Maloney rose to speak on behalf of Leonard Jackson. It was his contention that Jackson was not a party to anything Suchan did the fatal day. He reminded the jury that Jackson had testified, "I did not fire my gun."

Maloney paused dramatically between each point. The jury listened carefully. Jackson was not asking for anything more than his life, said Maloney. "He will not walk from this courtroom a free man, but he does deserve to live."

Maloney spoke for twenty-five minutes, then the judge called a short recess. Jackson and Suchan, still handcuffed together, barely looked at each other. "There were no bad feelings between them," remembers Robinette, "yet there seemed to be no great bond." They seemed almost indifferent to the fate which was so shortly to be decided.

At one minute before three, W.O. Gibson began his address to the jury, presenting the Crown's case against Suchan and Jackson. Gibson dismissed the notion that some sort of divine intervention had saved Suchan from death. He cut through the emotional pitfalls that Robinette and Maloney had laid out for him, presenting the accused as a pair of killers who together planned to evade the law and who should be found guilty of murder.

Gibson's blunt, common-sense approach impressed the jury. He mocked the idea that Tong's death was accidental. "When you ask Suchan, 'Did you intend to kill Tong?', well what else would he answer? 'No!' Yet he shot from an angle of forty-five degrees. He hit him. He killed him."

After his thirty-five minute speech, the jury was sent out of the courtroom, while both sides conferred with the judge on the finer points of the law.

It was Robinette's contention that since neither Tong nor Perry were attempting to apprehend or arrest the accused but merely to investigate, there was no resistance of lawful apprehension. The judge agreed that Robinette had a point, and decided not to raise that particular charge in his speech to the jury. By now it was late afternoon, and the judge asked the jury to decide whether to proceed or to continue in the morning. There was general agreement that they should carry on, now that they were so close to the end.

Chief Justice McRuer spoke for about an hour. He tried to present both interpretations of the story fairly, and clarified the jury's position in making judgements. "It is not necessary," he said, "that you find both guilty or both not guilty. You may find Suchan guilty, and Jackson not guilty." However, he did not give the jury the option of finding the accused guilty of two different offences. "I cannot see how you can find in law Suchan guilty of murder and Jackson guilty of manslaughter, because his [Jackson's] guilt depends on your view of Suchan's act."

The Chief Justice summed up his charge:

Each and every one of us has a high responsibility to an ordered society in which we live. We live by rule of law, and not by rule of force ... You will do just what defence counsel asked you to do, —do justice. That means justice to the accused, and justice to the society in which we live.

At 5:40 p.m. the jury retired.

But there were still further objections from Mr. Robinette. While pressing for the best possible case for his client, he was careful to be respectful to the judge. He said, "I do not mean to be critical, my lord —" but the judge interrupted, "I want you to be critical." Robinette's objection was that the jury had not been adequately instructed on their alternatives.

It did seem to me, my lord, that in discussing the alternatives between murder and manslaughter, they should be told that if they are in a state of doubt, they should bring in manslaughter, and not murder.

His Lordship: "I think that is a proper observation."

The judge called the jury back into the courtroom, and charged them further. Finally, at 5:55 p.m., they were sent to the jury room to deliberate the verdict.

According to the trial transcript, they were out for one hour and forty-five minutes. Somehow, during this time, the crowds of curious people seemed to lose interest. Perhaps they went home for supper. Perhaps they thought the jury might be out for days. By the time the jury returned at 7:40 p.m., there were only about thirty or forty spectators in the courtroom.

Throughout the trial, Jackson had kept his eyes on the floor most of the time. Suchan's expression was blank, emotionless, almost disinterested. Now both of them watched the jury, their attention focussing on the foreman as he rose to give the verdict.

The courtroom was tense as the registrar asked the formal questions.

"Do you find the prisoner at the bar, Steve Suchan, alias Victor J. Lenoff, guilty or not guilty of murder, as charged?"

The foreman's voice was shaky and dry. In his nervousness, he called Suchan by his alias.

"We find Victor Lenoff guilty of murder as charged."

There was absolute quiet and attention as the registrar asked the second question.

"Do you find the prisoner at the bar, Leonard Jackson, alias Fred Wilson, guilty or not guilty of murder as charged?"

The foreman regained his composure, and spoke in a level voice.

"We find Jackson guilty as charged."

All eyes turned to the prisoners. If the spectators expected to see a display, they were disappointed. There was no reaction at all. Suchan and Jackson continued to look straight ahead, their faces impassive.

Chief Justice McRuer thanked the jury, agreed with their verdict, and discharged them from further jury duty for five years. The Crown attorney, Mr. Gibson, moved for sentence.

For the first time throughout the trial, McRuer showed a trace of emotion. His head lowered, his voice quiet and trembling, he sentenced each prisoner in turn, as was his duty:

> You . . . shall be taken to the place from where you came, and there kept in close detention until the sixteenth of December, 1952, and thence you shall be taken to the place of execution, and there hanged by the neck until you are dead. And may the Lord have mercy on your soul.

Robinette turned to Maloney. Both of them were filled with great emotion. "My God," whispered Robinette, "I've never heard those words before."

DEATH ROW

20

The courtroom emptied quickly. Only the cleaning women remained when the prisoners were escorted outside. As they walked into the warm night air, Suchan mumbled to Jackson, "And they call that justice!"

Gently chiding him, Lennie Jackson turned to Steve. "Of course that's justice," he said. "We killed a man, didn't we?"

Across town, Ann Jackson sat with her husband's half-brother, Sam Stone. Both of them were bitter and angry. "I don't see that Lennie should hang for something he didn't do," said Ann. "It was the newspapers that convicted him." Sam Stone agreed with her. But for the moment they felt helpless and alone. How could you fight the judge and the jury and the whole legal system?

Steve Suchan didn't seem to care one way or the other. As he and Jackson were led to the patrol wagon, photographers' flashbulbs popped and reporters crowded in for the last bit of news. Police officers held machine guns at the ready. Just before the doors of the wagon closed on the two prisoners, Suchan yelled out to the press, "Have fun boys!" With a wave of his arm, and a wisp of a cynical smile, he was gone.

There were no good-byes among the members of the Boyd Gang. As soon as Suchan and Jackson were sentenced, Boyd and Willie Jackson were moved out of death row. Just as the penal system had thrown them together, now it separated the men whose lives had for a time intertwined so dramatically. There were few regrets.

Boyd had his own trial to think of. Throughout most of the Crown's evidence, Boyd sat quietly reading his Bible. His interest was sincere, but police were sceptical. They remembered the notorious "Red" Ryan who, pretending to be converted to religion, had escaped custody to commit more crimes. They were taking no chances with Boyd. He was heavily guarded at all times.

Each night, the prisoners were taken back to the Don Jail. For the notorious Boyd Gang, there was no bail. Now Edwin Boyd was in a cell by himself, with little to do but read the Bible. He remembers the cell vividly:

> They put me in there and gave me a pail. That was my toilet. Twice a day they would open the door and take me out to the toilet at the end of the corridor. You were in view of the guard at the end, you were in view of everybody that was walking up and down. They would let you take the pail up twice a day and empty it. That was about the only contact I had with anyone. The guards stood in front of my cell and made sure nobody came near.

In the midst of the trials, Sam Stone arrived back in the Don. In a raid on his house, RCMP discovered 108 capsules of heroin and arrested Stone on two charges of illegal possession, and one of stealing. He was soon on his way back to Kingston Pen, and Ann Jackson was left to fend for herself.

Also fending for herself was the widow of the late Sergeant Tong. A member of provincial parliament claimed that Mrs. Tong had been promised her husband's full salary for the rest of her life. That would have been $4,500 annually, but the city had voted to give her $3,750 a year for ten years. The politician claimed that Mayor Lamport had given the impression that the city paid Mrs. Tong $9,000. This was not so. "The money was paid out of funds to which Tong contributed during his lifetime, except for a sum given her by the Canadian Bankers' Association," said the MPP.

Suchan and Jackson, on advice from their lawyers, had decided to appeal their convictions. The grounds for appeal would be the admissibility of Crown evidence on target shooting (specifically the dummy head and torso), and the evidence on resistance to arrest. Robinette and Maloney would argue that the evidence had no bearing on the case and had influenced the jurors.

Before the lawyers had a chance to file for appeal, officials of the Don Jail were in a turmoil. They discovered three saw blades on a window sill in the section of the jail where the Boyd Gang was held. One window bar had been cut and another partially cut, with the openings disguised with soap and shoe polish. A royal commission inquiry into Don Jail conditions was scheduled to begin in ten days, and there were rumours that members of the Boyd Gang would be called to testify about how they escaped. Police dusted the saw blades for fingerprints, but no connection with the Boyd Gang was ever proven.

The juries brought back a guilty conviction against Edwin Boyd, Willie Jackson, and Robert Boyd on the Leaside robbery. Bank robbery charges against Steve Suchan and Leonard Jackson were not proceeded with. In Judge Forsyth's courtroom, the attention now shifted to some of the minor members on the fringes of the Boyd Gang.

Mary Mitchell, looking blonde and beautiful in a gray calfskin cape, pleaded not guilty to the charge of hourbouring Edwin Boyd. Boyd was brought into the courtroom, handcuffed to a detective, and surrounded by policemen. Witnesses stated that Mary Mitchell had arranged and paid for motel rooms for Boyd on several occasions. There was evidence from the motel clerks and managers, and little evidence to the contrary.

Judge Forsyth ruled as admissible Mitchell's signed statement given to Sergeant Payne that she had lived with Steve Suchan and kept Edwin Boyd at their apartment in Montreal and in motels in Toronto. On the stand, Mitchell claimed that police had "twisted" her statement, and that she was upset when she signed it because police had told her they were going to hang Lennie.

Mitchell admitted that the statement was substantially correct, but that she had told police that she did not know that Thompson and Gibson were aliases for Edwin Boyd and Willie Jackson. "If I thought that the man I knew was anyone other than Jack Thompson, I think I'd probably have taken a trip to Alaska."

The Kozaks were also brought before Judge Forsyth on charges of harbouring, aiding and abetting. Their lawyers argued that Boyd and Willie Jackson had been brought to the Kozaks' house by their son. It would have been difficult for them to refuse him. "The Crown would agree to leniency," said the Crown counsel. Judge Forsyth was unmoved. Kozak had harboured two criminals, declared the judge. He knew what he was doing. Defence counsel spoke of Kozak's six-year-old son, Suchan's younger brother, Eddie. The child would have to be turned over to an institution if both parents were sent to jail.

However, juries found both Mary Mitchell and the Kozaks guilty. Judge Forsyth delayed sentencing until the end of all the Boyd trials.

The next robbery dealt with was the Lansing branch of the Dominion Bank. Edwin Boyd pleaded guilty to seven more charges against him. On his way to court, he had complained of feeling dizzy and sick. He had been unable to eat breakfast, and now stood in court, pale and ashen-faced. But the evidence that day was somewhat more heartening. Sergeant Payne was giving him a character recommendation:

> He had great opportunities to fire on me in the Heath Street apartment, and never did. I believe that Edwin Boyd, even if he has these guns and faces these charges, is a very safe man with a gun. He has less respect for his own life than for the lives of the people he robs, or the police.

For years after, Payne would say that Boyd had saved his life by not shooting him down when he had the opportunity.

Because Robert Boyd's other brother, Gordon, had testified that Robert was visiting him on the day of the Lansing robbery, and because the evidence against him was so weak, Robert Boyd was acquitted on this charge. It was the first acquittal in the Boyd trials. He decided to appeal the verdict on the Leaside robbery.

There were a few more small victories for the Boyd faction. Dorreen's case was dismissed and she was released. Police were forced to give her back her belongings, which they had confiscated at the time of the Heath Street capture. Dorreen walked away smiling, a free woman. She took with her $6,000 in hundred-dollar bills, rolled up in her Tampax box.

The other victory for the Boyds was the fact that two witnesses on whom the Crown was relying failed to identify Edwin Boyd in court. They were employees of the Bank of Toronto at Dundas and Roncesvalles in Toronto, and had been held up by Boyd almost a year before. One of them said that she had picked out a suspect from police lineups earlier in the year.

"How did you do that?" she was asked.

"I'm not sure. I saw so many pictures of Boyd in the papers that I'm not sure if I was influenced or not."

On October 15, 1952, the Boyd trials ended. The following morning, eight people stood before Judge Robert Forsyth to hear their sentences. In the front row of spectators, wearing her scarlet coat and no hat, sat Dorreen Boyd. With her was Flo Lamb, a friend with whom she was living at the time. The first three to be sentenced were the peripheral figures of the gang.

For harbouring their son's friends, Sam Kozak was given nine months, and Charlotte Kozak six months indeterminate. Mr. Kozak stared straight ahead, but his wife was nearly in tears as she was led out of the courtroom. Members of the Salvation Army took charge of their young son, Eddie.

Mary Mitchell's lawyer stressed that her involvement had been with Suchan, not Boyd, and that she had broken off all involvement with the Boyd Gang the February before. Solemnly, the judge intoned the sentence. "Six months indeterminate."

Dorreen Boyd and Flo Lamb exchanged hopeful looks. These sentences weren't so bad, they thought. Perhaps Edwin would get a lighter sentence than they feared. Dorreen smiled at Ed, and he smiled back wanly.

Handcuffed together in the prisoners' box, there was barely room for the five convicted men, Edwin and Robert Boyd, Willie and Joseph Jackson, and Allister Gibson.

For their part in the College and Manning robbery, Boyd's recruits were sentenced first. Joseph Jackson, Willie's brother, was given ten years. Allister Gibson, their brother-in-law who had bungled his first and only attempt at armed robbery, was sentenced to eight years. Robert Boyd, for his part in the Leaside robbery, was sentenced to three years, which he had already announced he would appeal. For harbouring his brother Edwin, Robert was given a sentence of nine months, concurrent with the three years.

Willie Jackson was the next to be sentenced. He was already serving seven years for previous offences before the jailbreak. Found guilty of armed robbery of the banks at Dundas and Roncesvalles, and Leaside, he was given twenty years on each charge, the two sentences to be served concurrently. He was also found guilty of escaping custody twice, and was given two consecutive two-year terms. The total of his time to be served came to thirty-one years. He was still to be lashed for his previous conviction.

Edwin's face was impassive. None of the prisoners had shown any emotion on hearing their sentences. Now it was his turn.

The jury had returned a not guilty verdict on the charge of armed robbery of the bank at Dundas and Roncesvalles, the same robbery for which Willie had received twenty years. Boyd could not be properly identified for that charge. But the list against him was impressive without it. He had been found guilty on eight charges of armed robbery, one charge of attempted robbery, two charges of jail breaking, two of escaping custody, and two of auto theft.

Now Edwin Boyd's cheeks began to twitch as Judge Forsyth quietly but authoritatively read the sentences.

"On counts one, two, three, six, seven, eight, thirteen and sixteen," said Forsyth, referring to all the charges of armed robbery, "the sentence is life."

Dorreen gasped and turned pale. This was far worse than she had expected. But she quickly recovered when she realized that Flo had fainted.

The life sentences were to be served concurrently. For attempted robbery, Boyd got ten years; his two jail breaks cost him five years, and each escape two; each auto theft resulted in a four-year sentence. His total time: eight life sentences plus twenty-seven years concurrent.

It was all over. Her friend recovered, Dorreen rushed to her husband's side. For a few brief moments they embraced. Then Inspector Nimmo hurried over. He couldn't allow this in the courtroom. Firmly he pulled Dorreen away from Edwin. She watched as they led him away, and the tears ran down her face as she wept unashamedly for the first time since the trials began.

Outside, the reporters were having a heyday. Willie Jackson claimed the cigar that Inspector Nimmo had promised him. The cameras clicked as Willie clenched the cigar in his teeth and puffed away. Both his hands were in use at the time, being cuffed to his buddies on either side, so he rolled the cigar around his mouth with his tongue.

Sergeant Payne reminded Willie that he had vowed to do whatever time they gave him standing on his head. "You're gonna have an awful flat head," laughed Payne. Willie just grinned. He could hardly wait to get back to Kingston. He knew a lot of guys at the Pen, and there was still time for a little baseball before winter.

Edwin Boyd, too, was in a laughing, jovial mood that day. He grinned his famous Errol Flynn smile for the cameras, and joined in the joking with the others. It was hard to believe that this was a man who had just been sentenced to spend the rest of his life in prison. But his real feelings were submerged that day. Twenty-four years later, he was still bitter about the trial.

> As far as the judge was concerned, he was as bored as it was possible to be, because he already knew what the final judgement was, and what it was gonna be. They had all worked it all out, and it was cut and dried. It was just a case of pleasing the newspapers and the publicity, that was all. They knew everything they were interested in knowing. They just went through the procedure.

Dorreen was bitter from the moment the sentence was passed. "Ed might as well have committed murder," she said. "For the children and myself, his sentence is a cruel blow." She left the courtroom by a side door, but not before she had received an assurance that she would be allowed to visit Ed at the Don Jail that afternoon.

Finally the men were all tucked away inside the paddy wagon. The doors were nearly closed when Inspector Nimmo came running over and threw them open again. He jumped inside and took a parcel from Willie Jackson who was laughing uproariously. The parcel contained fertilizer, and it belonged to the boy who ran the courthouse elevator. Willie had lifted it on their way down.

21

There was no time for good-byes. At six a.m., Edwin Alonzo Boyd, Willie R. Jackson, and Joseph Jackson left Toronto's Don Jail in a blue patrol wagon surrounded by police motorcycle escort. Boyd had signed a declaration that he had no intention of appealing against his life sentence. He had also signed confessions giving the details of his two escapes.

Boyd would not be asked to testify at the royal commission enquiry into the jail's administration; indeed, Mayor Lamport declared that if Boyd were going to testify, he (Lamport) would refuse to sit in the same witness box. Nevertheless, Boyd's confessions would be tendered as evidence at the enquiry.

Boyd was now telling the press that he would not try to escape from Kingston. "Two mistakes are enough," said Boyd. The leader of the now-defunct Boyd Gang had no opportunity to see Steve Suchan and Leonard Jackson before he left for Kingston Penitentiary. Boyd pulled a spare sock from his overcoat pocket and waved it at reporters and photographers. The doors of the patrol wagon clanked shut, and the notorious criminal was gone.

Within a week, Frank Watson was convicted and sentenced to twelve years in Kingston Penitentiary for bribing a Don Jail guard and for possession of counterfeit money. Watson had tried to assist his friend, Lennie Jackson, by giving a jail guard counterfeit money in the hope of facilitating an escape. Because of the Don Jail enquiry, the guard was called to testify and the whole story came out. The guard was sentenced to two years.

Another guard testified that Steve Suchan had tried to bribe him with $5,000 about two months before the September escape. The guard refused the bribe and reported the attempt to the governor.

The probe covered more than 3,200 pages of testimony and lasted twenty days. By the end of the enquiry, two questions remained unanswered: How did the prisoners get the hacksaw blades, and how did they get a key for their cells? The commission never did come up with the answers.

On November 12, 1952, the appeal court of Ontario heard Arthur

Maloney and John J. Robinette speak on behalf of Leonard Jackson and Steve Suchan. The lawyers were asking for a new trial on the basis of improper evidence and misdirection of the jury by the judge.

The courtroom was hushed. In the back row sat a group of law students who had been asked by their professor to attend the appeal hearing. One of them, a young woman, rushed in late, her yellow polo coat flying out behind her. She slid into her seat and looked up. The rostrum of five judges seemed to be looking at her. Her friends whispered that she should have been wearing a hat, a formality which had completely escaped her. Then another friend whispered, "That's Jackson's wife."

The friend pointed to a woman sitting on the right side of the courtroom, about half-way to the front. Ann Jackson was dressed completely in black. Her make-up was perfect. Her face presented an icy exterior. "She looked like a movie queen," recalls the former law student.

The lawyers presented their cases for appeal, then the five judges retired to discuss their decision. They were out for only fifteen minutes. Their verdict: "Appeal denied." Suchan turned a cocky head toward the spectators and seemed to smirk. He appeared to some like a child who instead of crying, decides to laugh.

Leonard Jackson made no such pretense. His face was brooding and intense. When the decision was handed down he looked dejected and defeated. Ann appeared frozen. She did not weep.

Shortly after the denial of appeal, Mrs. Kozak asked Robinette if her son could see a priest. Robinette was not Roman Catholic, but Arthur Maloney was. Maloney called on Reverend Father John Kelly, from St. Michael's College in Toronto.

Father Kelly protested. He wasn't the man for the job, he told Maloney. He had worked almost exclusively in education. "This is a pastoral job of extreme need," said Kelly. Maloney was persistent. Finally, Father Kelly accepted the challenge.

Suchan and Jackson were in adjoining cells in the Don Jail. They could not see each other but could converse easily. Maloney approached Suchan, whose initial reaction was hostile. He said that he wouldn't see a priest. Suddenly Lennie Jackson spoke up. "Mr. Maloney has done a lot in this case," said Jackson. "Couldn't you do this for him?"

Almost immediately Suchan's attitude changed. He agreed to talk with Father Kelly. Maloney is sure that Suchan wanted to see a priest all along but was afraid to say so in front of "Tough Lennie".

Father Kelly visited Suchan several times a week. He would stay two or three hours. He tried to develop an approach toward conversation. At first they avoided religion altogether. Suchan had read Tolstoi's *War and Peace*, a fact which impressed both the lawyers and the priest. Father Kelly discussed the book with him, and then they went on to sports and current events. Occasionally they talked about Suchan's family, but Father Kelly didn't press the issue. "He didn't even respond much to violinist talk," remembers the priest.

For the first five weeks, Jackson listened silently and sullenly to the conversations between Suchan and the priest. He did not participate in the talks, but he did not ignore them either. "After five weeks," says Father Kelly, "I felt I had accomplished nothing pastoral or religious." Suchan was always glad to see the priest, but only because it was a break in the boredom. Father Kelly was despondent.

One day Kelly went to see Father Basil Sullivan at lunch. "You're being too humanistic, too naturalistic," Father Sullivan told the younger priest. "You're not leaving room for divine grace." Father Kelly was taken aback. He asked what he should do. Father Sullivan told him to get two sets of rosary beads from the church, take them to the jail, and wait to see what would happen.

"Aren't those rosary beads?" asked Suchan.

"Yes they are," replied Father Kelly.

"Could I have a set of them?"

In stunned amazement, Father Kelly handed the rosary beads to Suchan. At that moment, the previously sullen Jackson wheeled around and faced the priest through the cell bars.

"Father," said Jackson, "could you get me a pair of those too?"

Father Kelly reached in his pocket and pulled out the second rosary that he had brought with him. From that moment on, the atmosphere changed. Jackson began to enter into the discussions, and the topics changed smoothly to religious matters. "Tough Lennie", born half-Jewish, raised in the Anglican faith, now took an interest in Roman Catholicism. Previous efforts by jail officials to get Jackson to see a Salvation Army officer and an Anglican minister had been to no avail. But time was running short for Suchan and Jackson.

At Lennie's urging, Kelly went to see Ann Jackson. She was carrying on bravely, raising the infant son for whom she and Lennie had such high hopes. She visited Lennie as often as she could at the Don, and finally pressured Maloney to try yet another appeal. Maloney and Robinette again went before a judge, this time Mr. Justice James Estey, of the Supreme Court of Canada, and requested leave to appeal the death sentences. Estey heard their arguments, but withheld an immediate reply.

For more than a week, the condemned men, their lawyers, Father Kelly, Ann Jackson, Anna Bosnich, and the Kozaks all waited and wondered. As long as Estey deliberated, there was still hope. In the meantime, a conversion was taking place at the Don.

Father Kelly was educating Suchan and Jackson in the tenets of Christianity. Both prisoners were profoundly interested. Although they never discussed the shooting of Tong, the priest felt they were now contrite and anxious to be forgiven, if not by man, then by God.

On December 12, four days before the scheduled hanging, Mr. Justice Estey emerged with his decision. Jackson and Suchan were refused a new hearing by the Supreme Court of Canada. There was little hope left. Leonard Jackson asked Father Kelly if he could be admitted to the Roman Catholic Church. Father Kelly replied that he could, but only on certain terms of conviction concerning the truths of religious beliefs.

The priest thought that despite the new denial of leave to appeal, both prisoners were more cheerful than when he had first come to their cells. Since Jackson's acceptance of the rosary beads, all three of them seemed to be on the same wavelength.

Suchan had been used to doing seventy pushups every morning in his cell, just for the exercise. "After he got holy," says Maloney, "he thought that was too worldy, so he quit." Then Suchan read about St. Augustine who, when asked what he would do if he knew the hour of his death, replied, "I would go on doing what I am doing now." This made sense to Suchan, and he continued his pushups.

Jackson had asked his mother for permission to receive instructions in the Catholic faith. He said that he wouldn't do it if she didn't want him to, because he had hurt her enough. Lillian Jackson agreed and Father Kelly began Lennie's lessons.

The prisoners had a few other visitors. Mrs. Kozak, now released after serving three months in reformatory, came to see her son. Anna Bosnich also visited Steve and told him about their infant son, now almost eleven months old. Ann Jackson visited Lennie, and a few times brought their baby with her. She was now living on welfare and missed Lennie desperately.

"Even if I'd known what the end would be," said Ann, "I'd still have married Leonard. Even if I had known he would be sentenced to hang, it wouldn't have changed me." She said that she understood the principle of a life for a life, but "two lives for one seems too many to take". She still wasn't giving up hope.

In a desperate last move, Ann went to Arthur Maloney and asked him to cable Queen Elizabeth an appeal for clemency. Maloney realized the futility and the impropriety of such a request, and quietly dissuaded her.

Suchan and Jackson were scheduled to be hanged December 16. On the fifteenth, Father Kelly went to the jail first thing in the morning. He felt that the two convicts were truly repentant, and decided to give them communion, in Jackson's case, his first. Father Kelly said Mass right outside their cells in an atmosphere of calm, resignation and reconciliation. They seemed now to have no great fear of death. Father Kelly left the jail, intending to go back in the evening.

That afternoon, the governor of the jail telephoned Kelly. There was, it seems, a small problem. Although not required to do so, officials traditionally allowed condemned men to choose what they wanted to eat at their last meal. Suchan had been no trouble.

"Fried chicken, mashed potatoes, and peas," said Suchan, "and for dessert, apple pie, ice cream and coffee. And two big cigars." The cigars were for Father Kelly and Suchan's favourite guard. Suchan didn't smoke.

However, Lennie Jackson, in his new-found religious zeal, wanted something special. For his last meal on earth he wanted to eat what Jesus Christ had eaten for *His* last meal. The governor was in a quandary. No one knew what sort of a meal that would be.

Father Kelly told the governor, "To the best of my recollection,

Jesus' last meal included unleaved bread, some herbs and wine." But the governor was under strict orders not to serve wine in the jail. Could Father Kelly please come out to the jail and talk to Jackson? Although he did not know what he would say to Lennie, Kelly agreed.

Lennie could see him coming along the corridor. In a tone of braggadocio, which was understandable to Kelly, Lennie called out, "Know what I did, Father? For my last meal I ordered the same meal as Jesus Christ had for His last meal!"

Kelly looked surprised and bewildered. He still didn't know what to say. Lennie asked, "Didn't I do right?"

"You did right," replied the priest. "But look, Lennie. The Mass is a re-enactment of the Last Supper, so this morning when you went to communion you had, with Christ, His last meal."

"I never quite thought of it that way," said Lennie. "That's good." Then with an abrupt about-face, he turned and yelled to the guard, "Cancel that order for my last meal! I'll have the same meal that Steve's having!" Mission accomplished, Kelly went back to the college.

About five p.m., the men who were no longer just their lawyers but their friends as well, Robinette and Maloney, went out to see Suchan and Jackson. All hope was now gone. Commutation had been refused by the Cabinet. The four men were in a sombre mood. They did not avoid the topic that was on all their minds.

"You've been my lawyer on earth," Jackson told Maloney. "I'll be your lawyer in heaven." Jackson had wanted to write to the press, apologizing for letting Maloney down at the trial. Maloney felt that these were two decent human beings before him. Did they really deserve to die?

Suchan read to Robinette a letter that he had written to his mother. The letter was in Slovak, and Suchan translated as he read:

My beloved dearest Momma,

I have just finished my supper, chicken, cranberry sauce, ice cream. I had my special order, and everything was good.

This morning at 6:30 we had Mass and last night I was to confession. I was to communion also.

I know that I'll join my two brothers who have gone before

me now, but I'm not afraid at all, and you, Momma, be strong and don't cry for me, I beg you.

How is it that all during my life, and even now, I've hurt you so, my Momma dear, Momma dear? If I had thought of you more, and a little less of myself, everything would have turned out well. Momma forgive me.

Now you have little Eddie. I pray to God that he will listen to you and love you with all his heart, that he may grow up to be a better man than I was.

Love him, Momma, for he loves you. If he does something wrong, don't spank him, Momma, but show him and explain to him what to do. He'll love you a thousand times more.

Anna is taking the violin for her son, she says, and I don't want any more misunderstanding or fights with her. Fighting will not help anybody.

If Eddie wants to play an instrument, then start him when he's young. Buy him a small violin, 'half-size', as a big one would not be suitable. But if he wants an accordion, then get him one, but don't have both.

Take him to the Toronto Conservatory of Music, as there he'll have the best of training. If he starts young, he'll be a better musician at 12 than I was at 22. I know a place where you can buy violins, Mr. Kindness' store at Walton Street and Yonge. $45 will buy a small one.

Ironically, Suchan was referring to the store where he had first traded his own violin for the .455 Smith and Wesson that had been the instrument of Tong's, and his own, destruction. He made a reference to Jascha Heifetz, the famous Russian violinist who was Suchan's own idol, and then went on with Eddie's musical training:

Let him begin right away, not in a year or two. He'll become a good musician if he wants to.

When you go to see Dad, send him my sincerest love and best wishes. If he sees it in his heart, I want him to pardon and forgive me.

Mr. Kozak was still in the reformatory, serving his sentence. Suchan had not seen him since the end of the Boyd trials.

Work never killed a man, but nerves have. That's what I've found out from books, and it is true.

Mother, be strong. Live for Eddie and for yourself. You're still young, and you were my true mother. Keep your head up, and look people straight in the face, because they are no better than you are.

Straight from my heart, I love you, Momma. And my small brother, a million times. Please forgive me, Momma, for bringing you so much sorrow.

Bye bye, Mother dear.

Your son,
Valent, xxxxxx.

Robinette's eyes were shining with tears. Suchan looked at him, and quietly said, "Don't cry for me, Mr. Robinette. I've never felt such happiness inside as I feel right now." Suchan felt that God had spared his life at the time of the Montreal gunfight so that he would have time to straighten out his affairs before his death.

In downtown Toronto, Mrs. Kozak and Ann Jackson were making arrangements for the funerals of two men who were not yet dead. Dozens of people had wired, phoned and written to the Mininster of Justice, asking that the death sentences be commuted to life. The two women were no longer under any illusion of hope.

About eight p.m., Father Kelly returned to the jail. Students at St. Michael's College were spontaneously organizing a vigil to pray for the two condemned men. For three hours Father Kelly led Suchan and Jackson in a private retreat. They were solemn and calm.

The condemned men had expected to be hanged at daybreak, but it had been decided without their knowledge that the execution would take place just after midnight. About an hour before the appointed time, Father Kelly could see a general gathering of coroner, hangman, and other officials ouside the cell block. Suchan and Jackson could not see them from their cells. When the coroner came in, they were surprised, but not disturbed.

The coroner asked Father Kelly whether he thought the men needed a sedative. Kelly told him to ask Suchan and Jackson. By now, Suchan and Jackson looked to the priest for guidance in all things. "Should we take it, Father?" they asked.

"Oh, I think you should, sure," said Kelly, smiling encouragement. The coroner produced a needle. The shot did not eliminate consciousness but produced a calm, almost euphoric state.

The priest had asked the jail governor if Lennie could have his wooden foot back to walk to the gallows. Even now, officials were worried about some slip-up or deception. The request was refused.

Outside the jail, a curious crowd had gathered. Word had leaked out that the execution was to take place at one minute after midnight. As the time drew closer, the crowd grew restive. Cars began to slow down near the jail. By midnight they were bumper to bumper. Eighteen policemen tried to control the crowd of about 400 people. There was no reason for the spectators to be there. They would see nothing, hear nothing, and know nothing when the actual moment of hanging took place. But still they remained.

Across town in St. Basil's Church, 100 students of St. Michael's College silently prayed for Suchan and Jackson. More and more were filing in, until some were kneeling in the doorways.

A raw wind made the 35-degree weather seem colder. Light skiffs of snow swirled through the jail courtyard. It was just after midnight, and the crowds were yelling now. Some seemed in a jubilant mood, as if they were at a football game. A few wept, and a few prayed. Inside the jail, all was quiet.

Suchan was the first to be led from his cell. He smiled wanly at the guards who accompanied him. He walked normally and did not hesitate when taken into the death chamber. The room was very cold. Suchan and Jackson wore only their blue denim trousers and open-necked jackets. Neither had shoes or shirt. "No one ever told me we'd be freezing to death," said Suchan. "I thought we were hanging." He called out, "Hurry up, Lennie. I don't want to freeze to death!"

Jackson was not far behind. He did not smile as he limped toward the chamber. Both men wore their rosaries around their necks. Father Kelly entered the death chamber with a handful of official witnesses, including the sheriff, the coroner and the guards.

Inside, the hangman stood waiting, his head shrouded in black. Two ropes coiled on beams hung suspended over the steel trap doors. Father Kelly annointed Suchan and Jackson with sacred oils as he murmured the Latin words of extreme unction. A moment before the hangman moved forward, Jackson extended his hand to the priest. Wordlessly, they shook hands, and Father Kelly turned to Suchan.

Clasping the priest's hand, Suchan saw the look in Father Kelly's eyes. "Don't worry, Father," said Suchan, "it won't hurt."

The hangman placed a black hood over each prisoner's head. They stood back to back on the trap doors. Father Kelly continued to pray. At 12:14 a.m., the hangman stepped to one side and pulled the lever. The trap doors sprang back, and Steve Suchan and Leonard Jackson dropped through.

Forty-five minutes later, after intermittent checks with a stethoscope, the physician pronounced them dead. It was one a.m., December 16, 1952. Steve Suchan and Leonard Jackson had paid the supreme penalty.

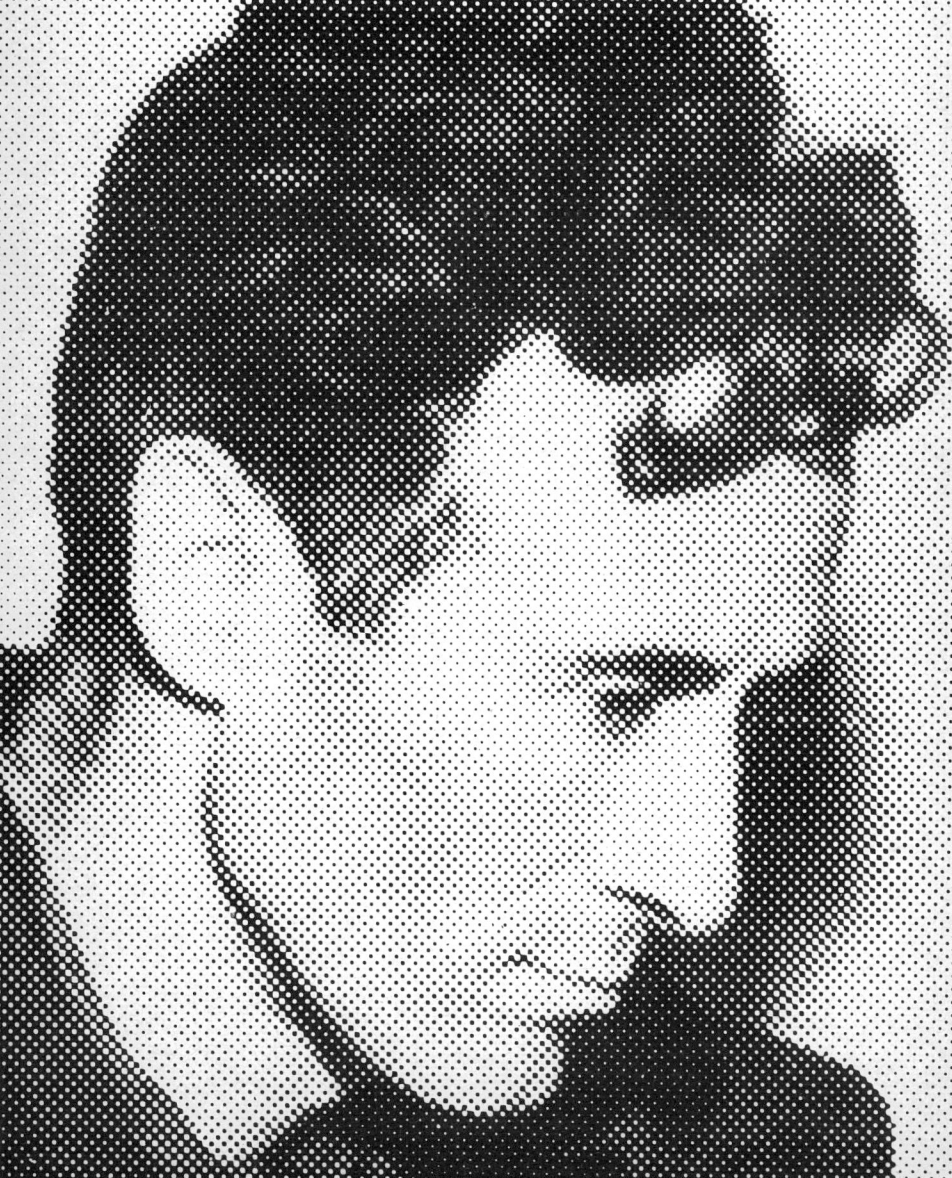

EDWIN

22

There was no vigil kept at Kingston Penitentiary. At the hour when Suchan and Jackson died, Edwin Boyd was sound asleep in his cell. Not far away, Willie Jackson dreamed like an innocent babe. Even Lennie's half-brother Sam Stone slept soundly that night.

Boyd's reaction to the deaths of his former accomplices was curiously detached.

"I didn't think too much about it for myself. It didn't touch me personally," says Boyd. "That was their problem." But Boyd was interested in the reactions of the other men in Kingston. "Poor Len, poor Suchan," said some of the inmates. Some of them idolized the men who had killed an old enemy, Sergeant Tong.

Many of the inmates knew Jackson personally, and felt sorry about his death. Len Jackson had been a member of the underworld group who had known, understood, and respected each other for a long time. Edwin Boyd, on the other hand, was a relative outsider.

"They couldn't understand why I was down there serving time," says Boyd, "and Suchan and Jackson were being hung. How come I wasn't being hung too?" Boyd explained to the inmates that they don't hang a man for robbing banks, and he was at the other end of Toronto when Tong was shot down. "Aw," said some of them, "you just had a good lawyer, or something."

Boyd didn't care too much what the other inmates thought of him. He was primarily a loner, the same as he had been before fate threw him together with the Jacksons in the Don Jail. Sometimes he would talk with Willie, now that they were together in Kingston.

Willie felt bad about Len, but he was glad that Suchan was dead. He had never forgiven Steve for refusing to split his share of the bank loot after Sam Kozak had disappeared to Florida with Boyd's and

Willie's. Referring to Suchan after the hanging, Boyd said, "Well, what do you think, Willie, your best friend is gone."

Replied Willie, "That dirty, rotten, two-faced, double-crossing—"

The era of the Boyd Gang was over. As television aerials sprouted on homes across Canada, people quickly forgot that their nightly entertainment for months had been the true-life serialized story of the most notorious bandits in the country. Now they had Howdy Doody in the afternoon and Tugboat Annie in the evenings.

Edwin Boyd passed his time like a good and obedient prisoner. In the riots that broke out in the penitentiary a few years later, Boyd made a point of standing in the middle of the exercise yard where he could be seen by the guards, as proof that he was not involved in the trouble-making and destruction.

Boyd was unencumbered by any troublesome feelings of guilt regarding his bank robberies. His attitude was, "They got lots of money, and I'm interested in getting it. So I'll try to out-think them and the police, and anyone else that's involved."

Looking back on the robberies, he says, "I enjoyed every minute of it. I got a good feeling when I was successful, and I got a bad feeling when I wasn't successful . . . I enjoyed the feeling of success and achievement."

Does he have any regrets, any feeling that he might have made a mistake choosing bank robbery as a career?

"Well," said Edwin Alonzo Boyd, in 1976, "if I hadn't taken Gault as an assistant, I'd still be doing it. That's how good it was."

EPILOGUE

Willie R. Jackson served fourteen years in Kingston Penitentiary. In 1966, he was released on parole and became a church janitor in Toronto. He is now believed living in British Columbia.

*Robert Boyd** served less than three months in Guelph Reformatory after successfully appealing bank robbery charges. Only the harbouring conviction stuck. He whiled away the time playing the tuba. When he came out, some influential people who felt he had been given a bad break helped Robert get a good job. He still works for the same company and lives with his wife and family in a comfortable home in Toronto.

Ann Jackson remarried exactly one year after Leonard was hanged. Later she became an alcoholic and her new marriage broke up. Her husband was awarded custody of Jackson's child. She died in the late sixties of cirrhosis of the liver.

Mary Mitchell served a few months for harbouring Edwin Boyd. She eventually went to London, Ontario, where she became involved in the body-rub and prostitution business. She died of a brain tumour in the early sixties.

Anna Bosnich raised Suchan's child alone. She supported herself very successfully with money she earned from her real estate and other business ventures. Now a well-traveled, middle-aged woman, her most recent trip was to Hawaii. She lives comfortably in a small house in a Vancouver suburb.

*Sam and Charlotte Kozak** live in Toronto and dote on their younger son Eddie, now a grown young man.

Dorreen Boyd brought up her three children alone while Ed was in the penitentiary. She worked in a lamp factory in Toronto, and eventually moved to British Columbia. Divorced from Ed in 1966, she has remarried. "I am leading a good life, still working hard," she says.

Allan Lamport is retired from politics and living in Toronto. The former mayor says, "I wish the death penalty would come back."

*Pseudonym

Jack Gillespie is retired from police work and owns a flower shop in Toronto. "Boyd," says Gillespie, "was a windbag."

Adolphus "Dolph" Payne rose to the position of staff superintendant on the Toronto Police force and retired in 1974 after forty-three years of service. "Most robbers," he says, "are dumb clucks."

John J. Robinette, Queen's Counsel, still maintains an active legal practice in Toronto. "I never knew where Suchan went wrong. I never thought of him as part of the Boyd Gang."

Arthur Maloney left law for politics and is now Ontario's ombudsman. Leonard Jackson "never struck me as a desperado or dangerous man. He was a small, slight man, polite and courteous," says Maloney. "He never really displayed remorse for the killing, but I felt he knew he had done wrong."

Edwin Alonzo Boyd was paroled in 1962, then sent back to Kingston Penitentiary for four more years for "violation of parole". Divorced after this stint, Boyd moved west, took odd part-time jobs, and eventually remarried. He dotes on his new wife who gets him to do little jobs around the house, at which he says he feels barely competent. The Parole Board gave him a new identity, and he now lives quietly in a western province of Canada.